Mysteries of the Bible

LIONEL AND PATRICIA FANTHORPE

MYSTERIES
of the
BIBLE

THE DUNDURN GROUP
A HOUNSLOW BOOK
TORONTO · OXFORD

Hounslow Press
A member of the Dundurn Group

Publisher: Anthony Hawke
Editor/Design: Jennifer Scott
Printer: Webcom Ltd.

Canadian Cataloguing in Publication Data

Fanthorpe, R. Lionel
Mysteries of the Bible

ISBN 0-88882-209-X
1. Bible — Criticism, interpretation, etc. I. Fanthorpe, Patricia. II. Title.
BS538.F36 1999   220.6'7   C99-932163-3

1   2   3   4   5   03   02   01   00   99

We acknowledge the support of the **Canada Council for the Arts** for our publishing program. We also
acknowledge the support of the **Ontario Arts Council.** We acknowledge the financial support of the
Government of Canada through the **Book Publishing Industry Development Program** (BPIDP) for
our publishing activities.

Care has been taken to trace the ownership of copyright material used in this book. The author and the
publisher welcome any information enabling them to rectify any references or credit in subsequent
editions.

J. Kirk Howard, President

Printed and bound in Canada.

 Printed on recycled paper.

www.dundurn.com

Dundurn Press
8 Market Street
Suite 200
Toronto, Ontario, Canada
M5E 1M6

Dundurn Press
73 Lime Walk
Headington, Oxford, England
OX3 7AD

Dundurn Press
2250 Military Road
Tonawanda, New York
U.S.A. 14150

This book is dedicated to all our friends
who are fellow members of ASSAP —
The Association for the Scientific Study
of Anomalous Phenomena.
It is a great honour and privilege to be your President.

Table of Contents

Foreword

by Canon Stanley Mogford, MA

Julius Caesar once described Cassius: "Yond' Cassius hath a lean and hungry look; he thinks too much: such men are dangerous."

If there is to be anywhere in this book a picture of one of the authors, the Reverend Lionel Fanthorpe, or if readers are familiar with him through his many television programs, such as *Nostradamus, Fortean TV, Stranger than Fiction, Stations of the Cross* and others, the term "lean and hungry look" will be misnomer indeed. His frame is robust and strong as might be expected of one who is both a weight lifter and martial arts expert. Lean and hungry he will never be! But he *thinks*. He may have the body of a pugilist but he has the mind of an academic. His intellect is equal to his frame.

This book shows him grappling with some of the dilemmas that have exercised biblical scholars for generations. His struggles with them will interest many, confuse others, and infuriate not a few. It will be a victory even to have attempted such a labour. We "lesser mortals," again to use some words from Shakespeare's *Julius Caesar,* can only marvel at his industry, his thoroughness, and, perhaps, (dare one use the word?) his ingenuity. Some will recognize and admire its daring; others may criticize and call it ingenuous.

In a concluding sentence, in a chapter in the heart of the book, the authors refer to the four keys that can unlock the great enigmas of the Bible. They will forgive me for changing the order in which they used them.

The first of these keys is investigation. We have to know the facts as they can best be discovered. The background will have to be identified and carefully researched, and comparisons made with what others, over the years, have deduced and formulated. Here, the authors are at their best. Their research is meticulous. The hand of the co-author is here clearly to be seen. Much has been looked at, tested, and refined and as a result, all who come to the book with open minds will find themselves infinitely better informed than when they started. As one who has had a life long interest in the Bible, not merely as a scholar, but as one for whom it is the "word of Life," I am indebted to them for the care they have taken, and the knowledge they have shared.

The second of the keys is interpretation. Charles Dickens makes Mr. Gradgrind say in his book *Hard Times:* "Now what I want is facts. Facts alone are wanted in life." This book is full of facts. There is the fact of the Flood, the ark, the Exodus, the Prophets and their messages, and the Gospels, and a host of others. Each chapter is full of them. The facts are then interpreted. What one person sees, another does not. The theory of one is academic to another. The authors have never lost sight of one great guiding truth. Whatever might be apparent, whatever common consent may be reached, no interpretation of any of these events will satisfy them if it conflicts with the love of God as revealed in our Lord Jesus Christ. They try to look at everything not with their eyes but His.

The third key that helps to open the doors to some of these mysteries is imagination. Here, as one who has known both the authors over many years, I see the hand of one rather than the other. Lionel has spent years of his life researching the paranormal. He has lived in the world of the supernatural, of the extraterrestrial, of alien technologists, genetic engineers and the like. He has lectured on it, made TV and radio programs about it, written books on it. Small wonder, then, if, in his wanderings in this world, some of what he has come to grips with, has pressed itself into his consciousness. Here, I find it harder to go with him. Fallen angels as genetic engineers and aliens as man's guardian angels are too much for me. A space craft as substitute for Elijah's winged chariot, and genetic engineers at work on Ezekiel's valley of dry bones are outside my prosaic, feet-on-the-ground, unimaginative existence. Nor is the writer himself, enslaved by his own theories. Theories they are and will remain. He dares us to think, to analyze for ourselves without bias or prejudgement. Any final solution, in a world so complex and intricate is yet to be found.

The last of the keys needed is tolerance. The writers of the book are committed Christians. Lionel has been a priest of the Church for many years. Their faith is rooted in the love of God as seen in Christ Jesus. As he puts it in one of the chapters: "In Christ God reached out and became human. Through Christ humanity responds to God." Love is never far from anything he writes. He loves God and he loves people and he longs for all men to know that love as richly as he does. All his questions, all his researches are done in that love. If anything fails that test he will discard it. He will not be ashamed of having examined it. At the very least, what he has written here will make us test our own beliefs.

Canon Stanley Mogford, MA
Cardiff, Wales, 1999

(Footnote: The authors are deeply grateful to Canon Stanley Mogford for providing this foreword. He is widely acknowledged to be one of the finest scholars and academics in Wales, and it is a real privilege to have his help here.)

Introduction

Darkness is afraid of light: truth fears nothing and welcomes investigation. The closed, prejudiced mind is fragile and brittle: the honest, open, receptive mind is always ready to consider new ideas and to evaluate them fearlessly, objectively, and rationally. The strictly traditional thinker is paralyzed and eventually fossilized by convention: the progressive thinker is dynamic, flexible, and always ready to think the unthinkable.

The Bible is a unique library of sacred books and collected oral traditions dating back over five thousand years. Some contain genuine history: others are mysterious myths, legends, fables, and poems. There are also books of law, ethics, letters, and prophecy. The Four Gospels describe the life and work of Christ. The Book of Revelation deals with eschatology — things which some Christians believe are yet to come: including the end-of-the-world and Judgement Day.

In our attempt to solve some of the Bible's intriguing mysteries, we have taken it down from its previously inaccessible sacred pedestal and treated it as objectively as any other piece of valuable research data: no more — and no less.

We've tried to assess whether there was an actual geographical location for the Garden of Eden, and what went on there. We've attempted to solve the strange problem of what Rahab the Harlot did when the Israelite spies went to Jericho. We've looked into the mysteries of the Nephilim; the destruction of Sodom and Gomorrah; and the dangerous powers concealed within the Ark of the Covenant. We've also speculated about its present whereabouts.

It seems *possible* that Moses brought some priceless artefact out of Egypt with him when he led the Israelites to freedom: was that why

Pharaoh pursued him so recklessly and lost his chariots in the Red Sea? It's equally possible that the prophet Ezekiel saw a spaceship, and witnessed a modern DNA-style medical miracle when he reported the resurrection of the dry bones in the valley of death.

Was Daniel protected by a force field which saved him from the lions — and did a similar shield save the lives of Shadrach and his friends in the furnace?

What were Urim and Thummim — the mysterious, decision-making stones — and how did they work? We've put forward a number of theories about them, and we've also speculated about their present location.

There's a major problem over Jesus's marriage: was the wedding at Cana where he turned water into wine his *own* marriage to Mary of Bethany? If so, was she the *same* lady as Mary of Magdala, the "woman taken in adultery," *and* the woman who anointed his feet with the expensive ointment of spikenard? Did Jesus *really* walk on water, feed thousands with a handful of bread and fish, calm the storm, cast out demons, *and rise from the dead after his crucifixion?*

These are only a few of the mysteries we've investigated in this volume. We greatly hope that they'll interest and intrigue our readers as much as they've interested and intrigued us.

Lionel & Patricia Fanthorpe
CARDIFF, WALES, 1999

Chapter One

The Garden of Eden

The Book of Genesis gives an account of the Garden of Eden which suggests a realistic description of an actual historical and geographical location — a real, solid, physical place, rather than the colourful dream landscape of myth or legend. George MacDonald, C.S. Lewis, and J.R.R. Tolkien all had the gift of creating imaginary landscapes which possessed uncanny realism — as if they had visited and subsequently described actual locations. Terry Pratchett's "Discworld" is even more fantastic than theirs, but every bit as coherent, consistent, and pseudo-realistic.

By contrast, the biblical description of Eden seems to possess a sturdy, time-defying realism, a sense of historical and geographical *actuality* which makes the quest for it well worth pursuing.

The first biblical clue is that the Garden of Eden spread over the sources of four rivers: the Tigris, the Euphrates, the Gihon, and the Pishon. The first two present no difficulties on a modern map, but it's helpful to note that the Hebrew Hiddekel is the same river as the Tigris. The River Aras was called the Gihon-Aras until relatively recent times. To find the fourth river, a little inter-lingual manipulation is needed. Within the area of the Tigris, Euphrates, and Gihon-Aras there is another river named the Uizun. An old scholar named Walker made an interesting etymological suggestion about this a few years ago.

He argued that in Hebrew pronunciation, the labial *u* became the labial *p* instead. The *z* of Uizun slides into a sibilant *sh* and the final syllable can interchange a *u* and an *o* without difficulty.

There are other possibilities for the Gihon and the Pishon, of course, and these include the theories of Josephus, Eusebius, and Augustine that the Pishon was the Ganges. Jarchi, Gaon, and Nachman argued that it was the Nile because the etymological root meant "to fill" or "to overflow." Chesney's research in Armenia led him to argue that the Pishon is now called the Halys and the Gihon has been renamed the Araxes.

So the geographical problem posed by the identity of the four rivers of Eden may well be solved eventually, but what of the ancient lands which were said to surround it?

After Abel's murder, his fratricidal brother, Cain, went to the east of Eden to an area known as Nod as far as the author of Genesis was concerned. Not far to the east of Eden, where Nod was once said to lie, is the small contemporary settlement of Noqdi. Could the modern village of Noqdi be all that remains of the ancient, biblical Nod?

The great riddles of Eden, however, are theological and philosophical enigmas rather than geographical and historical ones. If the biblical account of creation is *literally* true — despite the enormous weight of scientific evidence which suggests that it is not: and, after all, even evolution's staunchest supporters will readily refer to it as a *theory* — then the philosopher and theologian are left asking *why* God chose to create our universe in the way that He did, and then to populate it with intelligent, observant beings.

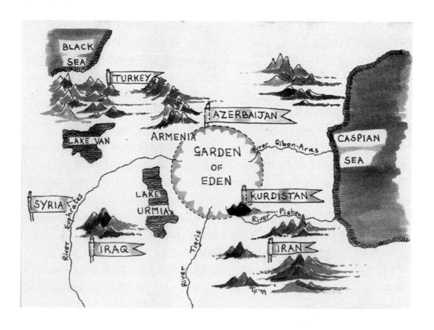

Map of the Garden of Eden. Drawn by Theo Fanthorpe.

The Yahweh of the Old Testament is described by many of its writers as a jealous guardian of his own power and glory: dominant, majestic, aloof, frequently awe-inspiring, and terrifying. Even many centuries later when Christ portrays him as a benign, loving Father, the threat of judgement and condemnation to the everlasting tortures of hell still seems to be there.

The Graeco-Roman pantheon was comprised of gods with human characteristics, separated from us only by their longevity and superior powers. Human suffering could then be explained easily enough by their capriciousness, jealousy, anger, competitiveness, and frequent quarrels. There was no insoluble paradox for the Graeco-Roman theologian when good people suffered. The difficulty of trying to reconcile the existence of a totally benign and loving God, who also enjoyed absolute power, with medieval torture and burning, the unspeakable horrors of the Nazi holocaust, the atrocities in Kosovo, or the fiendish terrorists in Sierra Leone hacking off innocent victims' limbs to impose their reign of terror, could not exist for them. But it is an unavoidable, mind-splitting dilemma which confronts every honest theist who tries to explain the contradiction of God and human suffering.

There is some useful mileage left in the argument which centres on the essential nature of free will. It can readily and universally be accepted that true and spontaneous love is the greatest good and the greatest joy in the whole of human experience. It is equally true that such genuine love cannot exist without real free will. Love cannot be bought. It cannot be compelled. It cannot be commanded. It can only be given and received *freely* by independent minds, hearts, and spirits. Love is like respect: it can be stimulated, earned, and attracted by kindness, gentleness, mercy, and altruism.

Free will can provide the good, rich, fertile soil in which true love grows. It can also be the toxic waste in which unspeakable evil is spawned. Hitler *could* have chosen goodness. Free will allowed him to choose the darkest form of evil instead.

If the free will argument is valid, God could not prevent Hitler's evil without depriving him of his free will.

But what about hindering or preventing the consequences of Hitler's evil choices? Suppose God had allowed Hitler to think and plan his evil, but had then inspired and empowered heroes to thwart his plans and rescue his victims before that evil could be put into effect. Suppose that this pattern had recurred over and over again since the very beginning, since Eden.

But is free will itself diluted or destroyed if the *consequences* of evil choices are neutralized? What if every evil thought is prevented from expressing itself in evil action? Does evil then become an illusion, a hollow sham? Does the would-be murderer look round at the world and say: "There is no point in my shooting, stabbing, strangling, or poisoning my victim because whatever evil I *try* to do will not have any *real* effect. God will simply intervene in some marvellous way: my gun will jam, the shot will miss, my knife will be deflected, my hands will be paralyzed just as they encircle the victim's throat, or the man will develop a sudden mysterious immunity to the cyanide capsule I've just dropped into his whisky glass." If good thoughts and good actions can produce good, solid consequences, while evil thoughts and actions are ineffectual, then there is no true freedom of will. The realities of the consequences of good and evil actions must be equal, if the choice between them is to be a genuine choice. If God is totally benign and totally powerful, there can be no room for equivocation or prevarication. The absoluteness of divine goodness must include absolute honesty. A benign God cannot be a cosmic stage illusionist or a celestial confidence trickster.

There is also the argument of stability and consistency. If everything is arbitrary and uncertain, if cause and effect are not parent and child, then learning is impossible and progress non-existent. If two plus two make three when they feel like it and five when they don't, if gunpowder explodes one day and not another, if arsenic kills today but not tomorrow, if affectionate embraces and a dagger in the heart come arbitrarily from the same unpredictable person, then life is impossible. So dare philosophers and theologians assume that God has made their universe consistent? Humanity can learn and develop only in a consistent environment. We can discover and eventually master the Laws of the Universe only if those Laws remain faithful to themselves and to our powers of observation and objective experiment. If *consistency* is as important as *free will,* have we taken the first faltering steps along the road to a partial solution of the problem of suffering and death in a universe ruled by a caring and omnipotent God? Is this the first tentative answer to the Eden problem?

Obsessively puritanical, fanatical, religious sects have almost invariably connected original sin with sex. Phrases like "forbidden fruit" have been understood by them to refer symbolically to sexual activity — often sex in general, sometimes a specific sexual activity or orientation of which cult members disapprove. The curious and irrational belief that total celibacy or, failing that, varying degrees of sexual abstinence or self-denial, are in some inexplicable way pleasing to a loving, joy-giving and creative God, may also be traced back — at least in part — to this confusion of sex and original sin. It hardly requires the wisdom and courage of Sigmund Freud, or some other pioneering psychoanalyst of his calibre, to suspect with good reason that the most strident advocates of sexual denial and restriction are likely to be those people with the most serious sexual hang-ups and misconceptions. Sex is as good, as natural, and as benign as eating, drinking, breathing, and sleeping. It has its safety parameters, of course, just as they have. The wise man or woman does not knowingly eat or drink anything toxic, nor any food infected with salmonella. Neither is it acceptable to steal a neighbour's food. The sensible man or woman does not breathe contaminated air. But to imagine that God *wants* people to give up eating, drinking, or breathing, or wants them to feel guilty about those good and natural biological activities seems as far from the truth as the east is from the west.

So if the "forbidden fruit" has no sexual connotations at all, what might the author of Genesis mean by it? What exactly *was* the "Tree of the Knowledge of Good and Evil" which stood in the Garden of Eden?

Serious students of morality and ethics come up with a number of tantalizingly different answers. The famous Farmingdon Trust which did outstandingly good work in the field in the late sixties categorized three types of moral character and attitude. The first was the *psychotic*, whom the Farmingdon researchers described as an "emotional moral cripple." According to them, such people were cognitively aware of good and evil, but could distinguish them only in the way that normal people distinguish colour, size, weight, or shape. The psychotic would know that attacking elderly victims with an iron bar and stealing from them was "wrong" or "bad." He or she would know that housing the homeless or feeding the hungry was "right" and "good." The psychotic's problem is that "right" and "wrong" or "good" and "bad" have no more *emotional* meaning for him or her than "left" and "right" or "up" or "down." Such distinctions as the psychotic makes are totally devoid of emotional context.

The second Farmingdon category was the *authoritarian moralist*, the man or woman of the sacred book, the unquestioning followers of the guru, of the official rules and regulations, or of the party manifesto. This attitude goes back to — or even far beyond — the days of the ancient Medes and Persians "whose law altereth not." Authoritarian moralists, despite all their inflexible faults and bureaucratic problems are still morally far ahead of the psychotics. Authoritarians are often deeply emotionally involved with their ethics. Good and evil matter to them. Their central weakness and their main focal problem is their inability to understand that what they regard as the ultimate and infallible source of moral authority can often be *wrong* — sometimes so hopelessly wrong that it disguises good as evil and evil as good. The famous Ten Commandments and the ancillary religious laws of the Old Testament — written on their literal and metaphorical tablets of stone — are the classical example of what typical authoritarians would recognize as an infallible and immutable ethical source. Tragically, in the name of such laws, authoritarians will resolutely and implacably imprison, torture, stone, or burn those who dare to disagree with them — and will then self-righteously convince themselves that the horrendous and inhuman evil which they are perpetrating is *good.* Matthew Hopkins, the Cromwellian Witchfinder General, was just such a man: as were the Witchfinders of Salem.

The third Farmingdon type was referred to as the *autonomous moral thinker.* This is the man or woman who judges every moral situation on its merits, who refuses to jump on any particular ethical bandwagon — however popular, or however traditionally revered — without reserving the inalienable right to jump off again, if, in his or her opinion, the wagon appears to be rolling the wrong way. The autonomous moral thinker takes a *general* attitude of "Is this loving? Is this kind? Is this helpful? Will this give pleasure to someone while hurting no one else? Would I want this for myself?" The autonomous moral thinker takes all that or she regards as best from every guru and from every rule book, while reserving the intellectual right to disagree. For the autonomous moral thinker, the ultimate source of ethical authority is *his or her own judgement* about whether a word or an action is acceptable to a God of love and mercy, whether a thought, word, or deed is kind, supportive, and benign. The autonomous moral thinker has the courage to go it alone, to accept full personal responsibility for his or her decisions. There is no rule book to hide behind. There is no guru to ask. You decide for yourself whether a thing is right or wrong — and then you speak or act accordingly.

So how does the Farmingdon analysis relate to the Tree of the Knowledge of Good and Evil in the Garden of Eden? What moral and ethical approach does that tree represent? What does it symbolize? Did the literal or metaphorical eating of the fruit of that tree take Adam and Eve, as the literal or metaphorical parents of the human race, into a different moral dimension — something beyond a state of young, amoral innocence? Did it mean that after a certain point of development was reached they had to take on the moral responsibility of thinking for themselves — becoming autonomous moral thinkers instead of obeying

20

unquestioningly, conforming unquestioningly? That raises the great philosophical, theological, moral, and metaphysical question about whether simple obedience and unquestioning loyalty are "better" — more moral, more likely to produce inner peace and happiness — than wanting to think for yourself, and make your own independent decisions. If an all-powerful God had wanted obedient robots, androids, or beings incapable of thinking for themselves, it would have been a very simple task to produce them. But if God chose to create free and autonomous beings who could genuinely accept or reject Him because they *wanted* to, who could genuinely choose between good or evil because they understood them, then the tree and its fruit have profoundly deep meanings. Was that first choice the prototype of all truly autonomous choice? Was it the choice of whether to accept the terrible responsibility of having free will and the power to choose?

Who or what was the literal or metaphorical serpent and its fateful role in the Eden drama?

In early Hebrew thought of the kind that must have been familiar to the author of Genesis, the serpent was a subtle, cunning, wily creature — like the fox in western medieval folklore. To what extent was the serpent seen as Satan himself, and to what extent was it thought of as being merely one of his agents or messengers of evil? The talmudic authorities give the evil spirit, or demon, which tempted Eve a name: they call it Sammâel.

An Adder.   A Viper.

The Phoenicians, however, held the serpent in the highest esteem, and the ancient Chinese regarded it as a symbol of superior wisdom and power. Their early artwork depicted the kings of heaven (*tien-hoangs*) as having the bodies of serpents. The Egyptians represented the eternal spirit *Kneph,* whom they regarded as the source of all good, in the form of a serpent. Paradoxically, *Tithrambo,* their god of revenge and punishment was also represented in serpent form, as was *Typhon,* the terrible god of evil and immorality — who also appears in early Greek mythology as the son of Hera.

The serpent was frequently tamed and mummified in ancient Egypt, where it also has a role in the alphabet as a symbol of subtlety, cunning, and sensual pleasure.

An Egyptian serpent, denoting immortality.

The Greeks associated it with Aesculapius and healing, with Ceres, the good provider, and with the swift and benign Hermes or Mercury. On the opposite tack, they also linked it with the evil Furies, and in its Python form as a terrifying monster that only the arrows of the gods could bring down.

It is particularly interesting to note a parallel between the Eden account and the doctrine of Zoroaster, which relates how the evil god Ahriman appeared in the form of a serpent and taught humanity to sin.

In the writings of those researchers who wonder whether the ancient sacred texts like Genesis were partial recollections of extraterrestrial interference in human history, considerable emphasis is placed on the idea of possible rivalry or conflict between two distinct groups of technologically advanced aliens visiting Earth simultaneously. If one such rival group were physically serpentine in form, or, more probably, used a winged serpent as an emblem, information and instructions given to human beings by the *other* group would condemn the serpent as evil. The argument goes on to suggest that genetic engineering by the alien visitors

— rather than a natural, Darwinian, evolutionary process — was responsible for the quantum leap in the development of the human mind and brain. Is it also possible that the record of Eve being created from one of Adam's ribs is a dim memory of a very advanced rapid cloning process?

If the Eden narrative is rewritten in terms of a genetic engineering laboratory, and the "forbidden fruit" is seen as exposure to some form of genetic contamination, then the expulsion of the contaminated breeding pair from their original, idyllic, garden laboratory into the dangerous world outside becomes a logical consequence of the contamination.

If one of their offspring, Cain, then demonstrates part of this hypothetical, genetic foul-up by murdering his brother, Abel, that would also seem to harmonize.

The idea that Eden was some sort of isolated, experimental, bio-engineering reservation run by extraterrestrial, alien technologists, gets around the problem of where the other people came from among whom Cain went on his wanderings. It also goes some way towards offering one possible explanation of the mysterious identity of the "sons of God" who were said to have mated with mortal women in Genesis 6:2, and whose offspring grew up to be "mighty men which were of old, men of renown."

Eden is a garden of mystery in every sense. Some recent DNA research suggests that humanity did perhaps have just two ancestors. Were they God's deliberate, miraculous, and specific creation, as Genesis records, and as several other ancient sacred texts partially reinforce? Were they the work of extraterrestrial genetic engineers, and, if so, *why?* Are they likely to come back to see how their experiment is getting along? Or are we under constant observation already? The Eden narrative leaves vast questions unanswered — especially the problems of whom God was talking to when He said: "Let *us* make man in our own image" (Genesis 1:26); the identity of the "sons of God" and the origin of the people of Nod among whom Cain wandered, and from whom he presumably took his wife, the girl who became Enoch's mother.

It is perfectly possible that the Supreme God of the Universe may have chosen to use his genetic engineers from another planet to create intelligent life on this one, just as it is perfectly possible that he used Darwinian evolution — or a modification of it — as one of his instruments. Neither concept raises the slightest theological difficulty nor does it present any challenge to faith: if anything, it makes God more awesome and powerful than the ancient authors, editors, and translators of Genesis realized.

Chapter Two

The Sons of God

Genesis 6:2 records that the "sons of God" married human girls and produced remarkable, superhuman offspring from them. Who were these sons of God?

One of the mysteries of the Bible concerns the plural *Elohim* which is frequently used instead of the singular *Eloah*, meaning simply *God*. One linguistic theory suggests that the use of the plural — like the royal "We" of the traditional English monarchy — indicates power and majesty. The term *Elohim*, however, is used occasionally in other contexts in the ancient sacred writings. It is occasionally applied to Chemosh, the god of the Moabites, to Astarte the Sidonian goddess of love and fertility, with similar attributes to the lovely Greek goddess Aphrodite, and to powerful, supernatural angelic beings.

In some ancient esoteric belief systems like Gnostic dualism that have survived in vestigial form into our own time, there was a suggestion that these angelic Elohim were powerful, supernatural beings who had control over different regions, or zones, through which an escaping soul had to pass — a celestial version, perhaps, of *The Running Man*. According to these belief systems, it was vitally important to know the names of these Elohim and the spheres which each controlled: no game can be won unless the player knows the rules. The escaping soul could not achieve union with God — the Ultimate Spiritual Reality — unless he, or she, travelled through all these regions.

C. S. Lewis's epoch-making science fiction trilogy contains one story, *Out of the Silent Planet*, in which the angelic planetary regent of Mars — who could easily be construed as one of the Elohim — is functioning correctly as a servant of God and a caring supporter and sustainer of the

Winged deity or angelic figure from Assyrian-Babylonian tradition.

Ancient winged globe symbol.

intelligent Martian life-forms. In Lewis's story, Satan, or Lucifer — who should have occupied a similar positive role for us as God's regent on earth — rebelled and became evil — hence earth was the silent planet of the title, not in communication with the other Elohim and their protectorates. In the old Gnostic texts, the seven Elohim ruling their respective zones included Gabriel, Ariel, and Adonai. To early Gnostic thinkers, matter was *evil*, and in a curiously inverted way they regarded Yahweh (whom they also called the Demiurge) as evil simply because he had created matter. This idea of matter itself — and the many good and wholesome pleasures which it brings — being *evil*, seems to belong on the same garbage heap as the morbid, anti-pleasure, pseudo-religious concepts of the grimmest puritan fanatics.

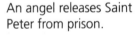

An angel releases Saint Peter from prison.

Ancient winged figure.

Manichaeism may also have a little light to shed on these mysterious superbeings known variously as angels or sons of God. Mani, its founder, was an Iranian prophet who lived and worked in the third century A.D. In his mind, the cosmos was split into two spheres. Light was good and darkness was evil. In the material world, he said, these two had become entwined together and the path to salvation consisted of untangling them. Once the believer had succeeded in separating them, absolute goodness — and presumably absolute happiness — could be achieved. Mani taught that the Great Father was served by twelve diadems of light known as the Aeons. They were the firstborn, and in groups of three they eternally surround and serve the Great Father, the Supreme Being.

According to Manichaean theology, the Prince of Darkness, the Devil, seeks to conquer the Kingdom of Light. The resulting and continually ongoing battle mixes good and evil, light and darkness, in our world of matter. Human beings — like the Ugly Duckling in the Hans Christian Anderson story — are unaware of their true nature as creatures of light and spirit, and are continually tempted and led astray by the Prince of Darkness and his demons. Fortunately, the evil done by the minions of darkness is counteracted by the benign and powerful Friends of the Light: a great Living Spirit and his five assistants named the Holder of Splendour, the King of Honour, the Light of Man, the King of Glory, and the Supporter.

The mystical and esoteric strands of Judaism can be traced back to the first century A.D., but it was only after the twelfth century that what might be termed proper esoterism really emerged as a distinct school of mystical Jewish thought. Following the nation's return from the Babylonian Exile during the sixth century B.C., there was massive speculation about the cosmic role of supernatural beings of extraordinary power who filled the strange realm between God and humanity. Both angelology and its opposite sphere of study, demonology, became subjects of great interest to mystical scholars. Angelologists speculated about the nature and powers of the angelic hierarchy, and one particularly powerful benign being known as Metatron was also called Little Adonai, meaning Little Lord, or Little God.

It is necessary to address the question as to whether the mysterious *sons of God* of Genesis 6:2, who sired children on human wives, were the same *type* of beings who are also referred to as angels. Their ability to enjoy sexual relationships with human beings suggests that the mysterious, superhuman species described as sons of God enjoyed a substantial level of material physicality which is not normally associated with traditional angels. This can be considered alongside the basic physical strength and agility of the angel who wrestled with Jacob in Genesis 32:25 "and prevailed not"; does the record here suggest that the purely human Jacob was a match for the superbeing? Jacob's antagonist ends the bout by resorting either to some type of martial arts move to which Jacob knew no counter, to some esoteric power or, perhaps, to technology. By one means or another, it appears that Jacob's hip was dislocated or severely sprained by his strange opponent. There are anecdotal rumours today of mysterious, highly advanced martial artists

Guardian angels.

Angelic figures.

— practising mainly in Asia and the Far East — who can concentrate the whole of their dynamic *ky-ai* power into one finger and so render catastrophic damage to an opponent at a single touch. Was Jacob's wrestling angel a being who possessed that extreme kind of *ky-ai*? Some traditional religious researchers into Jacob's wrestling episode might prefer to suggest that the whole contest was a psychic or spiritual one, not to be taken literally. It is also interesting to speculate that the Hebrew word Jabbok, or Yabbok, suggests that the name of the waterway near Penuel where the incident occurred actually implies the idea of wrestling.

Another line of argument which can be put forward for the existence of angels, Elohim, sons of God, or whatever title we choose to give to such real or imaginary semi-divine beings — and even for hierarchies of demonic beings — is similar to the argument which suggests that extraterrestrial life forms must exist simply because the universe is so enormous and our planet Earth so small. The universe is, in fact, so incalculably vast that the probability of our being the *only* intelligent life form within it is tantamount to zero.

If we apply a similar argument to the vast range of organisms inhabiting the biosphere of this minute planet, we can begin with viruses and bacteria and ascend to dolphins, whales, and anthropoid apes who score only marginally below Homo sapiens in IQ tests. There seems to be a steady continuum of ability rather than a series of discrete steps. Why, then, should there be such a huge gulf between Homo sapiens and Almighty God the Creator? The gulf is immense: infinitely greater than

Angel releasing Peter — second version.

the gulf between humanity and the jellyfish. If there is a gently sloping ability continuum from the amoeba to the aardvark, and from the aardvark to the anthropoid apes and us, why doesn't such a continuum extend from us to God? Who lives in the cosmic chasm? Angels, Elohim, djinn, elementals, or even, perhaps, some of the demons? Both demonologists and angelologists would undoubtedly like us believe that this strange gulf is densely populated — just as the medieval schoolmen delighted to argue about the number of angels who could dance theoretically on the head of a pin.

If we can go along with the *"if-there's-a-gap-there-must-be-something-in-it"* argument, then what type of beings are these celestial Elohim, angels, or sons of God likely to be? What is their nature? What is their purpose? How does their existence affect ours? What sort of communication can we hope to have with them?

If they are primarily beings of spirit, or pure, disembodied intellect, references to their activities suggest that they seem to have the power to assume additional physical attributes as and when required. There are close parallels here between the attributes of the biblical angelic beings and the powers ascribed to the pantheon of Greek and Roman deities, who could, in the stories, become indistinguishably and hedonistically human when it suited them.

It also seems highly likely that they enjoy the same degree of free will as human beings can exercise — perhaps rather more. The biblical allusions to "war in Heaven" and "fallen angels" points to their ability to choose between loyal obedience to God or selfish rebellion against the Divine Goodness. When we think what horrendous evil a mere psychotic human tyrant can unleash here on earth, the potential consequences of an angelic being turning away from God's goodness are almost unthinkably appalling. And what if there is a complete hierarchy of such malevolent demons and "fallen angels"?

From all the visions, dreams, and biblical accounts of the appearances and activities of angels and demons, the strong possibility of their existence needs to be taken seriously — yet, like all unexplained phenomena, the possibility of their existence also needs to be examined cautiously. We are never so helpless, nor more in danger, than when we believe in something passionately and uncritically. Religious fanaticism is an addictive opiate from which reason rarely breaks free. The human mind can be an excellent safety filter when its objective, analytical powers are harnessed to a resolute, rational will and used properly; when allowed to jump freely to conclusions, it tends to land in the emotional equivalent of an intellectual sewage pit.

According to the Gospel accounts, Christ accepted the existence of both angels and demons. He gives us the clear impression that He knew what He was talking about.

Chapter Three

The Patriarchs

Following on from the references to Adam and Eve's immediate descendants as recorded in the Genesis story of Eden and continuing after their expulsion from the Garden, one of the great mysteries is the abnormal longevity attributed to these antediluvians.

There are two distinct lines of patriarchs in the Genesis account: Seth's line continues through Enos, Cainan, Mahaleel, Jared, Enoch, Methuselah, Lamech and Noah. Cain's semi-parallel line includes Enoch, Irad, Mehujael, Methusael, Lamech and the sons of Lamech — Jabal, Jubal and Tubal-Cain. The members of this second patriarchal line are credited with pioneering mechanical and technical skills, building cities, and organizing society.

In Enoch and Noah, they undoubtedly showed examples of high morality and religious ethics — but in general the Bible account criticizes them. Their biblical redactor traces their failure to the mysterious intermarriages between the "sons of God" and the "daughters of men" in Genesis 6:1–4, which have already been referred to briefly. But it is interesting to note that "daughters of men" is rendered much more precisely as "daughters of *Adam*" in the early Hebrew versions.

In some research quarters, this detail has given rise to daringly imaginative speculations about Adam and Eve being the work of extraterrestrial genetic engineers, who wished to keep their experimental breeding lines separate. As a consequence of the lines being united, this theory continues, the controllers of the experiment had their worst fears realized. The hybrid humanoids expelled from the sterile Eden complex soon developed severe behavioural problems.

This, of course, seems to contradict much contemporary scientific study of human gene pools. Such evidence as there is suggests that inbreeding like that between the Egyptian Pharaohs and their sisters tended to cause certain genetic weaknesses, whereas the introduction of new blood gave fresh strength. Certainly, it is clear from the Genesis account that the result of the union between "Adam's daughters" and the "sons of God" produced outstandingly powerful and physically courageous children: the "mighty men of valour" of the Genesis account who performed outstanding deeds. Mental images of mythical warrior-heroes from the golden age — like Conan the Barbarian and Deathstalker fit snugly into this context.

Whatever their alleged moral and ethical failures, these antediluvian patriarchs and their contemporaries seem to have enjoyed remarkable longevity. At the age of 365, Enoch *seems* to have ended his earthly life prematurely by the standards of that semi-legendary epoch — but then, there is much about Enoch himself which is a signpost to several intriguing mysteries of a different kind. As with Elijah and Melchizedek, for example, it is reported that Enoch *did not die*.

Essential clarification of the biblical nomenclature reveals *two* patriarchs named Enoch. The first (also spelled Henoch on one occasion — meaning *dedication* in Hebrew) is listed as Cain's eldest son. The city he built was named after him, and pioneering scholars like Ewald have tentatively identified it as the Phrygian city of Iconium. Certainly there is an Iconian legend of a co-founder named *Annakos* in Greek, which is etymologically close to the biblical name *Enoch*. Claims have also been made for a settlement called *Anuchta* in ancient Susiana, as well as the Caucasian city of *Heniochi*.

The second Enoch, the more famous and mysterious one, is listed in the patriarchal chronologies as the son of Jared and the father of Methuselah — longest lived of all the mysterious and shadowy antediluvian patriarchs. This second version of the name means *descent* in Hebrew.

Ancient sheep of a breed that would have been familiar to the earliest patriarchs.

In the Epistle of Jude, Enoch is described as the seventh from Adam. This seven may simply be one of the popular "magical numbers" or "mystical numbers" which appear from time to time in the scriptural records: the seventh day was traditionally a symbol of divine completion and a time of sacred rest.

The remarkable early Christian Bishop and commentator, Irenaeus, seems to have regarded the mysterious, deathless patriarchal Enoch as a type of perfect humanity. Irenaeus writes of him: "a man pleasing to God who raised him to Heaven, while angels fell to earth by transgression. "

Irenaeus himself is worth a brief digression. His parents were Greek, and he was born at some time between A.D. 120 and 140 in Asia Minor. Either as a child or a very young man, Irenaeus met the great martyr Polycarp, who died in A.D. 155, and had in his youth enjoyed a direct link with the apostle John himself. Irenaeus became bishop of Lugdunum after Pothinus (the previous bishop) was martyred.

Irenaeus was a constant opponent of the Gnostics, whom he regarded as heretics. In the sense that Polycarp knew John who had been a leading disciple of Jesus, and Irenaeus knew Polycarp, it could be said that there were only three metaphorical "generations" between Irenaeus and Christ.

Irenaeus and Clement of Alexandria were leading opponents of Gnosticism in the second century, but Irenaeus had a fair mind as well as a keen one. In refuting Gnosticism, he described it clearly prior to attacking it. Consequently, when the ancient Nag' Hammadi Gnostic library was discovered in Egypt during the 1940s, it soon became evident that Irenaeus's comments on Gnosticism were accurate and fair — despite his dislike of Gnostic beliefs.

It was partially Irenaeus's determination to defeat Gnosticism, that led him to work for the establishment of a set creed and a canon of scripture — one that would exclude all the Gnostic writings which were so popular and well-known among his contemporaries.

Fair and honest even to what he regarded as the spurious arguments of his most bitter opponents, Irenaeus's views on Enoch, the Patriarch of Mystery, deserve consideration.

Enoch's 365 years may have numerical significance as well. Ewald suggested that he might have been some sort of "god of the New Year." Certainly, ancient traditions regarded him as a pioneer astrologer and astronomer — possibly one whose teachings formed the basis of that esoteric Chaldean sky-knowledge which led the Magi to Bethlehem millennia after Enoch's time. Eusebius and Eupolemus are involved with passing references to Enoch, and refer to his being identified with the giant Atlas. Josephus wrote that Enoch "departed to the Deity."

However, after the birth of Enoch's son, Methuselah, the Genesis account says simply that Enoch "walked with God ... and he was not; *for God took him.*" What precisely do those very mysterious words *mean*?

Both the early Greek and Latin church fathers derived doctrines of bodily resurrection from the biblical accounts of the deathless states of Enoch and Elijah. The Gospel account of the experiences of Peter, James, and John while they were with Jesus on the Mount of Transfiguration attests to the presence of Moses and Elijah centuries after they had left this earth.

The book bearing Enoch's name is almost as mysterious as its alleged author's life. The majority of published scholarly opinion seems to be on the side of the *Book of Enoch,* otherwise known as *I Enoch,* having been written only a century or two before the birth of Christ, during the period when the Dead Sea Sect at Qumran was flourishing. This would put the book several millennia after the historical lifetime of Enoch the patriarch. Aramaic fragments of the *Book of Enoch* were discovered among the Dead Sea Scrolls, substantial extracts of its start and finish were found in Greek versions, and one entire copy was saved in Ethiopian — a copy which seems to have been translated from Greek. Hebrew portions of the *Book of Noah* were also found among the Dead Sea Scrolls, and several scholars acknowledge that this work was either the source of the *Book of Enoch* or a parallel version of its main theme and message. As well as the material in the *Noah* volume there are five major sections in *Enoch.* The first one centres on the downfall of the vulnerable angels in antediluvian times, and concentrates on Enoch's journeys to celestial destinations where he learned many strange wonders and divine secrets.

Patriarchal herdsmen with their flocks.

The most significant aspects of *Enoch's* second section are the three profound parables dealing with the end of the world, and especially his intriguing references to "The Son of man" – a title which Jesus used during his earthly ministry. In *Enoch,* this Son of man title undoubtedly refers to the Messiah, the Great Leader appointed by God, whom the Jews hoped was coming to deliver them. There are some curious passages in Chapters 70 and 71 (which look suspiciously like later additions) in which Enoch, the mysterious deathless patriarch, is identified with the messianic Son of man.

In the third section, the angel Uriel shows Enoch many astronomical mysteries, which read like a truncated list of the wider range of wonders contained in *The Book of the Heavenly Luminaries.*

The fourth section reveals Enoch to the reader as both prophet and seer. After an introductory passage about the flood, this section launches out into a discourse often referred to as *The Vision of the Seventy Shepherds.* Like Aesop, the author of the *Book of Enoch* describes characters by using animal symbols. The gifted Victorian religious writer, George MacDonald, had a character named Curdie in several of his children's books. This young hero was given the gift of being able to feel the animal shape which denoted the person's character when he shook hands with a stranger. For example, a loyal and faithful person would have a hand that felt like a warm and friendly dog's paw. A potentially dangerous enemy would feel like a snake slithering through Curdie's fingers. This kind of animal symbolism runs right through the fourth part of *Enoch.*

The fifth and final section resembles a greatly expanded version of the speech which Shakespeare put into the mouth of Polonius in *Hamlet.* At its best, this section of *Enoch* comes close to Christ's moral teachings in the Beatitudes, or Sermon on the Mount. Enoch's work here has a high moral and social content, and although he was in partial agreement with some of the teachings of the Qumran Sect, he veered away from them significantly over the doctrine of predestination: they were for it — the writer of *Enoch* was against it.

Another curious feature of *The Book of Enoch* is the *Apocalypse of Weeks.* The main purpose of this remarkable little interpolation — which, oddly enough, may actually have been the work of the main writer — was to divide the history of the world into ten metaphorical periods which he called "Weeks." Seven of these had already gone at the time when he was writing: three were yet to come.

At first sight, this book — apparently written a mere two centuries before the start of the Christian era — cannot have any connection with

Enoch the mysterious patriarch who spent 365 years on earth and then went directly to be with God without first undergoing the formality of human death. But what if the wildest and least probable hypotheses are *true*? What if Enoch the patriarch *was* taken by God into a timeless, dimensionless, arcane paradise, and returned from there after several millennia of human time to write his strange books? What if his longevity greatly *exceeded* that of the other patriarchs? What if the greatest enigma of the sect who used the secret caves of Qumran *was Enoch himself* — an incredibly ancient, holy hermit, toiling away at the sacred volumes that bear his name?

Once more the challenging mystery of patriarchal longevity presents itself. If it *was* real, how did they manage it? Modern medical science suggests three tentative explanations: it was genetic; it was cultural — the result of a totally benign diet and a pollution free environment; or it was sheer will-power and pure *faith* — an indomitable, psychological refusal to succumb to the ageing process. We are only now in the twenty-first century beginning to paddle in the shallowest margins of that infinite cosmic ocean of what human mental power — genuine mind-over-matter — can hope to achieve. It is possible, of course, that any two of the three suggestions are true and in tandem. Perhaps all three may be involved.

Consider the genetic possibilities first. If Eden *was* an extraterrestrial genetic engineering complex, would not the project leaders have been interested in discovering a longevity gene? Is that what the "Tree of *Life*" symbolized? If one set of genes conferred higher cognitive abilities — symbolized by the forbidden "Tree of the *Knowledge* of Good and Evil" — did another set confer extreme longevity? Was Enoch testing out as a very successful longevity specimen, and as such was he removed from the Eden complex to test his new abilities in deep space, or on another habitable planet?

It also has to be remembered in this context that Enoch's *son* was that same Methuselah whose name has since become something of a byword for longevity. Was it not only Enoch but his *son as well* who were tested — to see how successfully the longevity gene had been passed on? Did the genetic engineers need to carry out further tests on Methuselah to find out if the longevity gene was easily and naturally transmissible before they could regard their Eden experiment as a total success and fly home again?

Had those hypothetical Eden managers set up their genetic engineering complex because they were vaguely humanoid themselves?

Could the phrase "*in our own image*" imply that the Eden managers *were* anthropoids? Was the whole basic idea behind the Eden scheme to discover which genes would increase intelligence and longevity, to test the terrestrial specimens thoroughly, and then for the complex managers to use the proven genes themselves?

Seen in this light Noah's universal flood provides a sinister nerve-tingling corollary. If Eden *was* a genetic engineering complex and something very undesirable *had* got out and run amok across the face of the earth, did the alien controllers deem it necessary to wipe out that undesirable and potentially highly dangerous modified humanoid strain? Were Noah and his family free from the genetic problem? Is that why they and they alone were preserved in the ark while the catastrophic floodwaters destroyed almost everyone else?

The genetic engineering theory also sheds an entirely new light on Cain's mysterious mark — was he let loose only after being carefully tagged first?

Consider, too, the relevance of the angelic being referred to as Uriel in this context — and the weird *celestial journey* on which he acted as Enoch's guide. Is it possible that when Enoch was taken on the fascinating trip which he described in his book, he really did make those epic journeys — but by spacecraft rather than by direct Divine intervention?

Which raises the vexed theological problem of: "If Eden was created by extraterrestrial genetic engineers, does God the Creator exist?"

There's no real problem there. The engineers merely become intermediaries. The universe is so vast and almost certainly so full of habitable planets that on statistical grounds alone it must contain many intelligent races easily capable of reaching Earth and being the Eden engineers. God is the Universal God. He is by no means confined to this insignificantly tiny planet in the way that we terrestrial humanoids are — *albeit just for the moment.* We can scarcely begin to guess what his other inter-stellar and intergalactic "children" look like — or what they can accomplish and achieve. But there is no need at all for cautious, traditional theologians to be distressed by our aliens' highly probable existence. The idea of aliens in Eden poses no threat to the truth of God's primal, creative initiative: they merely widen our intellectual horizons, increase our sense of awe, and enable us to wonder at the power of the Maker of Makers. Their hypothetical existence also goes some way towards providing an explanation for events like Noah's Flood which are not otherwise reconcilable with a God of love and compassion. The Eden engineers were not necessarily compassionate or loving — perhaps they were just scientists like us exercising their free will and their supposed right to do what they wanted with primitive laboratory animals. Their moral justification to themselves would have been vast advances in intelligence and longevity for their people — provided that their Eden experiment worked satisfactorily.

If it wasn't genetics, was it an ideal environment, free of all pollution? Possible, of course: medical statistics show that other things being equal clean air and pure water are great reinforcers of longevity, but could they reinforce it enough to reach the enormous life spans that the patriarchs enjoyed? Faintly possible, perhaps, but it hardly seems likely.

Then what of mind over matter? Here another possible solution may lie: the human mind is undoubtedly capable of far more than we normally give it credit for. Christ himself said that faith could move mountains — if only we knew how to use that mysterious faith capacity at its optimum level.

Living life to the full, tackling every day as a fresh opportunity to do something good, something worthwhile and exciting, while keeping the mind eternally young and optimistic, are all very useful and effective defences against the ageing process. *Refusing* to slow down, *denying* the crippling lie that you are not every bit as good in mind and body as you were yesterday, or last week ... or last year ... are powerful counter-attacks against ageing. But it has to be a very strong mind indeed that can prolong the fight for centuries.

The mystery of the great longevity of the biblical patriarchs remains largely unsolved: theories abound, but definitive solutions still remain elusive.

Chapter Four

What is Phrophecy?

Prophecy differs significantly from precognition in that the prophet believes himself, or herself, to be the messenger or mouthpiece of a god, a demon, or some other powerful form of supernatural entity. Prophecy, as distinct from precognition, characteristically contains an ethical element: usually a warning of some description — *unless A, then B....*

In the story of Jonah, for example, the reluctant prophet was told to go to Nineveh, confront the Ninevites with their sins, and prophesy the doom that was about to descend upon them as a result of their unacceptable behaviour. The story goes on to say that because Jonah was convinced that they would not listen to him, he promptly boarded a ship going in the opposite direction. After his encounter with the gargantuan fish, however, Jonah changed his mind and went to Nineveh as instructed. To his great surprise the citizens listened to him and repented.

As a result of their repentance, the doom which had been threatened in Jonah's prophecy was averted. The story goes on to relate that instead of rejoicing in the lives which his preaching had saved, Jonah was angry because God had *not* wiped out the Ninevites as the original prophecy had threatened. Mere precognition would simply have shown the destruction of the city as a future event: Jonah's prophetic preaching was both ethical and conditional.

If prophecy and precognition are simply glimpses of one inevitable future, they raise insurmountable metaphysical questions about the relationship of cause and effect. They also destroy the concept of human autonomy and free will. Morality and ethics slide out of the frame altogether. Surely, there has to be another explanation?

The biblical evidence seems paradoxical at best, and sometimes downright contradictory. When Kish's young son, Saul, went to consult the prophet Samuel about some lost asses belonging to his father, Samuel anointed the boy as the first king of Israel. Samuel also told him — apparently using some sort of preternatural vision — that the lost asses had already been found. This relatively trivial piece of psychic information about the missing animals comes into the category of mere precognition; anointing young Saul as king, however, could be classified as a form of *real prophecy* — something vitally important for the future constitution of the nation of Israel, and something which would turn out to have strong ethical connections. Saul's later failures were seen essentially by the author of the Books of Samuel as *moral* failures, failures to obey God's commands as interpreted and relayed by the prophet.

A similar example of precognition *and* prophecy occurring in close proximity is found in Christ's meeting with Nathanael. In the Gospel account (John 1:43–51) when, through Philip's prompting, the prospective disciple first meets Jesus, he salutes Nathanael as "an Israelite ... in whom [there] is no guile." Nathanael asks how Jesus can possibly know this, to which Christ replies: " Before ... Philip called thee ... I saw thee under the fig tree." This relatively basic, paranormal knowledge of Nathanael's previous whereabouts is enough to convince him of Christ's power and divine status. From this simple precognition, however, Jesus proceeds to tell Nathanael that he will witness far greater, *spiritual* things — including the ascent and descent of angels in Christ's presence. This latter statement is considerably more powerful than simple precognition: this is *prophecy* with its essential ethical and moral ingredients.

There is also Christ's clear identification of Judas Iscariot — one of the Twelve — as the man who will betray him. This identification again raises the vast underlying question of prophecy and predestination. How far — to what *extent* — was Judas *cast* in this role? Did he not have a choice? Did the inevitability lie in the weakness and temptation of such a man in such a situation, rather than in the removal of the man's will power and freedom of choice? The compulsive gambler in Las Vegas? The alcoholic in a well-stocked bar? The gambler and the alcoholic *could* both find the strength to say to say "No" *if they really wanted to.* Choice is the inalienable right of the strong.

Judas's behaviour towards Christ is in itself one of the deepest mysteries of the Bible — just as Rahab's behaviour was at Jericho.

Some biblical scholars and historians have attempted to explain the problem by suggesting that Judas's surname "Iscariot" was a corruption of

"Icarius," a nickname meaning "the man with the knife." They surmise that if Judas had been a Zealot, a patriotic Jewish extremist who was prepared to try to drive out the occupying Romans by terrorism if necessary, then a nickname such as "Judas the Knife" would have been appropriate for him. If he had joined Jesus in the hope that Christ was going to be the militaristic Messiah the Zealots were hoping for, he might well have grown impatient with his master's refusal to lead an armed revolt against Rome and re-establish an independent Jewish state, as the indomitable Maccabees had done. According to this Zealot theory, it was Judas's impatience rather than his treachery which led him to try to force the pace. Did he argue within himself that if Jesus was arrested and threatened with death, he would be forced to use his divine powers to bring the Romans down? Does that explain the meaning of Judas's subsequent suicide? Did he realize *too late* that Christ's Messiahship was a Messiahship of peace and love, not of hatred and war? A mere traitor betraying his leader for money, would scarcely have felt driven to suicide over what he had done, as Judas was.

The great prophets of the Old Testament had far more morality and ethics in their messages than simple foretellings of the future. Amos denounced evil and injustice in all its forms, but his prophecies of doom on the offenders all had strong moral connections.

Amos was a simple herdsman from the mountain village of Tekoa. He was a tough, outdoor man, to whom what he regarded as the vice and luxury of the idle rich was total anathema. His first chapter begins with a powerful denunciation of Syria and Damascus. Their palaces will be destroyed, and their people will be led away into captivity. Amos gives *an ethical reason* for the forthcoming doom of Damascus: their people had

Architecture from the ancient city of Nineveh where Jonah the prophet was sent to preach.

43

transgressed in treating the Gileadites with brutal savagery. Amos goes on to prophesy doom and disaster for the cities of Gaza, Ashdod, Ashkelon, and Ekron. He foretells doom for the Philistines, and the inhabitants of Tyre because of what they have done to the people of Edom.

Finally, the ferocious herdsman-prophet turns his attention to the Israelites themselves. They will suffer similar disasters because they have turned away from God's laws. In Amos's own inimitable prose: "They have sold the righteous for silver, and the poor for a pair of shoes." The morality and social responsibility of prophecy is nowhere expressed more clearly than in the Book of Amos. Because of the people's failure to show compassion to the poor and needy, the prophet predicts the destruction of their holy places, and their luxurious ivory palaces. They themselves will be "led away with fish-hooks." According to some ancient inscriptions, at a time when iron was too rare and expensive to be wasted on chains, the Assyrians economized by running fish-hooks through their prisoners' flesh and leading them away with cords attached to the hooks.

The moral element of this awesome ethical prophecy is clarified in Amos 5:14: "Seek good, and not evil, that ye may live: and so the Lord, the God of hosts, shall be with you."

Just as with Jonah's visit to Nineveh, Amos declares that the peril which has been prophesied for Israel and Judah *can* be averted — if only the people will behave ethically towards those in need.

Ancient ship of the type on which the prophet Jonah would have sailed.

In Chapter 8:5, Amos thunders against dishonest trading practices. He has seen unscrupulous corn merchants "making the ephah small and the shekel great, and falsifying the balances by deceit." The *ephah* was the measure: the *shekel* was the price. As a result of this dishonesty, declares the prophet, God will "cause the sun to go down at noon." There will be great sadness, and a terrible famine. Yet at the end of all these tribulations, there is fresh hope, says Amos. In Chapter 9:14, he writes: "They shall build the waste cities, and inhabit them; and they shall plant vineyards, and drink the wine thereof; and they shall also make gardens, and eat the fruit of them."

It is highly probable that Amos's personal background and life style as a rugged and hardworking herdsman, and a gatherer of semi-wild sycamore figs, gave him his clear perspective on social responsibility, and his puritanical hatred of luxury.

Sycamore figs of the type which were gathered by the prophet Amos.

Just as Amos was the outstanding prophet of social justice, so Hosea, by virtue of his very different life experiences is generally regarded as the prophet of love and forgiveness. Just as Amos forged the grim hardships of his life experience as a tough mountain herdsman into his detestation of urban greed, injustice and luxury at the expense of the poor, so Hosea took the tragedy of his marriage to Gomer and turned it into a parable of God's relationship with Israel.

The early part of the Book of Hosea tells how he felt compelled to marry Gomer, how she had numerous adulterous affairs, and conceived various children who were not his. When her numerous lovers no longer found her sufficiently attractive, she ended up in the slave market — where Hosea found her, bought her back, and took her home again. From these experiences he produced a set of prophecies which in his mind paralleled God's relationship with an unfaithful and religiously adulterous nation. Just as Gomer had been tempted away by rich lovers, so, in Hosea's eyes, Israel had been tempted away from her original God by Baal and other pagan idols.

Once again, as with Amos, the prophecy of Hosea has a distinctly conditional ethical tone. If Israel and Judah give up their "adulterous" relationships with the other gods, then Yahweh, the One True God, will take them back just as Hosea, his prophet, has redeemed Gomer from the slave market and taken her safely home again. The quintessential heart of Hosea's message is to be found in Chapter 6:6: "For I desired mercy, and not sacrifice; and the knowledge of God more than burnt offerings."

It is, in principle, the same vital moral message that James encapsulated in Chapter 1:27, of his Epistle in the New Testament: "Pure religion and undefiled before God and the Father is this, to visit the fatherless and the widows in their affliction, and to keep himself unspotted from the world."

New Testament James can be regarded as yet another important moral writer in the broad prophetic tradition of Old Testament Amos and Hosea. The core of his message is virtually the same as theirs: true religion is kindness and mercy — it has very little connection with ceremony, liturgy, and ritual. It is essentially active and pronomian, not antinomian.

If most of the richest biblical prophecy is more concerned with morality and ethics than with foretelling future events, where does futurological biblical prophecy come in? There are numerous rather strange apocalyptic passages — largely to be found in books like Daniel and Revelation — and these are examined in detail in later chapters. There are also the mysteries of prophetic revelations in visions or dreams, such as those of Pharaoh's butler and baker, and of Pharaoh himself in the time of Joseph.

The mysteries of Urim and Thummim as a means of foretelling the future are also dealt with in detail in their own chapter. What were these mysterious devices which the High Priest used primarily in order to ascertain the will of God, or to find answers to such questions as which way the army should move against the enemy, and when? They, too, in a sense, were instruments of prophecy, just as the living, breathing, human prophets were. Lots were also drawn to decide similar questions.

Prophecy and prognostication, whether derived from human sources, or from instruments and artefacts, are undoubtedly among the most intriguing of all biblical mysteries.

Chapter Five

The Tower of Babel

Genesis 11: 1–9, gives the biblical account of the Tower of Babel. At the heart of the story is one of the many quaint and colourful, aetiological or explanatory myths which purport to give reasons for various natural phenomena: thunder is the laughter of the gods — or their game of celestial skittles; the rainbow appeared after the flood as God's promise that the earth would never again be destroyed by water; the robin has red feathers on its breast because it attempted to take out the crucifixion nails to end Christ's suffering.

The story of the Tower of Babel begins with the assertion that there was only one universal language in the beginning. In the course of their wanderings from the east "*they*" (an intriguing use of the plural pronoun, which the author of this section of Genesis may well have intended to include all of Adam and Eve's descendants, via Noah and the survivors of the Flood) arrived at the Plain of Shinar. It was a pleasant enough spot, and they elected to stay for a while. It was then decided that it would be a good idea to build a permanent city there, and accordingly they set to work. The Genesis account says that they used brick for stone and "slime" for mortar. There is general agreement among scholars specializing in the period that the word translated "slime" here probably refers to pitch or bitumen.

The Tower of Babel does not provide an explanation for the origins of language but for the differentiation of language. The origins of language do not seem to have concerned the authors, compilers, and redactors of Genesis. It seems probable that the writer's natural assumption was that language had been built into Adam and Eve along with their basic understanding of themselves and their environment.

Palaeolinguistic studies seem to suggest that language and thought patterns evolved in mutually reinforcing roles — like acrobats who raise themselves on piles of wooden blocks by adding a block at a time to each pile on which their hands balance alternately.

Hunting, especially with primitive flint weapons, was likely to prove most successful when groups of hunters co-operated. Co-operation — unless we consider the theory that our earliest ancestors were telepathic — was almost certainly improved by language. The earliest aural signals may have conveyed basic, but vital, hunting messages such as: "Go forward. Go back. Move towards me. Move away from me. Keep still and silent. It's coming towards you."

The technique of a skilled shepherd controlling his dogs with simple sounds, elementary proto-words, or whistle signals could be similar to the proto-words with which Palaeolithic hunting parties co-ordinated their movements.

The authors and editors of Genesis probably felt that they had to try to provide an explanation for the apparent anomaly: if all persons were descended from Adam and Eve, why did Babylonians, Israelites, and Canaanites speak different languages?

There is an interesting and mysterious connection between the Babel story and the apostles speaking in tongues. On the day of Pentecost, all those to whom the apostles preached heard the words in their own language — yet the apostles were Galileans. Some analysts of this

Ruins on the site of ancient Nineveh. Was the Tower of Babel once in this area?

"speaking-with-tongues" phenomenon have wondered whether the apostles were using Koine Greek — a simplified version, which resembles classical Greek in much the same way that pidgin resembles standard English, and which was widely used and understood throughout the Roman Empire.

Psycholinguistics experts have investigated numerous cases of glossolalia, a state in which a subject with no conscious knowledge or recollection of another language can apparently speak it fluently. In the most interesting reports of glossolalia, some subjects have been able to *speak* their mysterious unknown language but have not known the *meaning* of the words they were saying. At other times subjects appear to have been able to understand the *meaning*, but have not been able to *reply* in the strange language.

The precise nature of the neurological and physiological processes involved in speaking and understanding a given set of audible signals (or visual symbols in the case of a written language) is complex and controversial. Most linguistic scientists would probably agree that the process is basically an associative one: a distinct, discrete sound, or sound pattern, becomes associated with an object (noun) or an activity (verb). If different human groups evolved at different sites at different times, their chosen sound patterns for denoting different actions and different objects would in all probability be totally arbitrary, with the exception of certain onomatopoeia.

If, however, the Eden origins of Homo sapiens are to be taken literally and historically, then a single "language of Eden" would be the logical sequel.

Investigation seems to suggest, rather tantalizingly, however, that the oldest roots of modern languages *do* tend to converge in the remote past. DNA investigations have also indicated the possibility of a common ancestor — maybe from the vicinity of the Olduvai Gorge.

The word Babel seems to have been derived from an ancient Hebrew root meaning "to confound" or "to confuse" and would seem to refer to the story of the tower which was never completed because its builders lost the power to understand one another's languages.

It has been suggested that slaves taken by the Babylonians to carry out their grandiose building projects were dependent upon interpreters among the Babylonian overseers. If a slaves' rebellion, or an outbreak of plague, led to the deaths of these interpreters, almost total confusion would have ensued, leading to probable abandonment of the site.

The Babylonians themselves referred to their city as Bab-ili, Babila, or Babilam, meaning "the gate of God." It was also known as Babilani "the gate of the gods." The ancient Akkadians called it Ka-dingira, which also meant "the gate of god" as well as Tin-tir "the seat of life." Its other titles included E or E-ki, meaning "house" or "hollow place." Yet another ancient title was Su-anna, meaning "the city with the high defence." The mysterious "they" of Genesis 2:2–9 may refer solely to the Cushites, followers of Nimrod, the much acclaimed "mighty hunter" of Chapter 10, listed in the ancient genealogies as the great-grandson of Noah through Ham's line. They seem to have referred to themselves as the people of Kingi-Ura, and are known in some scholarly circles as the Sumero-Akkadians. It is likely that they migrated to Shinar from some original location in the north-east of Mesopotamia.

Their building materials were mainly bricks and bitumen, and their earliest city layout seems to have been a relatively basic collection of dwellings scattered around a central temple-tower which they called the Zikkuratu.

Artist's impression of the Tower of Babel. Drawn by Theo Fanthorpe.

Part of the mystery of the city of Babel and its vast tower is its great age. It is mentioned before Erech, Akkad, and Calneh in the account in Genesis 10, and almost certainly predates them by many centuries. The Greek historians of Alexander's time questioned the Babylonians about it, and were given a nominal date of 2230 B.C. The city is undoubtedly much older than that.

The principal god of Babylon was known as Merodach and the city was regarded as his sacred dwelling in a very special and particular way. It was often referred to as "Babilu mahaz Marduk" which translates as "Babylon the stronghold of Merodach."

This Merodach had a consort called Zir-panitum, the principal goddess of Babylon. Innana, Nana, or Ishtar was also regarded as one of the most important patron deities of ancient Babylon.

The great Hammurabi, known in Babylonian as Kimta-rapastum, was king of Babylon round about 2120 B.C., and was a clearly established member of the Babylonian dynasty.

Throughout the ensuing centuries, there was continual war between Babylon and Assyria. The great city and its magnificent temples were destroyed and rebuilt on numerous occasions, almost any of which could have been the inspiration of the Tower of Babel story.

Nebuchadnezzar was a particularly vigorous rebuilder and restorer, as Daniel 4:30, clearly indicates. Antiochus Soter was probably the last Babylonian king to carry out any restorations. The bold and decisive Xerxes plundered Babylon and intrepidly carried away the golden statue from the Temple of Belus, which Darius had hesitated to remove for religious reasons. By the time Alexander the Great got there, the city was in ruins once again. He originally decided to restore Babylon's former glories, but even Alexander's brilliant imagination drew back from the awesome logistics of a task that would have needed ten thousand labourers simply to clear away the rubble before the rebuilding began. After the death of Alexander, the decay and desolation of Babylon continued for many centuries.

The biblical mystery of the Tower of Babel, and its alleged consequences for global languages remains unsolved. It is not that there are no ruined Babylonian towers to which archaeologists can refer: there are, if anything, rather too many.

Chapter Six

The Mystery of Rahab

Alongside the high profile magical, miraculous, and historical mysteries recorded in the Bible, there are some equally intriguing low profile, behavioural mysteries. The strange sequence of events in the exotic house on the walls of Jericho is one of these.

At first glance the story is straight forward enough. Joshua, the brilliant Hebrew general who took over their leadership when Moses died, wisely decided to send two spies to the Canaanite city of Jericho before attacking it.

In Middle Eastern cities of that period, inns, taverns and brothels tended to be situated near the gates so that travellers arriving in the city could locate them easily. A scarlet cord hanging from a window and a scarlet lamp above the door would indicate the nature of the premises.

As the Hebrew spies approached, they saw at once that this particular brothel situated on the city wall would be an ideal place from which to carry out their espionage mission. Once inside, they meet Rahab and arrange to stay.

Nerves are on edge in Jericho. News of Joshua's previous military successes against the neighbouring Canaanite strongholds has already reached the city. The arrival of the Hebrew spies has been quietly observed. Information about their arrival reaches the king. He sends for Rahab and demands to know where these two dangerous men are.

She reports that they were there earlier, but had slipped away at dusk just before the gates were due to be secured for the night. She assures the king that a swift patrol would almost certainly be able to overtake them.

Meanwhile she hides them in the flax in case she is not believed and a search party is sent to the house. She begs them to save her and her family when the Hebrew army storms Jericho.

They make her a solemn promise, and instruct her to bring her family together into this house on the wall when the attack starts. They explain that it is vitally important for her to mark the window as usual with the scarlet cord of her profession so that the house can easily be identified.

At the first opportunity, Rahab lowers them down the wall on that same life-saving scarlet cord and advises them to make for the mountains and hide there until the king's patrol gives up the search for them.

The plan works. They remain in the mountains for a day or two, then return safely to the Hebrew camp and report everything to Joshua.

When the attack on Jericho takes place, they go swiftly to Rahab's house while the carnage rages all round it. No one else is spared. Jericho, is devastated and destroyed but their vow to Rahab and her family is faithfully kept.

Intriguingly, Joshua 6:25, records that "Rahab is with us to this day" indicating that she married a Hebrew and that their descendants were still thriving in the Hebrew nation when the Book of Joshua was written.

The story as it stands, however, raises several challenging behavioural mysteries. *Why* did the spies feel sure that they could trust Rahab? *Why* did she feel certain that she could trust them? They literally trusted one another with their very lives. Do strangers of different nationalities normally offer and accept that kind of ultimate trust?

Their trust was not only mutually offered and accepted: subsequent events proved that it was totally justified by the solid gold integrity of both parties. Spies and prostitutes both live in convoluted serpentine worlds where honesty and integrity are rarer than lap-dancers in a monastery. Rahab herself had no difficulty in telling the king of Jericho a yarn that would have done justice to Baron von Munchausen.

Despite the nature of her work, Rahab was undoubtedly deeply devoted to her family. It wasn't solely her own life she begged for: she wanted to save her parents, brothers, and sisters as well. Why, too, were the spies so determined to keep their word to her? It's easy enough under the stresses of war for integrity to be the first casualty. Promises are even more vulnerable than flesh and bone when bloodstained swords are swinging in the desperate heat of battle and the only law is kill or be killed. Yet their promise to Rahab and her family was sacrosanct to the two Hebrew spies? *Why?*

Is it possible that *Rahab was a Jewish girl?*

The well known account of Joseph and his coat of many colours is a stark reminder that Canaan was infested with opportunist slave traders of the kind who sold Joseph in Egypt.

Captive Israelites: is this how beautiful young Rahab was taken to Jericho as a slave girl?

The Hebrew families who straggled out of Egypt with Moses easily became separated from their main column.

It would have been the easiest thing in the world for slave traders to abduct Rahab and her family under cover of darkness. But how to get the best price for them in Jericho? Beautiful young Rahab is undoubtedly the jewel in the crown: and the slavers know exactly where to take her. The proprietor of the house on the wall begins the long, inevitable haggling. No, he has no interest in the others. They might just be worth a handful of silver as domestic servants.... It is only Rahab who is worth gold because she can earn gold. The others are practically a liability. The parents might just as well be killed now. They will not really justify the price of feeding them....

If the girl proves difficult and uncooperative even she may not be worth anything. The slavers understand the haggling arguments only too well.

Then to everyone's surprise, the spirited and intelligent slave girl intervenes. She understands perfectly well what is going on, and what their problems are. Perhaps she can help them all?

The proprietor and the slavers listen attentively. What if she is willing to be totally committed to her work? She could earn far more for him than three or four desperately unhappy girls who have to be starved and beaten into reluctant, passive submission. Her vivacious enthusiasm will attract many extra customers for him. In return, will he allow her family to stay too, as domestic servants, to gather wood, to fetch water, to prepare flax for linen, to spin, to weave, to clean...? One price for the whole family and she promises to be the best and most exciting harlot in Jericho.

If he doesn't believe her, would he like to prove it for himself? She will sleep with him here … now … then he can decide if she's worth what she's asking. There are nods and smiles....

The proprietor leads Rahab to his couch.... Soon he is more than satisfied that she can honour her bargain. Money changes hands. She has won. The family who mean more to her than her own life are safe.... Just as important, she has kept them together.

As long as they are alive and together there is always hope of rescue. Joshua will conquer this land before long. They will go back to their people. Her life in this house on the wall will be like a nightmare that fades when the sun rises.

One day two strangers come in. Something about them makes her wonder. Dare she ask them who they are and where they're from? Could they possibly be Joshua's men?

She dare not speak to them in Hebrew. The house is full of local clients and local girls. One wrong word and the strangers — if they are Joshua's men — will be captured. Her persistent hope of rescue will be disappointed. One of the men beckons and smiles. Money changes hand. She takes him to her room. As they undress she sees that he is circumcised. Now they are alone she dares to whisper in Hebrew. His eyes brighten. He smiles warmly. He answers her in Hebrew. She tells him her story. He tells her why he and his brother are there.

The attack on Jericho will not be long delayed. They talk urgently about the present danger to him, and the imminent danger to her and her family when the great attack begins. In the heat of battle, no Israeli soldier will have time to stay his sword stroke at the urgent pleading of a girl dressed as a Jericho harlot.

Rahab is already very concerned that someone will have reported their presence in the city … even reported that they are in her house on the wall.... It will be best if she hides them among the flax....

Harlots in Jericho.

The walls of Jericho are mysteriously destroyed. Drawn by Theo Fanthorpe.

They are no sooner safely hidden than messengers arrive from the king. She plans her story quickly. We've already noted that she's brave and quick-witted as well as beautiful. That's what saved her family after the slavers brought them all to Jericho. Yes, of course, the men were here. One of them was her client. They went away soon afterwards. She's almost certain that they've left the city. If the king's soldiers pursue them swiftly it should not be difficult to overtake them. It is an honour to be of service to the king.

As soon as it is dark enough, she lowers the men down the same strong red cord which hangs from the window to tell the world what the house on the wall has to offer, the same scarlet cord which is destined to save her life....

Rahab's integrity is absolute and so is theirs. It is a life for a life, an infinite trust for an infinite trust.

The collapsing walls leave Jericho totally vulnerable. The invincible Israeli army storms through from all directions. The two spies race for the house on the wall. Rahab's family are gathered with her. All are safe. Her courage and intelligence have saved them a second time. The spy she spoke with has his arms protectively around her lovely young shoulders — but not for money this time. There is a powerful bond between people who have saved each other's lives.

So there is a fairy tale happy ending. They marry. They raise a family.

And at the time when the Book of Joshua was written, Rahab's descendants were thriving among their fellow Israelites. We hope they still are.

Chapter Seven

Noah's Ark

The story of a vast flood and a holy, boat-building hero who saved not only himself and his family but many animal species as well is known throughout the world. The biblical account of Noah seems to be based on three distinct, ancient texts which scholars refer to as the Yahwist, the Elohist and the Priestly versions. The first two are very similar as far as the Flood narrative is concerned, but are easily distinguished by the words which the writers have used for God. The Yahwist version calls him Yahweh; the Elohist version calls him (or *them?*) Elohim. The Elohist text seems to be the oldest of the three, and probably goes back as far as the ninth century before Christ. The Yahwist narrative is generally agreed to date from about 800 B.C. — around the era when Hosea and Amos were writing their great moral prophecies. The Priestly version is the result of editing, redacting, and refining which went on in the sixth century B.C. — during, or shortly after, the Babylonian captivity, when the Jewish priests had more time on their hands than they wanted — time which they turned into an opportunity to edit and revise their sacred texts.

Non-Judaeo-Christian accounts of the Flood, which nevertheless bear close resemblance to the biblical versions, come from Mesopotamia, the Land of the Two Rivers — the Tigris and Euphrates — and date back to about 3000 B.C. A wide, flat valley floor with great rivers on either side of it might well have been vulnerable to a flood great enough to convince its Mesopotamian chroniclers that it was universal.

The Sumerian version begins with the gods deciding to destroy humanity with a great flood. There are protests from Nintu, on humanity's behalf. A benign and devout hero named Ziusudra fills the dual role of king and priest: in this he bears a remarkable similarity to the mysterious

Melchizedek, the powerful priest-king of Salem, to whom Abraham gave gifts, and from whom Abraham received a blessing. Melchizedek was said to have neither beginning of life nor end of days: what kind of being was he? And where was he from? Were he and Ziusudra *similar* beings? Or were they actually the *same* being known by different names to different peoples at different times and in different places? Was the Egyptian "god" Thoth, alias Hermes Trismegistus of Emerald Tablet fame, yet another member of that same group of mysterious super-normal beings? Or was Hermes, perhaps, yet *another* alias for Ziusudra and Melchizedek?

Warned by Enki in a dream, Ziusudra embarks in a huge ship, which survives the terrible seven day floods and storms. The good and pious Ziusudra offers the appropriate sacrifices to the sun-god while still on board his ship. He is rewarded with the gift of immortality.

The Babylonian version also begins with the gods threatening to destroy humanity by water. This time it is Ishtar who lodges a protest on humanity's behalf. The hero of this Babylonian version is Utnapishtim: Ea warns him in a dream that the flood is on the way. Utnapishtim's gigantic ship has seven storeys and nine divisions: both important "sacred" numbers. Every conceivable type of animal is taken on board, and the flood arises as the result of heavy rain and storms. It lasts for barely six days, and the great ship which Utnapishtim has constructed comes to rest on Mount Nisir. He sends out three birds: a dove, a swallow, and a raven, and then offers appropriate sacrifices on Mount Nisir. The gods gather round to enjoy the sacrifice, and reward Utnapishtim and his faithful, hard-working wife with immortality. They join the deities. The lapis lazuli necklace of Ishtar becomes a memento of the great occasion, rather as the rainbow does in the Priestly version incorporated into the amalgamated biblical accounts.

In the Yahwist version in Genesis, God announces that humanity will be destroyed because of sin. The God-fearing, righteous Noah becomes the hero of the Yahwist account, and is duly instructed to enter the ark along with seven pairs of every ritually clean beast and only two of the others. It is God himself who shuts the ark after Noah and the others have embarked. The Flood lasts for forty days, but in Hebrew "forty" and "many" are frequently synonymous. It subsides after either two or three periods of seven days. The "magical" or "sacred" numbers (3 and 7) are coming into play again here. Like Utnapishtim, Noah sends out birds — in his case a raven and a dove. When the ordeal is over, Noah offers sacrifices, and Yahweh accepts the "sweet savour" of them. In this Yahwist account, God resolves never again to destroy humanity with a flood.

Did Noah include venomous creatures such as the scorpion?

The Priestly version of exilic times begins with God's decree that all flesh will be destroyed because it is corrupt. Noah, again the hero of the Flood narrative, is described as a uniquely righteous man, and is accordingly favoured with God's personal warning. The ark is built in the ratio of 30:5:3 which is, incidentally, particularly seaworthy and hydrologically sound. It has three storeys. One breeding pair of each type of animal is taken on board. The exact dates of the beginning and end of the Flood are given, and it is attributed to the fountains of the great deep being broken, and the windows of Heaven being opened. The Flood has a duration of 150 days and takes a further 150 days to subside. The ark comes to rest on Ararat, and God makes a covenant with Noah that floods will never again destroy the earth: aetiologically, the rainbow becomes the sign, or symbol, of this divine promise.

Noah plans and builds the ark. Drawn by Theo Fanthorpe.

The flood story from tablet eleven of the Assyrian form of the Epic of Gilgamesh tells how Gilgamesh himself, a semi-mythical, semi-legendary king of Mesopotamian Uruk, actually *met* Utnapishtim, referred to as "Utnapishtim of the Distant Horizons" or "Utnapishtim who is Afar." These Gilgamesh tablets were actually unearthed from the ruins of what had once been the very impressive library of Assurbanipal, the last great king of Assyria. The amazing eleventh tablet actually contains Utnapishtim's own account — his personal journal, or diary — of his adventures during the flood. As analyzed earlier, it seems very similar to both the Priestly and Yahwist versions as they are intertwined in the Bible.

The Gilgamesh version refers to the world as teeming with human activity and clamour to such an extent that Enlil and the other gods were unable to rest. The Assyrian flood was, therefore, intended more as a silencer than a punishment for wrong-doing. Enlil's motivation seems to have been similar to that of the angry, night-shift neighbour who bursts in on the teenagers' party and destroys their amplifier when he cannot sleep because of the music.

Taking all the Middle Eastern accounts together, it certainly seems *possible*, if not probable, that several millennia B.C. a hero saved himself, a small group of people — probably his immediate family — and their essential livestock, by building a large vessel to ride out a flood which at the very least devastated Mesopotamia, and may well have reached much farther afield.

What is to be made of the numerous reports of sightings of what purports to be the remains of a large wooden vessel — certainly the biggest in the ancient world as far as is known — on or near Mount Ararat? A great many expeditions to the Ararat region of Turkey — many of them manned by enthusiastic American Christians — have claimed to see what they reported to be the remains of a huge ancient ship partly buried in ice. The biblical dimensions roughly translated into modern measurements suggest that the ark was about 13.5 metres high, 135 long, and 22.5 wide. There is reference to some sort of "window" or opening at the top.

Where the biblical account mentions Ararat, it may well be referring to a *region* rather than just one specific mountain. Certainly there was an ancient *kingdom* known as Urartu in the vicinity of modern Ararat.

Once the great ship had served its purpose as far as Noah and his family were concerned, it was to all intents and purposes left to lie derelict on the mountain. Or was it? There is no reference to the fate of Noah's ship as such in the work of any later biblical writers. Nowhere do we find a passage suggesting that if the faithful make their

Mount Ararat — did the ark land here?

pilgrimage to such and such a place, they will be able to see the great
old ship for themselves. Although the biblical writers seem to be very
reticent about what finally became of the ark, there are references
dating from about the three hundred years before the birth of Christ,
which give the impression that its remains were still clearly visible on
Ararat. Recent expeditions have variously reported coming across the
ark, not on the summit of Ararat, but well above the three 3,000 metre
level. According to their reports, it appears to be partially encased in
snow and ice most of the time. The reports suggest that when there is
an unusually warm summer, however, the mysterious structure can be
seen, even accessed. Some explorers claim to have walked across the
frost preserved timbers of its ancient roof; others recount that they
have actually been inside it.

Former NASA astronaut James Irwin raised the public profile of the
ark hunters in the 1980s when he participated in expeditions to Ararat.
With the break-up of the former USSR, the cold war tensions of the
Russo-Turkish border where Ararat is situated were lessened. Western
expeditions to the mountain were no longer seen as a major threat to
Russian security.

One of the most interesting archaeological explorations of the Ararat
area was undertaken by Sir Leonard Woolley in 1929. Believing that he
was working in the area which he described as Ur of the Chaldees, in the
south of Mesopotamia, and north of the Gulf, Woolley had successfully
excavated what he believed to be the graves of the ancient kings of Ur, the
tombs of Sumerian aristocrats dating back some five thousand years — at
least a full millennium before Abraham's epic journeys. Delighted as he
was with these discoveries, Woolley's enquiring mind took him farther

and deeper. Below the ancient tombs he discovered a layer of alluvial clay, which he was convinced had been deposited there by a flood of significant proportions. Below this clay, he found evidence — mainly in the form of potsherds — indicating that an advanced stone-age culture had once flourished there. Not surprisingly in the circumstances, Woolley sent home the now famous telegram: "We have found the flood."

Woolley may or may not have found evidence for the Flood, but there is an interesting case to be argued for the ark having come to rest other than on the mountain which is currently referred to as Ararat.

The biblical references, when studied closely, suggest that the ark settled (Genesis 8:4) "on the mountains of Ararat." *Mountains* is plural, and *Ararat* is better understood as a geographical *region* rather than as one individual mountain. When the Genesis account was first written, Ararat would have been understood as the region around Lake Van, and so was then well to the north of ancient Assyria.

During Templar times in the thirteenth century, Mount Ararat became the favourite site for the ark's last resting place, but much earlier traditions had favoured a different mountain some 322 kilometres away — although still within the boundaries of the *Kingdom of* Ararat. This rival site is known by a variety of names: to a few of the ancient chroniclers it, too, was called Ararat, which may well have accounted for some of the understandable confusion. It is, perhaps, most widely known as Cudi Dagh, or Khudi Dhagh. Close to the Iraqi-Syrian border in southern Turkey, it is roughly 320 kilometres south of the famous Mount Ararat. Cartographers place it at approximately 37° north, and 42° east. The River Tigris is not far away, and the Turkish city of Gizre is relatively close.

The intriguing Khudi Dhagh has more names than the elusive count of Saint Germain. In various accounts it is called: Mount Judi, Cardu, and Quardu, which is particularly interesting when the mystery of Rennes-le-Château is recalled. One of the mountains near Rennes, and one which has traditional connections with the deeper, darker strands of that enigma, is also called Cardu. Khudi Dhagh is also referred to as Mount Goryene or Gordian, Karduchian, and Kurdian. The ancient Assyrians called it Mount Nipur.

Although the summit of Khudi Dhagh would struggle to reach the 3,000 metre mark, it is nevertheless snow-capped during the cold months.

There are a number of interesting pieces of evidence by early writers like Josephus, concerning the ark's landing place. Josephus, it must be remembered, was Jewish by birth, but Roman by inclination. He lived at the same time as Saint Paul, and was an official Romano-Jewish historian. This privileged position gave him access to a great many important book collections and unique, ancient archives.

In his own book, *Antiquities of the Jews,* Josephus wrote:

"The Ark landed on an Armenian mountain peak. Noah, aware now that the Earth was safely through the flood, waited for seven days more. Then he released the animals and went out with his family. He offered a sacrifice to God and then celebrated with a family feast. "

(The Armenians apparently named the spot *The Landing Place,* or in their own language *apo bah tay reon* which literally means *The Place of Descent.*) Some linguistic and historical analysis has been done on this place name by William Whiston in his translation of Josephus. Whiston argues a case for the modern city of Nakhichevan, about 100 kilometres south-east of Ararat. Josephus, himself, however, rather seems to be referring to a mountain in the Gordyene district, and there is evidence that the early Armenian historians thought that *Gortuk* or *Gorduk* (their name for Gordyene) was the landing place.

Josephus also quotes from Berossus, a Chaldean historian and priest, who was active approximately three centuries before the start of the Christian era. Unfortunately, his original work has been lost, and what is known of his writings is what survives in quotation in Josephus and Polyhistor, who wrote during the first century B.C. Berossus said that the ark was still to be seen in the Gordyene mountains in Armenia (Urartu) and that those who knew of its whereabouts scraped pitch from its ancient timbers and used it to make amulets.

Apart from Josephus and Berossus there are interesting references to the ark in a document generally referred to by scholars as *The Samaritan Pentateuch.* This is a version of the first five books of the Bible used by the Samaritans, who had been separated from mainstream Judaism in the fifth century B.C. The Assyrians had deported many of the inhabitants of the northern Jewish Kingdom of Israel, and had replaced them with Assyrian colonists. These intermarried Assyrians and non-deported northern Jews became the Samaritans. Their Pentateuch differs significantly from the traditional, orthodox version, because of their tendency to make amendments which smoothed out difficult passages.

There is also evidence about the ark in the *Targums.* These are Aramaic paraphrases written for the Jews who came back to Jerusalem after their captivity in Babylon, and had difficulty with the older, purer Hebrew writings. According to the Targums, the ark came to rest somewhere in the Mountains of Cardu or Quardu. Once again, there is this tenebrous link with the Rennes-le-Château enigma, and the esoteric Mount Cardu overlooking that mysterious French village.

Yet another passage from Josephus refers to a ruler of Adiabene named Monobazus who gave his son, Izates, a smaller country, a region or principality named Carron which was supposed to have contained the remains of the ark. As far as ancient history cartographers can decipher its whereabouts today, this ancient land of Adiabene, which must have *contained* Carron, had the Tigris as its western boundary and the Upper and Lower Zab Rivers to the north and south of it.

Eusebius of Caesarea was a Christian historian who flourished during the fourth century. He was a pupil of Pamphilus, from whom he learnt a great deal, and to whom he was loyally devoted. Pamphilus was martyred in A.D. 310, and Eusebius himself was probably imprisoned at the same time.

The best known of Eusebius's works was his *Ecclesiastical History,* which set out to be a fully documented account of the Christian Church up until Eusebius's own time. Unfortunately, he was not the greatest of historians, and his account of heresy left much to be desired. His knowledge of the western church was scanty, but he did, however, make an important reference to the ark. According to Eusebius, a fragment of the ark still survived in the Gordian Mountains.

Yet another interesting piece of evidence about the ark's final resting place comes from the *Pershitta.* This document is a version of the Bible which was translated especially for the Christians in Syria. The earliest known copy seems to date from around A.D. 390–410, and cites the Mountains of Quardu as the site of the ark's landing, as the Targums do. It may be that the Pershitta is based on the Targums — at least to some extent.

The fourth century Byzantine writer, Faustus, was an Armenian historian although he was Greek by birth. Unfortunately, his original work has vanished, but parts of it are still extant in translation. Faustus tells of a pious monk named Jacob, who was obsessed by a desire to climb the mountain and see the ark for himself. After many unsuccessful attempts, this Jacob met an angel, who took pity on him and rewarded him with the gift of a piece of timber from the ark. Faustus's story of Jacob the monk, seems to have become the foundation of several later references to the ark's preservation on Ararat. However, in Faustus's original account, Jacob the monk is also the bishop of Nisibis, situated only 100 kilometres from

Khudi Dhagh. Mount Ararat would have seemed a long distance from Jacob's home ground, whereas Khudi Dhagh was eminently reachable.

If Faustus had actually meant Mount Ararat, he would probably have referred to it as Masis, its Armenian name — as he does elsewhere in his writings.

An early ascetic bishop of Salamis, or Constantia, in Cyprus was the fanatical and dogmatic Epiphanius who went after heretics like a wild pig after truffles. Born in Palestine around A.D. 315, he was profoundly influenced by the extremes of Egyptian monasticism. He founded and ran his own stern little monastery near Eleutheropolis and devoted much of the rest of his life to spreading his quaint ideas and attacking worthier men like Origen who fell within his definition of heretics.

Epiphanius died at sea in 403, and so was practically a contemporary of Faustus of Byzantium. Like Faustus, he put in his five cents worth of contributions to the probable location of the ark. According to Epiphanius it was resting somewhere in the Gordian Mountains, and was still being exhibited to interested pilgrims. He went a stage further and declared that Noah's altar could also be seen there by those who took the necessary trouble to look for it.

Two or three centuries later, Isidore of Seville is alleged to have provided similar evidence for the ark being on the Gordian Mountains.

An interesting and informative twelfth century Jewish source, Benjamin of Tudela, apparently provides evidence that the ark had once been on a mountain named Ararat, but that Omar ben al-Khatab had taken it down and made it into an Islamic mosque. The ruins of an old city known as Jezireh ben Omar, were said to lie at the foot of Khudi Dhagh, and, according to Benjamin, some remains of the ark were still to be seen there in the twelfth century.

The reference to Omar ben al-Khatab is not the only Islamic reference to the remains of the ark. The Holy Koran itself records that the ark came to rest upon Al-Judi. Other academic Moslem authorities suggest that the records intimate that it landed at Khudi Dhagh, or that Mohammed was actually referring to the Judi Mountains in Saudi Arabia. Two tenth century writers, Al Masudi and Ibn Haukal, both refer to sites which strongly indicate Khudi Dhagh. Two thirteenth century Moslem authorities, Ibn Al-Mid and Zakariya ben Mohammed al Kaswine, the celebrated geographer, tell of a seventh century emperor who climbed the mountain to see the remains of the ark, and of wood from the ark being used to build a monastery.

There is an account of five Turkish soldiers struggling home from Baghdad after the First World War ended in 1918, who came across the remains of the ark by accident. If they had followed the course of the Tigris, it would have brought them to Khudi Dhagh. The presence of formidable British Forces in Syria would have made it prudent for the small Turkish cadre to detour well away — hence, following the Tigris home would have made good sense.

What is to be made of an earlier account by Jan Struys, a Dutch adventurer who had the misfortune to be captured and enslaved by Armenian bandits in 1670? Struys testified that on Ararat, he met a sick, elderly hermit, whom he was able to heal. For some curious reason, the Armenian bandits believed that their enslaved Dutchman possessed paranormal healing powers, which was why he had been ordered to treat the revered hermit. In gratitude for being restored to health, the pious old man gave Struys a piece of extremely hard, black wood, which he said was a genuine piece of the ark. He also gave the Dutchman a precious stone, which sparkled brightly, and which the hermit claimed to have discovered underneath the remains of the ark.

In 1876, Oxford University explorer, James Bryce, reached the peak of Great Ararat — around 5,100 metres — and discovered an anomalous old piece of wood about 1.5 metres long. Bryce was convinced that it had once been part of the ark. Bryce's relatively modest discovery was surpassed by the claims of the remarkable John Joseph, prince of Nouri.

Born in Baghdad on February 7, 1865, and duly baptized on the fourteenth, John Joseph's prodigious titles included such notable achievements as: "His Chaldean Excellency, the Venerable Monsignor, the Zammorian, Earl of the Great House of Nouri, Grand Archdeacon of Babylon, Discoverer of Noah's Ark."

Tragically, there are all too many pompous little ecclesiastical bureaucrats and control freaks in our churches today who secretly envy John Joseph's resplendent ranks and titles, and see themselves as "Princes of the Church" rather than as servants of God and of people in need.

John Joseph, who was also referred to as "The Most Venerable Prelate," made three attempts to climb Ararat in 1887. He reported that on the third attempt he found the ark; it was almost completely exposed — only the central portion was covered with ice and snow — and remarkably well-preserved for its age. Nouri reported that the beams were very thick, reddish brown, and fastened together with long, broad nails.

John Henry Barrows was president of the World Parliament of Religions at the Chicago World's Fair in 1893. He invited The Most Venerable Nouri to come to Chicago and tell everyone how he had found the ark. Nouri duly arrived and spoke so convincingly that a group of wealthy Belgians offered to finance an expedition to bring the ark back down the mountain and rebuild it for exhibition at the World's Fair. The scheme collapsed when the Turkish government understandably refused to give permission for the ark to be moved should Nouri and his team succeed in relocating it. When the final report of the World Parliament of Religions was drawn up, no mention was made of Nouri and his alleged adventures on Ararat.

Towards the end of the First World War, the Armenians naturally sided with the invading Czarist Russians against their traditional enemies, the Turks. It was bad luck for the Armenians when the Bolshevik Revolution took Russia out of the war and left them at the mercy of the understandably vengeful Turks. Many Armenians fled across the River Aras into what later became Soviet Armenia. Others escaped to any hospitable country that was willing to accept them: a significant number reached the United States. One such refugee was a fascinating character named George Hagopian. Born in the late 1890s, young George had an uncle who was deeply religious and, according to George's own account given some sixty years later, took the boy to see the remains of Noah's ark. This had happened not once but twice, first in 1908 and again in 1910. George said that he had grown up near Lake Van, where his grandfather had been the minister in charge of a large church. His uncle — the one who took him to see the ark — was a shepherd who grazed his flocks on the lower slopes of Ararat.

They began by approaching the mountain from the south, and passing through the town of Dogubeyazit, circled round half the mountain so that they could approach it from the north. The boy was riding a donkey until the going became too steep for it, and at that point his uncle placed George and the provisions on his broad, powerful shoulders and climbed up towards the ark. They spent two or three hours exploring it in detail, and were still able to get back to the foot of the mountain before dark.

In 1908, the weather was unusually dry. Little or no snow had fallen on the mountain, and there had been similar conditions for the past three or four years. These would be almost ideal climatic conditions for viewing the ark. George recalled that it was very cold and foggy up there, and the ark seemed to be resting on a great, bluish-green rock. To one side lay what looked to the boy to be an unclimbable precipice, or cliff face. He looked over the edge and found it difficult to see how deep down it went because of the swirling mist.

George reported that the ark itself was long and rectangular. It was flat bottomed, but the sides curved out slightly as they rose, so that the decks would have been broader than the base. The roof was almost flat, and possessed a row of several windows — George reckoned there were fifty or more — and they in turn were covered by a sort of shield or awning. Each window was about a metre long and half a metre wide. The sides as far as he could see had no doors, windows, or other apertures. There was a large opening in the roof, and a gangway, ladder, or staircase descended from it.

Very significantly, George reported that to his inexperienced, boyhood eyes, the ark had appeared to be made of *stone* rather than wood. He expanded this statement by saying that when he was able to observe it more closely, he could see that it was wood, but the wood was petrified, and exceptionally hard. He recalled that his uncle had been unable to get so much as a knife blade into it, and that when he had fired his musket at it to demonstrate its hardness, the flattened ball had simply fallen to the ground below the point of impact. When George attempted to feel a seam, or ridge where the planks joined, he could feel nothing except a completely smooth, flat surface. The joints and grain of the petrified timber were clearly visible, he said, but they *felt* totally flat.

Something like green moss or lichen covered the roof of the ark, and this scraped off very easily. Underneath it, as George described it, lay more of the same, dark brown, incredibly hard and resistant, petrified wood.

When George returned home and told friends in his age group of his exciting adventure, he discovered that several of them had also seen it, and that their descriptions of it tallied closely with his.

He died in 1972.

A remarkably colourful account of yet another ark sighting is found in the so-called Roskovitsky Report. According to the account that bears his name, Vladimir Roskovitsky was a White Russian pilot, working for the Czar prior to the Bolshevik Revolution of 1917. He was sent up near Ararat to test out aircraft number seven which had just had its new supercharger installed. With one companion on board, he took off as ordered and flew the few miles from their airfield to Ararat. On circling the mountain, the two men were amazed to see what appeared to be a large ancient ship partly submerged in a small lake on the side of the mountain. On returning excitedly to their airfield, they reported their sighting to their commanding officer. He in turn contacted HQ, and an expedition was sent up the mountain to examine the strange craft which the two aviators had spotted.

According to the Roskovitsky Report, the soldiers found the ark in an amazing state of preservation, and there was clear evidence of doorways and cages — some of which looked as though they had been constructed to house far larger animals than anything living on earth in 1916. At this point it is important for the researcher to bear carefully in mind that the so-called Roskovitsky Report did not see the light of day until 1940, when it was published by Floyd Gurley in a Los Angeles magazine called *The New Eden.* Gurley was an enthusiastic Christian, who had received the rudimentary essence of the story from Ben Allen, a retired lawyer, who was a keen student of creationism, the deluge, and related topics. Gurley's article attracted worldwide attention both from interested readers and the media, and he passed all the material he received to Ben Allen.

Ben was not happy.

He said that Gurley's account was wildly exaggerated — only about 5 percent of it could be substantiated and that was the least sensationalized 5 percent which Allen had given him in the first place. In Ben's disclaimer he said that many years after the alleged event, the relatives of some long dead Russian soldiers had told him that while their relatives were serving in the Czarist Army, there had been an episode in which an aviator had reported something strange — possibly a large boat — partly submerged in a lake on Ararat. Infantrymen were sent to examine it. They and their officers thought that it might have been the remains of Noah's ark. Those were the only facts that the Russians had given.

So the reports and counter reports of suspected sightings and refutations continue: there are enough of them to fill several volumes. Is it Mount Ararat that we should search, or "the *other* Ararat" known as Khudi Dhagh? Is it possible that the Ark — even if frozen and/or petrified — could have survived so long? Did George and his uncle really find a vast, ship-like structure in 1908 that was too hard for musket ball or knife to penetrate? If it was that hard and that smooth, *where did it come from in the first place? Who brought it to the mountain? And why?*

If George was telling the truth, and if his memory was still accurate after so many years, was the ship which he and his uncle inspected one which had travelled *much farther* than the biblical Noah and his family did?

Something that can be said in favour of that line of enquiry is that *if* Atlantis once existed, and *if* its citizens once possessed much higher technological skills than their neighbours, the mysterious craft on Ararat or Khudi Dhagh might well have been one of their escape vessels. If it came from farther still, what of the semi-aquatic "gods" like Dagon, or the mysterious intelligent marine creature, the Quinotaur of the Merovingian legends? Is it remotely feasible that the inhabitants of that remarkable vessel were extraterrestrials, or favoured (righteous?) humans in the care of benign extraterrestrials? There are details of the size, the shape and the divine sealing of the ark, which might just raise an eyebrow or two. Close attention to the details of the story, its worldwide ubiquity, and the careful, environmentalist preservation of so many animal species, do just make the open-minded and imaginative researcher wonder whether the biblical account of Noah's ark is only the tip of an amazing iceberg.

Chapter Eight

The Mysterious Power of Prayer

There are many occasions recorded in the Bible where prayer works swiftly and effectively. The prophet Elijah challenges the priests of Baal to a great contest on Mount Carmel. The servants of Baal become hysterically excited: they scream and shout, and exhort Baal to grant their request using every trick they can think of, but nothing works for them. Elijah mocks them unmercifully. He suggests that they shout louder because Baal may be asleep. Perhaps their god has gone hunting? Maybe he's been on a long journey and will soon be back? Baal does not answer the frantic prayers of his desperate worshippers.

Finally, it's Elijah's turn. His prayer, by contrast, is short, quiet and simple:

"Lord God of Abraham, Isaac and of Israel, let it be known this day that thou art God in Israel, and that I am thy servant, and that I have done all these things at thy word. Hear me, O Lord, hear me, that this people may know that thou art the Lord God, and that thou hast turned their heart back again."
(I Kings 18: 36–37)

Like Elijah, many prophets, priests, holy men and women — as well as ordinary believers — throughout the biblical narrative have clearly had their prayers answered. The deep and troubling mystery remains: some equally worthy prayers offered by equally devout and deserving people are not answered. *Why?*

How much do we actually *know* as researchers into paranormal and anomalous phenomena about the amazing — and as yet largely unexplored

— powers of the mind? Jesus himself said that prayers must be uttered in *faith.* The man or woman of prayer must *believe* in the power and reality of prayer, if that prayer is going to be answered.

If we begin with the premise that God has absolute power, limitless wisdom, and total knowledge, that his Divine Nature is boundless and unending love, and that He is omnipresent in every nook and cranny of his universe, then we must utterly discard the suggestion that he answers prayer in a whimsical or arbitrary way. God does not have moods. There are no times or seasons when he is unapproachable. His suprapersonal consistency is as great and unbounded as his love for us all. So why does one terminally ill patient experience a miraculous recovery when his loved ones pray for him, while another, who is equally loved and prayed for, does not? Why does one soldier come safely home from battle when his family and friends pray for his safety, while another is blown to hell beside him on the enemy beaches? God is not selective in his love. He does not favour one life at the expense of another. Every sick patient and every soldier in action is of equal value to the God of Love and Mercy who created us all: so *why* is one prayer answered where another isn't?

Can there be a clue somewhere in the essential *consistency* of God's Nature? We live in a mysterious universe. Not only are its observable externalities mysterious, but our inward experiences, what we choose to call our consciousness, our feelings, and our introspective thinking processes are mysterious as well. What we know of the observable universe, and what we know of ourselves and our personal awareness, suggests very strongly that there are discernible systems, patterns, and orders in both the internal and external universes.

If there were no consistency, if today's left were tomorrow's right; if this morning's up were this evening's down; if red were yellow on Mondays and green on Tuesdays — but not every week — we could *learn* little or nothing about ourselves or our environment.

If a fragile substance is struck with a heavy steel hammer, the fragile substance breaks. We are putting the consistent laws of physics into practice here. The fist of a powerful martial artist will smash a door panel. The tiny hand of a three-year-old child will not.

There are many natural laws of physics, chemistry, and biology which our ancestors did not understand. The quaintly erroneous phlogiston theory held sway until the role of oxygen in combustion was discovered. It needed Pasteur's genius to show that germs caused disease. It needed Harvey's discerning observations to demonstrate definitively that blood circulated around the body. The wisest men and women of ancient times were not able to understand problems which a secondary school pupil can solve easily enough today. Intelligence alone is not enough: we need the relevant data as well.

What if there is some secret that we do not yet know which points the way to unfailingly efficacious prayer?

Take the analogy of an advanced spread sheet or word processing system. If we know which keys to press, and in what order, the system will work superbly. If we miss a key, or press keys in the wrong order, the results will be disappointing. If we do not realize that we have made a mistake in applying the system, we are likely to blame the system rather than ourselves. Could the secret of prayer be something similar? We complain bitterly when things go wrong: "What's the use of praying? Prayer's a waste of time. It doesn't work." Shouldn't we be asking instead: "What's *wrong* with *my* prayer? What's *wrong* with *my* faith? What's *wrong* with *my* mental and spiritual prayer techniques?" A novice driver on his or her first lesson often finds a car hard to handle. But the gears, clutch, brakes, and steering work perfectly well in the hands of an experienced driver. The laws of locomotion remain constant, because if they didn't none of us would ever be able to drive. If today's clutch is tomorrow's accelerator and next week's brake, cars would be undrivable.

Can we begin to analyze prayer techniques in the way that we analyze computing methods and car driving? Can we monitor our progress in prayer much as we monitor our progress in acquiring any other knowledge or skill? There is nothing unworthy or irreverent in such an approach to prayer: it is infinitely worse to regard the God of Eternal and Consistent Love and

A devout eastern holy man at prayer.

Mercy as some sort of capricious tyrant who will answer prayers when he feels like it but not otherwise. That concept drags God's ethics down to well below the level of any morally mature and responsible human being.

If prayer is a natural process that works, it is a process that must work *consistently* in accordance with the God-given laws of prayer.

We believe that if anyone ever really knew what prayer was and how it worked, Jesus did. From his unique position as the pre-existent *Logos* or *Word* of God, from his sharing with the Holy Spirit in the triune nature of God, Jesus understood the nature and function of prayer perfectly. If any teachings on prayer — in the Christian Bible, or in any other sacred canon of scripture — are worth studying at all, then the teachings of Jesus are the clearest and most valid.

Jesus provided us with a number of vitally important clues concerning the nature and function of effective prayer. It is the ongoing tragedy of the Christian Church that its founder's wisdom in this area is so chronically ignored or deliberately disregarded and distorted. Christ's own prayers are free, spontaneous, and from the heart: there are no set forms, no liturgies, no dull and boring prayer rituals. Any location is sacred and suitable for prayer because it's all God's universe, and he is omnipresent within it. There are no set times or seasons for prayers: whenever a human heart feels the need to commune with God, that is the ideal time for that individual to pray.

Setting monotonous rules, routines, and special orders of prayers at strictly observed regular times is no part of Christ's teaching on prayer — and can be seriously counter-productive for most worshippers. The God of Ultimate Love is also the God of Ultimate Freedom, because freely expressed love is necessarily a voluntary and spontaneous thing. You can pray where you like, and when you like: your kitchen table or your favourite lounge chair, your garage or your garden shed — even the bathroom. God doesn't mind in the least where or when you pray — but he's always delighted to hear from you. The sincerity of your prayer is what matters to God.

Vast cathedrals and ornate churches are all very well for those who like that sort of religious art and architecture, but they are far from mandatory.

There is nothing so negative as the idea that prayer is a daily *necessity*, regularly *imposed* upon us, or *compulsory*, that it is some sort of painful and unwelcome *duty* which God expects us to perform regularly — or else — regardless of whether we really *want* to pray. Would you value a greeting, or a string of formalized compliments, from people who didn't really want to talk to you, but felt that they *had* to because you were their boss?

76

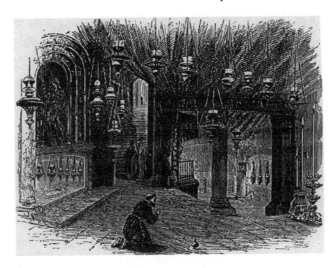

A holy man at prayer in the Chapel of the Nativity.

Take the analogy of loving partners, families, and friends. We don't expect them to trot up to us obediently so many times a day, favouring one particular "approved" holy place, in order to repeat certain liturgical words from a book.

As much as we love our nearest and dearest, and as much as they love us, our human love at its greatest and most altruistic is only a faint shadow of the immeasurably vast eternal love which God has for each one of us. If we don't expect our beloved partners, families, and friends to show their love by regular, ritualistic actions accompanied by repetitious liturgical words — *neither does God.*

Although God is undeniably and awesomely God, he is also a Person — being divinely suprapersonal makes him infinitely *more* of a personality than the most loving, charismatic man or woman who ever walked the earth. God is not an impersonal force, or a vaguely amorphous cosmic awareness hovering indistinctly amid the universe. God is the Ultimate Personality.

Jesus, who knew incomparably more about God than anyone before or since, expressed his deep knowledge of this suprapersonal concept of the Almighty by addressing him as *Father.* Furthermore, despite Christ's own unique, pre-existent, suprapersonal relationship with the God the Father, he clearly taught his followers to use the same form of address when they prayed. When Jesus teaches us to pray, he tells us to think of God as our own very special, personal, supremely loving, and transcendent Parent — not just *his* Father, but *ours* as well.

A loving parent does not set *routines* for contacting his or her children: they're *always* welcome — whatever they're doing, wherever they are, and whatever time it is. So it should be with the contact with God which we call prayer.

Christ also made it clear to the disciples that "vain repetitions" of the kind which the hapless priests of Baal practised were not an effective form of prayer.

Christ's clearest prayer teachings are to be found in *The Lord's Prayer* itself, and this deserves close and careful analysis, if we are to discover more clues as to what makes prayer effective. It starts with the vital reminder about the parenthood of God: "Our Father," and it proceeds to indicate the ultimate purpose of God and the universe in which he has placed his creation.

"Who art in Heaven" means what it says. Heaven may be succinctly defined as a place of unending and abundant delight. Think what you enjoy most on earth. Multiply that pleasure by a factor of infinity and a duration of eternity and you are paddling in the shallowest water at the edge of God's Ocean of Everlasting Happiness.

Human lovers who are truly in love want nothing more than to make each other happy. Individual members of loving families want to *share* their happiness with brothers and sisters, grandparents, parents and children, uncles, aunts, cousins ... neighbours, friends ... *everybody*. So does God — and he has the power to do it.

"Hallowed be thy name," speaks clearly of the reverence and respect duly and rightly owed to God by his creation, but in its fullest and deepest sense *hallowed* conveys a sense of someone or something which is honoured and respected *because it is truly loved as well as venerated.* Loving and honouring the *name* of God is to love and honour God himself. In ancient times, the *name* was believed to be a centre of power. Another piece of advice which Christ gives in regard to effective prayer is to ask for what we want *in his name:* that is, to invoke his power by the use of his name because the name is inseparably associated with the person. The same idea is contained in phrases such as: "In the name of the law."

"Thy Kingdom come," is another central part of this tightly condensed prayer model. Christ taught his disciples that the Kingdom of God was a threefold concept. There is the kingdom which is *within* us, experienced as a sense of peace, an awareness of tranquillity, of belonging to God, of being an integrated part of his creation and as such being fully aware of his love and his Fatherly concern for us. There is the kingdom on earth, which comes just a shade closer whenever we deal honestly and fairly with each other, whenever we treat others as we ourselves would wish to be treated, when we help the poor, the sick, the oppressed, the lost, and the lonely. Thirdly, there is the kingdom yet to come: the fulfilment of God's will on earth, when there will be peace and joy during this mortal life as well as in Heaven. It is not beyond the power of dedicated men and women to reform our earth as Wilberforce freed the slaves, and as Florence Nightingale improved the conditions of the soldiers who were dying in the atrocious Crimean military hospital. Every kind and generous thought, word and deed can help to bring this aspect of God's Kingdom nearer. This perspective of the Kingdom of God is like a glorious, indestructible bridge linking the eternal joys of Heaven to the transitory joys of Earth, so that they will be almost indistinguishable. Eternal and abundant life in this kingdom-yet-to-be will be the perfect expression of God's perfect love.

"Thy will be done," expresses the quintessential kernel of effective prayer. More nonsense has been talked about "submission" to the Will of God by well-meaning but hopelessly erroneous priests and religious teachers than about almost any other theological subject. If we stick with our earlier model of God as a suprapersonal, all-loving, and all-powerful parent, it becomes obvious that the concept of a dominating, dictatorial tyrant-in-the-sky who *demands* total obedience from everybody is irrelevant. The will of a loving Father God is for the eternal and abundant freedom and happiness of his creation. Petulant demands for obedience and conformity are symptomatic of inadequacy and psychosis. The most appropriate place for a querulous control freak is on a psychiatrist's couch. In praying that God's will be done, we are not abandoning our own individual wills — we are joyfully acknowledging that God's will is for our perfect freedom, happiness, and rugged individuality. In praying that God's will be done, we are praying most fervently for ourselves. God wants only what is best for us — when his will is done, we achieve that sublime freedom, personal development and happiness which he wants us to have.

"Give us this day our daily bread" is another vital indicator which guides us closer to the secret of effective prayer. "Give us" is a reminder that God is an inexhaustible source of everything we need, a divine cornucopia of all things good. There is no merit in poverty or self-denial for its own sake. There is no piety in deliberately going without when there's plenty for everyone.

To share a scarce resource with those in need is a truly holy and sacred action, an expression of real piety: to deny yourself something you really like when there's more than enough of it for everyone else to enjoy as well is not piety: it's a particularly damaging form of stupidity.

"And forgive us our trespasses" ("trespasses" here can also be translated as "debts") is another essential ingredient of effective prayer. Electronic equipment works best when its contacts are clean, when there's no dirt or corrosion to impede the flow. Does prayer work in a similar way? Does "sin" (to revive an unfashionable old word) interfere with the flow of prayer just as dust and oxidation interrupt and inhibit the flow of electric current in a circuit?

God's magnanimous and instantaneous forgiveness provides the ultimate spiritual refreshment and refurbishment. It is conditional only upon our honesty and sincerity when we request it. God's forgiveness can carry out its vital cleansing work for us only when we recognize our need of it and freely ask him for it. Forgiveness cannot be force-fed to an obdurate prisoner on a spiritual hunger strike.

Feelings of guilt are the emotional first cousins of masochism: the bizarre desire to experience pain, degradation, and humiliation. Guilt needs to be diagnosed, treated, and cleared neatly away, if prayer is to become truly effective.

Coleridge's *Ancient Mariner* — the unfortunate sailor who shot the albatross — provides a great object lesson in what prolonged guilt can do to an over-sensitive, introspective mind. At one point in the poem, the mariner is unable to pray because he feels the overwhelming weight of his guilt. Shakespeare makes a similar point in *Macbeth* where the regicide is unable to say "Amen" when he hears someone else praying.

All that Coleridge's mariner had to do was to feel genuinely — even though very briefly — sorry for the bird, and to resolve not to do anything like it again. Then he could have made a nutritious albatross pie from the edible bits, shared it with his shipmates, chucked the rest over the side and got on with his life.

It's a tough world. We have to be survivors. Guilt impedes survival. Lose it. God's forgiveness is the fathomless vortex of love into which guilt vanishes permanently. God's forgiveness also provides us with a permanent model for our own behaviour in that direction. There's an old Jewish phrase "seventy times seven" which means "without number, infinite" or "endless." Peter asks Jesus on one occasion how many times he should forgive his enemy, and suggests that as far as he was concerned seven times would be pretty magnanimous. Jesus tells him that seventy times seven, infinite forgiveness, would be closer to God's ideal. Yet again, Christ's irrefutable logic is unanswerable. The power of God's forgiveness washes over us and around us: it then flows from us to those whom we need to forgive. The most effective prayer flows from the man or woman to whom forgiveness is an integral part of existence.

"Lead us not into temptation" has suffered badly in translation: as much of the Bible has. God tempts no one. He sets traps for no one. To be a living, breathing, human being is to be vulnerable to temptation. It's a grim, associative fact of life: like cholesterol with heart disease, HIV with casual unprotected sex, and cigarettes with lung cancer. The subjunctive "Let us not be led into temptation" comes closer to the true meaning. "Protect us from temptation" gets nearer still. The things which tempt us away from all that is good, positive, and altruistic attenuate our lines of communication. We cannot pray as effectively while we are struggling with temptation as when we are not. To be effective at anything important, we need to concentrate our mental and physical powers on it: fighting, weight-lifting, shooting, filming, recording, or riding a big Harley Davidson through rush hour traffic all demand our full attention. So does effective prayer.

"Deliver us from evil." No one recognized the constant and sinister presence of evil in the universe more perceptively than Christ did. No one opposed it and defeated it more effectively than he did. We need to be delivered from it by God's power if our prayers are to be as effective as we want them to be — and as God who gave us our power to pray wants them to be. When we allow evil to get to us, when we are greedy, cruel, selfish, deceitful, treacherous, disloyal, or ungrateful, our power to pray effectively is negated by that evil. We become like gun barrels blocked with mud after falling into a ditch — more dangerous to ourselves than to the enemy until the mud is cleared. God can and will clear the muzzle for us, but we need to realize that it is blocked before we can ask him for help. Sinister, insidious, and pervasive as it is, evil can be overcome. The power of good is infinitely greater. We do not live in a dualistic universe where balanced powers of order and chaos wrestle eternally for a supremacy that neither can ever win. This is undoubtedly God's universe, and although this Earth which we live on is only a minute, almost infinitesimally small, fraction of it, it is still *God's* Earth. However large the power of terrestrial evil may loom as far as we're concerned, it is trivial and puny in the extreme compared to the infinite and absolute power of God. Every observation we make is a matter of perspective. A storm cloud directly over our heads seems sinister, while the incalculably greater power of the heat and light from the sun ninety-three million miles away doesn't seem relevant at that moment because the storm cloud has intervened. When we pray "Deliver us from evil" we are asking to see the sun again, and to be reminded of how trivial the storm cloud really is despite its unwelcome proximity.

Mysteries of the Bible

The central theme of our argument concerning the mystery of effective prayer is this. prayer is an immensely potent force if only its vast powers can be released. The mystery of prayer which confronts us in the Bible is that some prayers are answered while others are not. God is not whimsical nor arbitrary: all people are of equal value in his loving eyes. God is also totally consistent; the laws of nature which he laid down in the very beginning do not alter — but there are some deeper, less well known, less observable, *principles* which are at work at levels which are harder for us to observe. These *deeper* laws — sometimes thought of as being responsible for what we refer to as paranormal or anomalous phenomena — work just as consistently and logically as the clearly observable *surface* laws of chemistry and physics. These deeper laws act like trumps in a game of whist, or like machine code in a computer. They can do things which the surface codes can't, and they can also do them much faster. Effective prayer makes use of these deeper codes, which are just as natural and just as God-given as the rest. If this is true, then there is no more important area of study than the exploration of methods of accessing these fundamental codes. To be able to pray effectively all the time would be to realize the ancient dream of every magician, every healer, and every worker of miracles.

Chapter Nine

The Mysterious Queen of Sheba

Where *was* the ancient land of Sheba, and who was its exciting and adventurous queen? Was she genuinely historical or merely a romantic myth or legend? If she was real, why did she pay a state visit to Israel? Can she be identified as the same beautiful and sensuous, but *mysterious,* African, Asian, or Arabian girl who features so exquisitely in the controversially erotic *Song of Solomon*?

One important clue may lie in an earlier mystery associated with Solomon's mother. King David, his father, was a fearless warrior, a talented poet and musician, and — most of the time — a man of faith, integrity, and honour. While still in his teens, David had unhesitatingly accepted Goliath's challenge to single combat and killed him. It was the fearless and tireless David who led the army of Israel through long, arduous wars against the Philistines, and finally triumphed. Shrewdly, he saw the military advantages of Jerusalem, fortified it and made it his ideal capital city.

He endured a heart-rending civil war against his beloved son, Absalom, and almost died of grief when the boy was killed.

One sadly discreditable deed blighted David's otherwise great and noble character: the Bathsheba episode.

According to the straightforward biblical account, the outstandingly beautiful Bathsheba was married to one of David's loyal soldiers — not a Hebrew, but a Hittite named Uriah. He was away fighting for king and country, when David, chancing to look down from the palace roof one fateful evening, saw the exquisite Bathsheba bathing.

The sight of her was more than any red-blooded warrior-king like David could resist. Proverbially, power corrupts, and absolute power corrupts absolutely. David's power was as great as his healthy sexual appetite: he sent for Bathsheba. Not long afterwards, she informed him that she was pregnant. The Jewish law in those days was implacably brutal about adultery. Bathsheba's life was now definitely at risk.

Whatever David's other grievous faults during this episode, he was not prepared to abandon her, nor to have her killed quickly and secretly before the whispers of his involvement with her began to spread. He sent for Uriah — ostensibly to bring him news of the battle. After hearing the official war reports, David suggested that Uriah deserved an enjoyable evening at home with his beautiful young wife before going back to the battle zone. To the virile David's horror and incredulity, Uriah apparently suffered from a puritanical sense of duty which prevented him from enjoying the voluptuous delights of a night at home with the delectable Bathsheba while his companions were roughing it on the battlefield. David even ordered him to stay an extra day, and plied him with enough wine to drown the most buoyant conscience, but still Uriah refused to go home. That seemingly incomprehensible decision sealed his fate. Had he, perhaps, guessed *why* the king was suddenly so anxious to contrive a conjugal night for him with Bathsheba?

Wherever the truth of the matter lay, David felt that he had now given Uriah every chance. It may well have crossed the king's acute mind that if the obdurate Uriah already suspected something, then David's beloved Bathsheba was in double jeopardy — first from a vengeful,

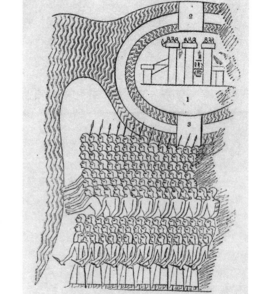

Hittite soldiers like Uriah in formidable military formation.

jealous husband, and secondly from a self-righteous mob of religious fanatics intent on stoning her as an adulteress. From then on, David could see only one way to save her.

Secret orders went to Joab, David's supremely loyal commander-in-chief. "Put Uriah the Hittite in the forefront of the battle — then withdraw and leave him to get killed." Joab's moral code began and ended with loyalty to David. Uriah duly died in battle as planned, and David married the pregnant Bathsheba.

Their first child died in infancy, but another of Bathsheba's sons grew up to become David's successor, King Solomon, reputedly one of the greatest and wisest men who ever lived. Under his guidance, Israel prospered greatly and his long reign was a time of almost legendary peace and plenty. Among the many interesting incidents which took place during Solomon's magnificent reign was that famous state visit from the queen of Sheba.

In Hebrew *bath* or *beth* means *daughter of* just as *bar* means *son of.* There is possibly some *deliberate confusion* in the biblical records over the name of Bathsheba's father. In the account in the 2 Samuel 11:3, his name is rendered as Eliam. So why isn't his daughter called Batheliam? In 1 Chronicles 3:5, he is called Ammiel. So why isn't she called Bathammiel? Both of her father's names have the same significance in Hebrew: the syllables have simply been reversed. Eliam and Ammiel can both mean "God is my people," and neither is a particularly typical Hebrew name. How relevant is it to note that Bathsheba's first husband was a Hittite?

There are several academic biblical researchers and historians who believe that there is evidence for regarding the Hittites as some of the very earliest occupants of Canaan. Genesis records that Heth, from whom the Hittites took their tribal name, was one of the sons of Canaan, who was

Co-author Lionel Fanthorpe beside the basalt head of a Hittite lion of the type that would have been familiar to Uriah, Bathsheba's husband.

himself the son of Noah's son, Ham. The Hittites are carefully distinguished from their Semitic neighbours in many of the old accounts of Middle Eastern ethnicity. Many experts associate the Hittites with the Cushites of Chaldea, among whom the great warrior Nimrod was a prominent conquering hero. Some ancient authorities linked the Cushites, Hittites, Egyptians, and Philistines. When Abraham first entered Palestine, he found that the Hittites were already well-established there.

Ancient historians and biblical records are in broad agreement that the Hittites were an old race, and not a Semitic one. Uriah was not a natural born Hebrew, but simply an ally of David's. He could even have been an itinerant, Hittite mercenary; there was plenty of work for such soldiers of fortune in that area in those days. As an itinerant mercenary, Uriah could well have travelled as far south as Sheba — wherever that elusive old kingdom actually was — and met and married his fatally attractive bride *while he was there.* So Bathsheba is named not after her father, but after her *birthplace*. She came from Sheba and is called the daughter of Sheba. Eliam or Ammiel perhaps accompanied them to Israel. There was a profound moral duty to care for parents and elderly relatives. How else could a professional soldier do it except by keeping them with him wherever his work took him? Hence the strange name of Bathsheba's father. He was a wanderer, with his son-in-law providing for him.

"Who are you? Who are your people?" ask his new neighbours each time the army moves on.

"God is my people," replies old Eliam (Ammiel), meaning that as he is a wanderer, with no permanent resting place, he regards himself as belonging to God rather than to any tribe or nation. Many of the new people he meets on his travels may not even have heard of his distant land of Sheba. Is it possible that Solomon, the greatest of all the Jewish kings, was partly Sheban?

What light does this shed on some possible additional reasons for the queen of Sheba's state visit to Solomon the Magnificent?

For the sake of pursuing the argument, suppose that Bathsheba, Solomon's mother, was, in fact, Sheban by birth. She is an intelligent and cultured woman as well as a very beautiful one, and, naturally, she tells her young son about her distant homeland, and her childhood there. The equally intelligent and sensitive young Solomon is deeply impressed. His mother's treasured memories go deeply into the boy's mind.

Years later, when he is king, Solomon talks to Bathsheba again about her former home. "Would you like to see some of your people again, Mother? I can invite them."

The royal invitation duly reaches the queen of Sheba. Oh, yes, indeed, Her Majesty has very definitely heard of Solomon, king of Israel: heard of his wisdom, his wealth, his armies, his navies, his prosperous merchant adventurers, his superb temple, and his royal palace. Her Majesty would be honoured and delighted to accept Solomon's invitation, and will bring with her a mixture of rich gifts and difficult questions so that she can experience Solomon's vast wisdom for herself.

The famous visit duly takes place. The attractive young queen meets Bathsheba as well as her illustrious son, King Solomon. As his mother was radiantly beautiful, so Solomon is irresistibly handsome. The spirited young queen can see his mother's Sheban blood in him and a sudden, wild, daring thought races through her mind.

Was the stirring love poetry of *The Song of Solomon* born from their encounter?

Let him kiss me with the kisses of his mouth …
I am black but comely …
He shall lie all night betwixt my breasts …
Our bed is green …
I am my beloved's and his desire is towards me …
His left hand should be under my head
And his right hand should embrace me …
Many waters cannot quench love,
Neither can the floods drown it …

There are various quaintly coy euphemisms for sex in the English translations of the more straightforward biblical records: she knew him;

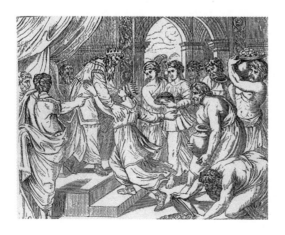

The queen of Sheba
visits King Solomon
the Wise.

she lay with him. What does 1 Kings 10:13 really mean? "And King Solomon gave unto the Queen of Sheba all her desire, whatsoever she asked." Did she dare to ask Solomon whether she could bear his child?

Although there are several possible locations for the land of Sheba, the Romano-Jewish historian, Josephus, locates it in both Ethiopia and Egypt. If he was correct about Ethiopia, that ties in with a very strong and persistent Ethiopian tradition regarding King Menelik I, otherwise known as Ibn al-Hakim, meaning *The Son of the Wise Man*. The Ethiopian Constitution of 1955 formally declares that their royal line "descends

Artist's impression of King Solomon's Temple. Drawn by Theo Fanthorpe.

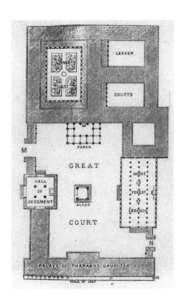

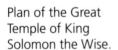

Plan of the Great Temple of King Solomon the Wise.

uninterruptedly from the Dynasty of Menelik I, son of the Queen of Ethiopia, the Queen of Sheba, and King Solomon of Jerusalem."

According to other strong and persistent ancient Ethiopian traditions, when the queen of Sheba (Ethiopia), whose name was Makeda, discovered that she was pregnant, she left Jerusalem so that her son and Solomon's would be born in her own Kingdom of Ethiopia.

When Prince Menelik was twenty years old, he set out to visit his illustrious father, and was very well received by Solomon. It is likely that his Sheban grandmother, Bathsheba, was also among those who welcomed him so warmly in Jerusalem. According to these Ethiopian traditions, Menelik was given so much honour and attention that the Jewish Elders, courtiers, and his numerous half-brothers began to grow jealous. They complained to Solomon about the length of Menelik's visit, and asked the king to send him home. Solomon reluctantly agreed, but laid down the condition that the eldest sons of all the prominent Hebrew families should accompany him.

Zadok, the High Priest, however, had a son named Azarius, who was one of Menelik's attendants on this voyage. Before they sailed for Sheba, Azarius used his special knowledge and privileged position as the High Priest's eldest son, to smuggle the Ark of the Covenant out of the Holy of Holies in the temple, and hide it secretly on board.

Menelik himself had no knowledge of what Azarius and the other young Jewish nobles had done until they were many miles away from Jerusalem. There is an interesting parallel here with the story of Joseph, who eventually rose to become Pharaoh's second-in-command in Egypt

Were the ancient ruins at Zimbabwe the site of King Solomon's mines? Drawn by Theo Fanthorpe.

Solomon in all his glory.

during the seven-year famine. The "stolen" cup in the Joseph story was hidden in Benjamin's sack, and neither he nor his brothers knew anything about it until they were arrested and searched by Joseph's soldiers.

Again according to Ethiopian tradition, the Ark was carefully preserved in the city of Axum. As far as can be ascertained, it is still there today. Tradition places it in the custody of a very ancient monk or holy man, whose sole duty is to guard it with his life. Up until comparatively recent times the Ark had been annually paraded during the January religious festival known as *Timkat*, but the hazards of the civil war were such that it has not been out of its ancient sanctuary for several years. Even when it was paraded publicly, it was always wrapped in thick cloths, not to protect the Ark itself, but to protect the onlookers from its terrifying powers.

It may be asked then, whether Solomon's mother really was at least partly Sheban, and whether Solomon and Makeda, queen of Sheba, produced a son named Menelik who founded the great Ethiopian Dynasty. Did the Ark of the Covenant find its way mysteriously from the Jerusalem temple to Axum, and is it guarded there still in a secret sanctuary? Bathsheba and Makeda are both women of mystery, but the history of the Ark and the riddle of its disappearance are part of a longer and more convoluted enigma.

Chapter Ten

Where is the Ark of the Covenant?

While the Israelites were undertaking their long journey through the wilderness after Moses had led them out of Egypt, their central place of worship was the Tabernacle, and the holiest object within the Tabernacle was the Ark of the Covenant, the Hebrew title of which can also be interpreted as the Ark of the Testimony.

Together with the Mercy Seat situated on its lid, this Ark was the centre of the Israelites' sacred mystery.

As far as can be ascertained from Exodus 25, it was cuboid in shape, 1.5 cubits wide, 1.5 deep and 2.5 long. The biblical cubit was approximately 45 centimetres or 18 inches — the length of a human forearm from elbow to fingertips.

It was made from acacia wood, which is a genus of the mimosa family, or Mimosaceae, found mainly in Africa and Australia as well as the Middle East. Finely divided leaflets give the stems a feathery appearance. Acacia flowers tend to be small and fragrant, and are almost always yellow or white. One variety found in the Sudan is the source of Arabic gum which is used in sweets, inks, adhesives, and, chemical products. The bark of most acacias is also a rich source of tannin. The acacias yield interesting and unusual wood, particularly appropriate for the sacred Ark of the Covenant.

This fine acacia wood was overlaid with gold on both sides.

The Mercy Seat was placed above the Ark, and supported a cherub at each end. It was regarded as the symbolic throne of God. When the Ark was in place within the Tabernacle, or later within the Holy of Holies in the temple, a luminous cloud known as the Shechinah was seen to hover above, and was clearly distinguished from the familiar smoke created by incense.

The word *Shechinah* comes from an old root meaning *to rest, to settle,* or *to dwell.* It is not found in the Bible itself. It was widely used, however, by later Jews, and borrowed from them by Christians. It signified the *visible* majesty of the Divine Presence, particularly when God was thought to be especially there in the area between the cherubim on the lid of the sacred Ark. The Shechinah was reported during the days of the Tabernacle, and while Solomon's Temple stood, but apparently it was no longer seen in Zerubbabel's Temple as it was one of the five things which some expert Jewish writers maintained were missing from this later temple. Dr. Bernard in his notes on Josephus disagrees. He argues from Josephus's records that as the mysterious *Urim* and *Thummim* were said to be in Zerubbabel's Temple, the other four significant "missing" things must have been there as well.

The first reference to the Shechinah is found in the Targums. A Targum in Aramaic literally means a *translation* or an *interpretation,* so the Targums were translations of portions of the Hebrew Bible — or, indeed, the whole of it — into Aramaic. At one time the word meant a translation of the Old Testament into any language at all, but was honed down over the years to refer specifically to a translation from the old Hebrew into the later Aramaic.

It was after the exile in Babylon that Aramaic became the preferred spoken language of the Palestinian Jews, and so replaced their original Hebrew. Just as Latin lingered among European academics and ecclesiastical scholars long after it had ceased to be spoken by Roman legionaries, so Hebrew lingered among Jewish academics and scholars until well after the first century A.D., although by then Aramaic was firmly established in the eastern Mediterranean area.

The Targums were produced to meet the spiritual and religious needs of the great majority of Jewish worshippers who found it difficult if not impossible to cope with ancient classical Hebrew.

The Israeli Ark of the Covenant. What ancient secrets does it contain?
Drawn by Theo Fanthorpe.

Where is the Ark of the Covenant?

When the Herodian Temple was destroyed in A.D. 70, the Targums came into their own. Synagogues had to replace the lost Temple, and the central readings in the synagogue services needed to be translated into Aramaic for the benefit of most of the worshippers. As time went on the Targums assumed the role of commentaries, and a special *meturgeman* attempted to explain away any confusions or doubtful meanings.

Wise sayings, proverbs, aphorisms, allegories, and legends crept into the Targums as time went on, so that the later ones were very different from the straightforward translations which had been the main purpose of the originals.

From its special use in the Targums, the concept of Shechinah came to signify the actual *presence* of God on earth as far as the early Jewish theologians and scholars were concerned. One reason for this was a fear on the part of the writers of the Talmud, Midrash, and Targums that some of the clearly anthropomorphic descriptions of God in the earlier writings might cause serious misunderstandings. The idea of a God who looked like an amorphous cloud of glowing mist — rather than a human being — undoubtedly seemed theologically *safer* to them than the earlier concepts of an undeniably humanoid God who walked in the Garden of Eden in the cool of the evening looking for Adam and Eve.

Some theologians have considered the existence of a parallel between the concept of the Shechinah and the idea of the Holy Spirit. Other, mainly medieval, theologians have tried to work out theories of the Shechinah as a separate Divine Being, someone or something created by God, perhaps a personified representation of Divine Glory or Divine Light.

In one of the sadder short stories of H.G. Wells a character goes in search of *Light*, and falls to his death in the process, but the Wellsian concept of *Light* in the mind of the tragic hero in this particular story comes surprisingly close to the medieval theological concept of the Shechinah.

Yet another Jewish idea connected with the Shechinah was that it would return when the long-promised Messiah came. In the Gospel account of the transfiguration of Jesus, when the disciples Peter, James, and John witnessed him shining with his rightful Divine Glory on the mountain top with Moses and Elijah, the Shechinah could well have been put forward as an explanation.

To what extent can this extremely mysterious and powerful Shechinah light be associated with the records of the Exodus? Many of the biblical accounts surround it with a cloud, so that the brilliant radiance of the Shechinah shines *through* the cloud. In the Exodus account "the Lord went before [the Israelites] by day in a pillar of cloud

... and by night in a pillar of fire." Philo interprets this as: "The fiery appearance of the Deity shone forth from the cloud" and Philo's ideas are always well worth considering.

Philo Judaeus, who was also known as Philo of Alexandria, was born in 15 B.C. and died in A.D. 50. He was a brilliantly intelligent, Greek-speaking, Jewish philosopher and theologian, whose great pioneering contribution to human thought was his attempt to reconcile faith with reason — an exceedingly difficult but supremely worthwhile intellectual task. Philo came of an extremely wealthy and influential family in Alexandria. He studied at one of the Greek gymnasiums where he mastered mathematics, astronomy, philosophy, grammar, and logic. He also made a deep study of rhetoric like all other young academics of his time and place.

Unlike his more ascetic scholarly colleagues, Philo had the profound good sense to *enjoy* life as well as to think about its meaning philosophically. He was a keen boxing fan, an enthusiastic theatre-goer, and a devotee of chariot racing. When he wasn't pursuing any of these sensible and healthy interests, he was enjoying an evening of good food and lavish entertainment; he was, in short, a practical *bon viveur* as well as a great thinker. Philo's love of a "middle way" between the extremes of Jewish scriptural fundamentalism on one hand and a liberal disregard of the old laws because they were considered to be "only parables" on the other, would have made him quite a comfortable member of the present day Anglican Church.

He is far and away our most valuable, reliable, and informative source of knowledge of the Hellenistic Judaism that was practised in Alexandria in his day.

The highlight of Philo's career, however, was an occasion in the year A.D. 39 on which he displayed great courage and integrity when he dared to lead a delegation of Alexandrian Jews to complain to Caligula about a recent pogrom in their city. The ignorant and prejudiced Greek orator Apion, who was opposing Philo, had just delivered a despicable racist attack on the Jews. Philo was on the point of refuting Apion's nonsense when Caligula decided he did not wish to hear any more arguments at that time. Philo, one of those rare beings who dared to risk the wrath of Caligula, told his colleagues not to be disheartened because God would very shortly deal with the insane Roman emperor. Shortly afterwards, to everyone's delight, Caligula was assassinated.

A man like Philo definitely deserves to be heard.

So what was this strange and mysterious Shechinah that was associated with the even more mysterious Ark of the Covenant?

Where is the Ark of the Covenant?

Looked at disinterestedly and objectively, the Ark was not an exclusively Jewish artefact. The ancient Egyptians used them for religious purposes as well, and there is a possibility that when Moses led the Israelite slaves out of bondage in Egypt, the Ark and its contents came with them. Had Moses with his secret inner knowledge of the Egyptian Court — he had, after all, been raised as an Egyptian prince — brought some great and powerful ancient treasure away with him? Was that why Pharaoh, on discovering its loss, launched his finest chariots suicidally across the treacherous bed of the Red Sea?

If distinguished researchers like Colin Wilson and Graham Hancock are right, and some of the technological wonders of very ancient civilizations escaped terrifying inundations or major disasters caused by ice and polar change, did any of those advanced artefacts find their way to Egypt? Was the dangerously powerful Ark of the Covenant itself one such object, or was it the carefully shielded and insulated *container* for such an object? Was it the spasmodic operation of a long forgotten technology rather than the presence of a deity which caused the Shechinah?

The 1999 discoveries by the *Joides Resolution* scientists drilling the bed of the Indian Ocean have tentatively indicated the ancient inundation of a huge land mass almost a third the size of Australia. Fifty million years ago it was a lush and fertile land. Dinosaurs grazed on the abundant vegetation which grew there. Twenty million years ago movement of the earth's crust started it on its long journey to the ocean bed. If one such great land mass could go down, why not others?

Whether it was the work of Egyptian craftsmen, Israelite craftsmen, survivors of Atlantis, or extraterrestrial aliens, the Ark of the Covenant was described as thickly covered with gold. Apart from its commercial and artistic value, gold has the great practical advantages of being easy to work and massively resistant to corrosion — *it also acts as an effective radiation shield.* If there was an artefact inside the Ark — some sort of weapon, perhaps — was it nuclear powered? Could the Shechinah have been a glow of pure energy, visible only when the machine was operating — in other words, when "God" was present and active?

An interesting case can be argued for the existence of *at least two Arks* and this, if substantiated, would go some way towards explaining the apparent existence of one Ark in Axum in the care of its holy guardian, and at least one other, now lost, or hidden elsewhere.

It may be suggested after close perusal of the biblical texts that Moses possibly received *different* items of the law on *different* occasions. Is it possible that these different portions were stored in *separate* Arks?

From Exodus, Chapters 20–24, it might even be inferred that the Ten Commandments and several important civil laws were proclaimed to the people directly by God himself, rather than to Moses as God's messenger. Exodus 20:1, clearly reads: "And *God* spake all these words." Was God speaking to Moses on Mount Sinai at that point, or is it remotely possible that the text means that the people themselves were being addressed directly?

The context certainly emphasizes God's strict instructions to keep the people and even the Priests *away* from the top of the mountain. Yet in Exodus 24:9–11, Moses and several of his companions actually *see* God, who is described as having "a paved work of sapphire stone" under his feet. In verse 12, God promises to give Moses the famous tablets of stone on which the law was to be inscribed. Verse 15 onwards of this same chapter refers yet again to what must be the Shechinah (although, as previously noted, as this is a biblical text, not a Targum, the word Shechinah itself is not used here). Moses goes up into the mount and a cloud covers it. The Shechinah radiates from within this cloud for six days, and on the seventh day God speaks to Moses from the cloud. The light gets brighter and more powerful. Later in the chapter it is described as "devouring fire" on top of the mountain — yet Moses enters it and ascends the mountain, presumably *inside* the Shechinah. He remains there according to the Exodus account for forty days and forty nights, but here again the Hebrew phrasing has to be considered carefully. Forty was an important number to the Israelites: it had the significance of an indeterminate "many" as well as its accurate numerical value of forty in the sense of four tens.

In Exodus 25:10–15, Moses is given instructions for building either *an* Ark like the ancient and mysterious one which he *might* have brought from Egypt, or *the* unique Ark of the Covenant, which is now being constructed for the first time. Hebrew stylists liked to rhyme their ideas in much the same way that some poets rhyme their words. The two accounts may represent no more than this linguistic preference — but they *might* just mean that there were *two* Arks.

Ancient Egyptian Ark. Did Moses take one like this with him when he left?

In verse 16, Moses is commanded to place the stone tablets containing the law into this Ark, and the following verses describe God's promise to "commune" with Moses from the gold-covered Mercy Seat on the lid of the Ark between the cherubim. The particular use of *commune* at this juncture has led some theorists to conjecture that the Ark was a communication device, one which has been picturesquely described as "a radio for talking to the Almighty." The omnipotent, omnipresent, and omniscient God would scarcely need one — an extraterrestrial mentor probably would.

When young Samuel was asleep beside it in the holy place at Shiloh, he heard what he believed to be the voice of God calling him by name. So clear and audible did this repeated call seem that the boy was convinced that it was Eli, the old priest whom he assisted in the sanctuary at Shiloh, who had called him. Eli assured him that he had not called and told Samuel to go back to sleep. When the call came again, Eli told the lad that it was God who was calling and instructed him how to answer. It remains a matter of speculation as to whether Eli had ever had a similar experience himself during the years that he had been in charge of the Shiloh sanctuary.

Suppose that the Ark really had been a strange, technological artefact from a civilization far in advance of anything in Egypt or the Middle East at that time, an unknown civilization that had been *almost* destroyed by some great natural disaster, but which had nevertheless left one or two survivors as well as a few of its artefacts. Had a handful of those knowledgeable survivors formed a secret organization of wardens or guardians, an elite cognoscenti of *those who knew the truth,* who saw it as their duty to protect the weird artefacts which had come from their drowned, or iced-up, lost culture and to teach a favoured few among their new hosts how that eldritch apparatus was operated? Was Moses, the Israelite–Egyptian prince, a party to that secret knowledge? Was his brother, Aaron in the know as well? What about his sister, Miriam, the prophetess? It is remotely possible that other secret groups — the legendary Priory of Sion, Alchemists, Cathars, or Albigensians, Templars, Rosicrucians, and Freemasons — all might have had an inner core who knew something about the secret powers and present whereabouts of these strange relics from a bygone age.

Exodus 34:1, records God's commandment to Moses to hew two further tablets of stone, like the first ones which got broken. The Book of Deuteronomy 10:1–5, contains an instruction to Moses to make an Ark of wood to hold these new tablets. This order is duly carried out. The mystery is whether these are simply two parallel accounts of stone tablets being placed in the same Ark. Are they merely co-existent accounts of the same event which are there because of the work done by editors and redactors during the exile in Babylon, or do they really refer to *two* Arks holding different sets of stone tablets containing the Jewish law? What may reasonably be inferred is the *possibility* that on the first day of the first month of the second year of the Exodus (see Exodus 40:1–2) the *first set* of stone tablets was placed in the elaborate golden Ark, while the later *copies* were kept in a simple wooden Ark.

In the turbulent eleventh century, shortly before William of Normandy invaded England in 1066, there lived in Troyes in Champagne, a brilliant Jewish scholar named Shlomo Yitzhaqi, or Solomon son of Isaac. He was a Rabbi and an expert commentator on the Bible and Talmud, who was best known by his acronym of Rashi. His superb mind enabled him to make the best of both worlds during his academic examination of the ancient texts. He combined literal and non-literal interpretations with an ideal mixture of grammatical and syntactical rigour married to a far-reaching and keenly perceptive imagination. He was meticulous, creative, and original. His wisdom and reputation still survive, and, deservedly, he still has many admirers among Jewish scholars almost one thousand years after his death.

Rashi was convinced that there were two Arks. The simple wooden one was taken into battle with the Israeli army. The elaborate golden Ark was not — except in the time of Eli, when it was captured by the enemy.

The Hebrew Bible is often called the Tanakh, sometimes rendered TaNaKh. Like Rashi's name it is an acronym, derived from Torah (Law), Nevi'im (Prophets), and Ketuvim (Writings). There are indications in it of an Ark being hidden under the temple: but which Ark was it, and did the Templars find it many centuries later? The golden Ark went to Egypt, according to the Tanakh, during the time of Shishak.

This Shishak, also known as Sheshonk I, was the first Pharaoh of the twenty-second Egyptian Dynasty. His ancestors were war-like Libyan aristocrats. There are no extant records of any great struggle, however, which brought Shishak to the throne, and his son, Osorkon married Psusennes, whose father had been the final Pharaoh of the twenty-first Dynasty. The First Book of Kings 14:25–26, describes how Shishak stormed Jerusalem and removed *all* the Jewish temple treasure. The relevant phrasing is emphatic and unequivocal: Shishak took *everything* — which looks as though the elaborate golden Ark containing the first set of stone tablets must have been included — unless it had already gone to safety in Ethiopia with Menelik, the man who was believed to have been the son of Solomon and Makeda, queen of Sheba (Ethiopia).

The next link in the mysterious and convoluted chain involves another Egyptian Pharaoh, Rameses III. Diodorus Siculus regarded this Rameses as the richest of all the Egyptian Pharaohs, but that could well have been an overestimation. Egypt was in dire trouble when Setnakht came along and founded the twentieth Dynasty in 1190 B.C. He was a strong and resourceful military leader, who pacified the land in time for his son Rameses III to take over as Pharaoh. Following in his father's footsteps, young Rameses smashed up a formidable invasion of the Egyptian Delta organized by an alliance of various Libyan chieftains, leaving most of them dead on the battlefield along with thousands of their troops. Following the fall of the once-great Hittite Empire to the north, further invaders, mainly sea-peoples, made their way south towards Egypt looking for trouble. Rameses met them head on in a great land battle in Palestine, and an even bloodier sea-battle in the Nile Delta. The would-be invaders went the same way as the Libyans, and these great Egyptian victories are commemorated in the carvings in the temple of Amon-Ra at Medinet Habu.

Most of Rameses' reign was spent in these defensive wars, but he was also noted for building a temple dedicated to the leading Egyptian god, the ram-headed Amon, in a remote and obscure village, Djahi Pakaanan (numerous spelling variations exist), on what would have been the direct mountain route from Egypt to Jerusalem. Amon was also identified with Ra, the Egyptian sun-god, and therefore known as Amon-Ra.

On leaving Egypt, crossing the desert and heading up the Judaean hills towards Jerusalem, the first village the traveller finds is Djaharya. It takes no great feat of linguistic acrobatics to suggest with some credibility that Djaharya could well be Djahi-Ra-Lya, meaning "The Village of Ra in Djahi." Was this the place where Rameses III built another great temple to Amon-Ra, one to which his subject peoples in that area could journey with their tribute — both to him, and to the head of the Egyptian pantheon?

The Harris Papyrus, one of the finest in the British Museum's excellent collection, purports to have been written by the son of Rameses III when his father died. It contains a reference to a "mysterious house" built in "the Land of Djahi" as well as to a location named as "Pekanan." But where *was* this place?

Another clue comes from records left by the valiant nineteenth century American explorer, Edward Robinson. Dr. Robinson made it on foot from Egypt to Jerusalem at about the same time as the young Queen Victoria was beginning her reign in the U.K. Somewhere between Beersheba and Hebron, he wrote of meeting a few Arabian people of the desert and one man on horseback. He was surprised on leaving the wilderness to come across green pastures and sleek healthy herds grazing there under the care of the people of a village which Robinson called Dhoheriyeh. Robinson thought these prosperous flocks were rather reminiscent of the days of the biblical patriarchs. He also said that the village was very high up and visible for many miles around. Most important of all, Robinson noted the presence of *a large ruin* (he thought it had once been a castle, or fortress) with the remains of a square tower still occupied as a home. It sounds very much as if Dr. Robinson *might* have rediscovered Djahi Pakaanan without realizing that he was looking at the remains of the temple of Ra which Rameses III had built there.

There are some biblical scholars and researchers who think it quite possible that when and *if* Shishak captured the golden Ark along with its precious contents, he may well have taken it to this temple of Amon-Ra at Djahi Pakaanan, or, as it is written on some of today's maps *Edh Dhahirya*.

It would have been far from impossible for a determined party of dedicated twelfth or thirteenth century Templars — like those who dug beneath *what they believed to be* Solomon's Temple in Jerusalem — to have gotten as far as Edh Dhahirya and dug with equal fervour there below the ruined temple of Amon-Ra. What, if anything did they find, and where did they conceal it? When their great and noble order was attacked and almost (but not *quite*) destroyed by the treachery of the despicable French King Philip IV in 1307, did some of their most precious treasures cross the Atlantic with their so-called "Lost Fleet"? Were the richest of those same treasures concealed in the mysterious, flood-guarded labyrinth below Oak Island off the coast of Nova Scotia? Were others hidden in the mysterious old French hill-top village of Rennes-le-Château, until a few of them at least may have been uncovered by the enigmatic priest, Bérenger Saunière, in 1885?

Were the Arks of the Covenant (if more than one existed) among the holiest of all holy relics, or were they merely strangely powerful technological artefacts from an ancient but sophisticated terrestrial culture? Was the awesome secret power, which at least one of them seems to have contained, due to the Presence of God glowing through the Divine Shechinah, or was it just the work of some brilliant, human or extraterrestrial artisan?

It seems extremely unlikely, downright impossible, in fact, that the Father God of Love, Mercy, and Compassion whom Christ revealed and demonstrated so clearly in his own Person could have been arbitrarily responsible for the death and disaster which so often accompanied the Ark. If it was *not* God's power that sprang so destructively from that inexplicable "sacred" box, then what *was* it, and *who* put it there in the first place?

Chapter Eleven

The Secrets of
Urim and Thummim

The three basic mysteries of Urim and Thummim are: what they actually *were*, how they were *used*, and whether they *worked*. Their first mention in the Bible occurs in Exodus 28:30, where there are, unfortunately, no references to what they are made of, nor to how they are to be constructed and used. All that it tells us is that Aaron, the High Priest, is to wear "a breastplate of judgement" into which the Urim and Thummim are to be placed. He will wear them "over his heart" continually while undertaking his priestly duties. The verse tends to give the impression that whatever the Urim and Thummim really are, they are small enough to be worn like pocket watches, or jewels, in a pouch or small bag which is part of Aaron's robes of office.

This absence of detail has led some religious historians to suggest that the Urim and Thummim were the direct handiwork of God, in the same way that the first tables of the law were "written by the finger of God."

Dr. Harold Browne, one of the learned contributors to Smith's *Dictionary of the Bible,* was of the opinion that because no description of them was given, and no directions for their use were added, their nature and function must already have been well known to Moses, to whom the authorship of Exodus was popularly attributed. Browne, and those researchers who shared his views, started looking for explanations of Urim and Thummim among the customs of ancient Egypt, Chaldea, and Babylon.

There are clear differences of opinion between Josephus and other Jewish historians about the details given in Exodus 28:16, which refer to the priestly breastplate being "double."Josephus argues that this "doubling" was done to give strength and stability to the fabric. Other commentators think that the idea of a bag, pouch, or container is intended — something to hold Urim and Thummim, as well as the other precious stones traditionally worn by the High Priest at that time. Josephus also argues stridently that the preposition "in" is not correct, and that "on" was intended. He thought that "on" was important because he believed that Urim and Thummim were worn on the High Priest's shoulder straps, rather than in some sort of container. Hebrew language experts are inclined to disagree with Josephus on the grounds that the same preposition is used in Exodus 25:16, where it clearly implies "thou shalt put *into* the Ark, the testimony which I shall give thee."

What is the real etymology and meaning of these two important Hebrew words: Urim and Thummim? Harold Browne and many Hebrew language experts regard Urim as the plural form of *or* or *ur*, meaning *fire* or *light*. It is exactly the same as the word used for *light* in Genesis 1:3: "Let there be *light*, and there was *light*."

The Septuagint is usually described as an early translation of the Hebrew Bible (largely corresponding to the Christian Bible's Old Testament) into the Hellenistic Greek that was used in and around Alexandria a century or two B.C. That suffices as a rough and ready guide to what it is, but scholars have argued over it fiercely for years, and will probably continue to do so for a few centuries yet. Traditionally, seventy-two of the leading Jewish scholars of their day were assembled in Alexandria by Ptolemy II Philadelphus, or his father, Ptolemy Soter during the years between 285 and 250 B.C. There exist copies of the Septuagint which are several centuries older than the oldest surviving copies of the Hebrew texts — and leading scholars like the late Dr. Ira M. Price recognized that that gave the Septuagint great research value.

One great problem confronting Hebrew experts is the existence of at least three major textual resources for serious academic study of the Hebrew Bible: the Septuagint, the Masoretic Text and the Samaritan Pentateuch. It is generally felt that all three need to be compared and contrasted rigorously in order to rediscover the original text.

Another great problem is that far from being the definitively accurate work of seventy-two great and careful linguistic scholars working assiduously at Ptolemy's bidding, as tradition suggests, there are parts of the Septuagint where the quality of the translation is little short of appalling.

Despite the doubts that surround it, however, the Septuagint is not entirely without merit, and it can shed some useful light on the problems of Urim and Thummim. If Harold Browne is right about Urim meaning "light" or "fire" then it would be reasonable to expect the Septuagint to translate it as "phos" — but it doesn't. In Exodus 28:30, and Leviticus 8:8, it uses "delosis" meaning "showing forth" or "manifestation." In Numbers, Deuteronomy, and 1 Samuel, it uses "deloi" meaning "visible" or "clear." In Ezra and Nehemiah it switches yet again and uses part of "photozein" meaning "to give out light" or "to shine."

If the Septuagint offers variety, the Latin Vulgate offers rather more. Jerome, its translator, lived from A.D. 347 until 420. He began the work in 382 and moved to Bethlehem in 386, where he worked mainly on the Old Testament. Having started by translating from the Septuagint, he changed his approach and worked directly on the Hebrew texts instead. By 405 he had completed the enormous task. Surprisingly, his work, although meritorious, did not achieve much popularity or recognition for three or four centuries, due largely to the survival of older Latin versions which were preferred at the time.

At one point Jerome translates Urim as "doctrina" which means "teaching" or "instruction"; elsewhere he uses the phrase "per sacerdotes" meaning "by priests" or "via priests." In yet another place he uses a phrase meaning "endowed with truth." Putting all Jerome's ideas together may produce a composite picture of Urim as something believed to be endowed with truth which was considered to be a means for giving learning or instruction via the hands of priests.

Thummim seems to present fewer etymological problems than Urim. There is fairly general agreement that it is derived from the Hebrew word "tom" meaning "perfection" or "completeness," something which is whole and brought to its proper finish." The Septuagint has "teleios" which also means "perfection" in Ezra; and "aletheia" meaning "truth" in all other instances. Jerome, in the Vulgate, translates these straight into Latin with "perfectus" meaning "perfect" and veritas meaning "truth."

What explanation is there for the use of the plural form –im which ends both words? As with the English royal "We" which was once used by the reigning king or queen to emphasize both the importance of the monarch and the identification of the ruler with his, or her, kingdom, so the Hebrew plural may also be used for emphasis, or to intensify meaning. Taken all in all, Urim and Thummim were probably understood by their contemporaries to mean a combination of light and perfection. The idea of *light* also reintroduces the mysterious Shechinah. Is there any possibility that Urim was an extension, or a relay, for the luminous power associated with the enigma of the Ark? If Urim and Thummim fell into disuse after the Ark disappeared, were they analogous to sophisticated electronic apparatus which could not function once its power source had gone?

The myths and legends surrounding the Emerald Tablets of Hermes Trismegistus (alias Thoth, the scribe of the Egyptian gods) may provide further clues to the mysteries of Urim and Thummim. Suppose that the Emerald Tablets themselves were not merely engraved records but powerful artefacts in their own right. What if the legend of Abraham's sister-wife, Sarah, disturbing the sleeping Hermes had some basis in fact, and what if she had actually dared to take Urim and Thummim — once part of the Emerald Tablets — from the enigmatic sleeper's cave? Did they eventually become part of the Jewish heritage?

Hermes Trismegistus alias Thoth Scribe of the Egyptian gods. What power lies in his enigmatic Emerald Tablets? Drawn by Theo Fanthorpe.

Did Sarah steal the Urim and Thummim from the sleeping Hermes Trismegistus? Drawn by Theo Fanthorpe.

The Secrets of Urim and Thummim

As the wheel of fate made its ironic turns, did they go back to Egypt with the slave-boy Joseph? Was it part of their weird power which enabled him to interpret dreams with such accuracy? When his adoring old father, Jacob, gave him the heir's "coat of many colours" were the Urim and Thummim stitched into it, and did Joseph manage to remove them and secrete them in his tunic before he was sold to the slave traders? When his favourite son's bloodstained coat went back to the heart-broken Jacob, did the old man realize that the vital stones were missing from it?

Had Urim and Thummim — originally strange artefacts which formed part of Thoth's Emerald Tablets — left Egypt with him? Had he subsequently lost them when the inquisitive Sarah ventured into the cave where he lay asleep — or in some abnormal state of suspended animation? Had they passed as precious, powerful heirlooms from Abraham and Sarah to Isaac, Jacob, and finally Joseph, and was it Joseph as a hapless slave who took them *back* to that same Egypt from which Thoth had brought them so many years before?

If their secret power was known to Joseph's Israelite family and their descendants during their long sojourn in Egypt, as well as to the Egyptian royalty who raised Moses as an Egyptian prince, would it not have been likely that Moses would have wanted to take those great treasures when he finally led his people to freedom? Was it Urim and Thummim inside an ancient *Egyptian Ark* which the escaping Israelites took with them to Sinai?

Yet none of this far out speculation reduces the omnipotent power of God by one iota. Nor does it diminish the concept of his benign concern with, and influence over, earthly events: apparent miracles of deliverance and positive plans for the future of his chosen people, can all be accomplished just as effectively via intermediaries as by direct intervention. If a drowning man is rescued via the intervention of a brave and powerful swimmer rather than by the shining hand of God appearing from a cloud and lifting him directly out of the water, the will of God has still been fulfilled. When a brilliant casualty surgeon saves a life by using the latest surgical techniques, God's will is being done through him just as surely as it is when Christ or a faith-healer touches a patient and prays effectively for a direct "miracle" cure. If the benign and powerful Hermes Trismegistus was an extraterrestrial alien, or a survivor of Atlantis or Lemuria, the humane acts he performed were just as surely part of God's will as if Trismegistus had been an angelic being with magical, miraculous powers.

If Joseph, son of Jacob, did God's will and saved many from starvation by virtue of his gift of dreaming and interpretation, it matters not a whit whether God spoke to him directly, or enabled him via the emeralds Sarah took from Hermes in the cave. God is pure goodness and that goodness can reach us *directly* from God himself, or *indirectly* via one of his agents. The light of the sun is much the same: it can reach us directly, through a transparent substance, or via a reflection.

God's benign power over the Urim and Thummim is not limited in any way by whether they were made by Moses or by Hermes Trismegistus, whether they came from Mars, Atlantis or somewhere much more distant.

There is a theory that they were *teraphim*, little idols or household gods as they were sometimes described. In the days of Laban and Jacob they seem to have been popular religious objects. Micah, as described in Judges 17:5 and 18:14, 20, has recourse to both teraphim and an ephod, or priestly apron.

Throughout the whole history of the northern kingdom, which became a separate state after the death of Solomon, the city of Dan was regarded as a sanctuary or holy place because of the presence of teraphim within it. Could they have been the original Urim and Thummim, or, more likely, *copies* of them?

Another interesting point concerning the origin of the Urim and Thummim is that nowhere in the Bible is there any reference to Moses, or to his great master craftsman, Bezalel, being told to make them.

So where did they come from?

Were they thought to have been made by God, as the first set of stone tablets of the law were said to have been directly engraved by him? Nachman and Hottinger seemed rather to favour this view.

A favourite theory put forward by both Christian and Jewish scholars was that the Urim and Thummim were the *whole* of the High Priest's breastplate, containing twelve precious stones — one for each of the

Playing pieces from the Royal Game of Ur. Were they related to Urim and Thummim?

traditional Jewish Tribes. The tribal names were engraved upon these stones, and when they became illuminated in succession, the Hebrew letters spelled out the answer — a technique that perhaps bears certain similarities to a modern spiritualist's Ouijah board. Josephus thought that the Urim and Thummim were the sardonyxes which were fastened to the shoulder straps of the High Priest's breastplate. Sardonyx is quite a remarkable stone. It is a translucent brownish colour, whose shades vary considerably. Sardonyx is a form of chalcedony, which is one of the silica minerals. Throughout history it has been one of the most widely used semi-precious gems. Sard and carnelian, which closely resemble it, have been used for engraved jewellery for several thousand years. Sard got its name from Sardis, the capital city of the ancient Kingdom of Lydia, which lay to the west of Anatolia. Its boundaries extended from the Aegean to the River Cayster. Most famous for its development of a gold and silver coinage system, and its great wealth, the Lydian Empire came to a dramatic end when its last ruler, Croesus, lost the war he had initiated against the Persians. At one time sardonyx (a mixture of sard and white chalcedony) was more expensive than gold, silver or sapphire.

There are also theories that the Urim and Thummim — whether made from sardonyx or some other precious stones — changed colour to reveal their message: bright and clear when all was well, cloudy or dull when there was a negative response to the question.

Another possible explanation which has been put forward over the centuries is that they were either a stone or a gold plate on which the sacred name of Yahweh had been carved. The cabalistic Book of Zohar suggests that the Urim has the name of God carved in forty-two letters and the Thummim has another, longer version of it involving seventy-two letters. According to this carved name theory, the High Priest had to stand before the Ark, or at least in front of the veil which concealed it, and stare at the engraved plate until he had entered a trance-like state. He was then able to interpret the answers which Urim and Thummim gave.

Psychologists and psychiatrists might have some relevant comments to make about this. If even a few of the Freudian and Jungian theories about the existence and function of the unconscious and subconscious minds are pointing in the right direction, by achieving an altered state of consciousness the High Priest could be doing one of two things. He might actually have manoeuvred his deeper mind into a position where its hypothetical hidden abilities would enable it to receive messages from some mysterious external source, or he might have opened a channel to it which would enable it to express its own ideas — some of which might have been deeply suppressed. The controversial and frequently challenged writer calling himself Lobsang

Rampa, nevertheless put up one or two interesting and provocative theories. One of these concerned his advice to give the subconscious a name, and regard it as a close personal friend, who would come and assist the conscious personality when called upon. Rampa also made the point that as the subconscious was busy doing other important things most of the time, it ought not to be called upon unless the subject was genuinely significant. Co-author Lionel was intrigued by this idea back in the 1970s and despite Rampa's warnings concerning trivia, gave it a brief, informal, practical test. He used *The Times* crossword as test material and found that the Rampa technique of asking the subconscious for help seemed to improve his performance. It must be emphasized, however, that the test was a short one, and by no means conclusive. Supposing that Rampa was broadly correct and that the vast repository of skill and knowledge allegedly lying stored in the subconscious could be accessed using his technique, then the High Priest might have been doing something similar when using Urim and Thummim. Was he calling on a reservoir of knowledge in his subconscious which was not accessible during his normal, waking state?

Some early Urim and Thummim theorists suggested that the voice of an angel spoke through them.

Dr. William Smith's *Dictionary of the Bible* includes an idea attributed to Michaelis writing in *The Laws of Moses*. He suggests that there were three stones, not two. One had "Yes" engraved on it, the second had "No," and the last one was blank. Objections to this theory include the argument that the Israelites of that period were perfectly familiar with casting lots, and that the absence of a person with the necessary "knowledge of Urim and Thummim" would have been highly unlikely if that's all the "knowledge" the stone's use had involved. Another objection is that Urim and Thummim were apparently capable of giving answers other than straightforward negatives and affirmatives.

Zullig suggested that Urim and Thummim were a set of engraved stones — he actually surmised that they were diamonds — and that only the High Priest and a close circle of his sacerdotal friends knew how to interpret them according to a special code of meaning. They were thrown on top of the Ark itself and the message was read from the pattern in which they landed. Zullig saw a parallel between this method and fortune telling using cards, tea-leaves, or coffee-grounds. Unsurprisingly, several of his contemporaries found his theory offensive. The tallest hurdle in its path is the idea that the stones used were engraved diamonds. It seems doubtful that any technique for engraving diamonds existed when Urim and Thummim were used, and equally unlikely that diamonds of a sufficiently large size were available. Of course, if there was a divine, an Atlantean, or an extraterrestrial origin for Urim and Thummim, those objections disappear.

The eminent Jewish interpreter, Kalisch, thought that Urim and Thummim were the twelve stones from the priestly breastplate, each representing one of the twelve traditional tribes of Israel. He found a linguistic explanation in a literary device known as a hendiadys (from a Greek phrase meaning "one from two") where two words are joined by a conjunction such as "and" to give a single composite meaning. Kalisch took Urim and Thummim to mean "light" and "perfection" and, therefore, as a hendiadys, to mean "perfect illumination." Kalisch then went on to his own version of the altered state of consciousness theory, suggesting that by concentrating on the stones, the High Priest was able to rid his mind of prejudice and selfishness and enter into a "perfect prophetic state."

A key point among the arguments raised by the various Urim and Thummim experts and theorists over the years is that as there is no description of them as such, and no account of their manufacture, they must have been well-known — at least to Moses himself — and that this suggests an Egyptian origin for them. Egyptian priestly judges wore a small image which personified Aletheia, or Truth, suspended on a gold chain around their necks. This was a permanent reminder to them of their duties to be fair and impartial in their judgements. The eyes of this image were closed, like the later blindfolded statues of Justice sometimes seen outside courts of law. It was customary for these Egyptian law officers to touch the lips of witnesses and litigants with this image, and require them to speak the whole truth.

When the Alexandrian Jews involved in the creation of the Septuagint translated Thummim as Aletheia, they could well have been asserting their belief that it was something very similar to the Egyptian truth images worn by law officers. Some old Egyptian monuments depict judges wearing an image of Thmei, the representative of Themis, which stood for both truth and justice, and there is a small but possibly significant connection between he words *Thmei* and *Thummim.*

A totally different idea connects Urim not with light, but with the word "arar" meaning a curse, and Thummim with "tammam" meaning to be whole. In this sense it has been suggested that they represented a sort of dualism, symbols of a hypothetical struggle between good and evil, between order and chaos, light and darkness. In this case, are they connected with the ancient Babylonian Stones of Destiny? One of these was called *Urtu* and the other *Tamitu.*

The use of the ephod, the priestly apron, is itself significant in the minds of some Urim and Thummim theorists. There were those who saw in it a miniature shrine or temple.

The glowing aspect of Urim and Thummim, along with the mysterious Shechinah, has also been associated with later descriptions of the quest for the Holy Grail by Arthur's Knights and others. In some variations of the legend, the Grail is not a cup or vessel at all, but a stone which glows mysteriously. Can the Grail be connected with Urim and Thummim?

There are also theories that the stone tablets housed in the Ark were pieces of a meteorite which glowed, and there are also references to accounts of a tube of fire, or jets of fire, which sprang from the golden cherubim on the lid of the Ark at certain times.

Do the controversial Dead Sea Scrolls provide any information about Urim and Thummim, and the previous idea associating them with a tube of fire, or jets of fire? There are two Dead Sea Scroll fragments designated 4Q375 and 4Q376 which refer to the test of a true prophet. The second one in particular, known as "The Ritual of the Three Flames," contains the information that the Urim was worn, or carried, in front of the anointed priest. The Qumran Sect, who were responsible for the Scrolls seemed to have worried a great deal about the nature of prophecy, and the need to be able to distinguish between genuine prophecy and pseudo-prophecy. It appears that they may have had an elaborate ritual of some kind involving the potential new prophet whose qualities were being tried and the High Priest standing near the Ark of the Covenant.

Fervent supporters of Joseph Smith, one of the founders of the Mormon Church, are convinced that he had gained access to the Urim and Thummim, and had been able to use them correctly and effectively. Born on December 23, 1805, in Sharon, Vermont, Smith was only 39 when he was killed by a mob while in prison — so becoming a religious martyr in the eyes of his disciples.

As a young man, Smith was a diviner, who dug for buried treasure. One day, when he was still in his early teens, he claimed to have had a strange religious experience in the woods. In 1827, at the age of 22, he reported that with the help of an angel he had been able to unearth some ancient and mysterious gold plates bearing strange inscriptions purporting to be the history of the indigenous North Americans. From what he read on those esoteric plates, Smith was convinced that their ancestors had been Hebrews who had sailed to North America via the Pacific Ocean many centuries ago. Smith also reported that these mysterious engraved gold tablets were in a language which he called "reformed Egyptian." All of which, strange as it sounds, may have more than a few strands of amazing truth in it.

The late Professor Barry Fell, one of the world's greatest experts on ancient languages and their scripts, and talented Nova Scotian paranormal researcher, George Young, both expressed the opinion that the weird tablet found at the foot of the shaft on Oak Island, off Chester, Nova Scotia, in 1805 (coincidentally the year that Joseph Smith was born) was written in an early Egyptian script and referred to a group of religious refugees from the Eastern Mediterranean. In the light of their theories, Smith's comments about a group of Israelites coming from the other direction are not totally impossible.

If such a group of Israelites actually arrived millennia ago and became the forerunners of the present indigenous Americans, there is no reason why the Urim and Thummim could not have come with them. Many of the so-called myths and legends of the indigenous Americans contain so many accounts of miracles and wonders that Urim and Thummim would not be out of place in their historic literature.

This riddle — like so many other biblical mysteries — remains largely unsolved. All that can be said with any certainty is that there were mysterious, ancient objects named Urim and Thummim which the High Priest of Israel used to answer difficult questions and to ascertain what he believed to be the will of Yahweh. What they really were, where they came from, and how they operated are still tantalizing, unanswered questions.

Chapter Twelve

What Happened to Sodom and Gomorrah?

The destruction of Sodom and Gomorrah is one of the best known episodes in the whole of Genesis. According to the biblical account, Lot, Abraham's nephew, was living in Sodom right up until the time when the cities were destroyed. Two mysterious visitors with what might have been paranormal powers, who are described as "angels" in Genesis, called on Lot, who lived up to the highest ideals of Middle Eastern hospitality. It is hard to overemphasize the near-sacred quality of a host's duties in that culture. If a man was your guest, then you had accepted the responsibility to die fighting in his defence should he be attacked. Macbeth makes this clear in Shakespeare's play, when he soliloquizes about his imminent murder of King Duncan. He knows perfectly well that the laws of hospitality in medieval Scotland make the same demands upon a host as the laws of hospitality in the ancient Middle East. His murder of the harmless old king who trusts him absolutely is therefore doubly treacherous and unwarranted. A million miles from Macbeth's treachery, Lot is prepared to go to any lengths to defend his guests. When the citizens of Sodom come and demand that he hands over his young male visitors for their sexual pleasure, Lot even offers them his two young virgin daughters instead. Instead of appeasing them, however, as Lot had intended, this merely infuriates the crowd, who then demand to know how Lot (who is only an-alien-in-residence, not a native-born citizen of Sodom) dares to set himself up as a judge of their behaviour.

When he went out to argue with the mob, Lot carefully shut the door behind him. He was in much the same isolated position then as the great, legendary, Roman hero, Horatius, who went out across the Tiber Bridge with Herminius and Lartius to hold off Lars Porsena's huge Etruscan army, while his fellow Romans hewed down the bridge behind him. Lot is never held up as a man of outstanding virtue in the Bible, nor is he praised for his heroism, yet in this Sodom episode he displays both virtues to a remarkable degree. It is now the turn of the mysterious guests whom Lot is defending to come to his rescue. They carefully pull him back inside the house and then blind the dangerous mob outside. It is, perhaps, significant to note that the mysterious "angels" clearly pulled Lot inside *well away* from whatever it was they were about to use to blind the men of Sodom *before* they used it. This together with their later devastation of the city sounds technical rather than magical. A truly supernatural being with the simple "*let-there-be*" powers of a real wizard could easily have blinded the mob *selectively* without injuring Lot's eyes. An extraterrestrial with hi-tech equipment of some sort, nerve gas, or laser weapons, would have had to get Lot out of harm's way before unleashing his power.

The extraordinary visitors then ask Lot whether he has any other relatives living in the city which they are planning to destroy. Angelic servants of an omniscient God would hardly have needed to ask. Lot is told to warn any such relatives of the impending doom, but when he carries out his instructions his sons-in-law refuse to take him seriously.

By early morning, whatever the "angels" had set up was becoming critical. Dissatisfied with Lot's progress, they take him and his family by the hand and *hustle* them out of the doomed city. The fugitives are warned not to look back, and to stop for nothing. Their mysterious protectors tell them that they can do nothing to the city *until Lot and his wife and daughters are well clear of the area which is to be destroyed.* Just as with the riddle of the blindness that struck the mob around Lot's door in Sodom, this extract seems much more closely related to the employment of some sort of advanced weaponry — perhaps nuclear explosives — than to magical powers in the hands of supernatural beings such as angels.

Lot surveys the bleak and inhospitable mountains, and begs to be allowed to go instead to Zoar, a small neighbouring town. Originally called Bela, Zoar appears to have been re-named to coincide with Lot's escape from Sodom. The biblical records show that originally, Zoar (or Bela) was closely connected with Gomorrah, Admah, and Zeboiim as well as with Sodom, and that this group constituted the semi-legendary "Five Cities of the Plain of Jordan."

It is now morning, and the destruction of Sodom and Gomorrah descends upon them as prophesied. "Brimstone and fire" rain down "from the Lord *and* from heaven." Sodom and Gomorrah are totally wiped out; but *why* does the chronicler carefully distinguish between the destruction that came generally from the sky and that which came distinctly and directly

What Happened to Sodom and Gomorrah?

"from the Lord"? Was a careful and observant onlooker describing the *two separate sources* of destructive power which he could actually see? Was one the weapon itself, or the alien ship carrying it, the place from which the destructive force was seen to be issuing? (Is this what he called "the Lord"?) Was the other the flying, burning debris being blasted up from the target and slowly raining down again? (Is this what he meant by "the sky"?)

Did a nuclear device destroy Sodom and Gomorrah?
Drawn by Theo Fanthorpe.

The tragedy of Lot's wife comes next in the recorded sequence of events. All around the saturated Dead Sea, there are curious configurations of marine salt which have moulded themselves into fantastic shapes like modernistic sculptors' portrayals of the human form. It takes very little imagination to turn one such natural salt pillar into the semblance of a woman. Is the story of Lot's wife being turned into a pillar of salt because she turned to look back at Sodom and Gomorrah merely an aetiological myth?

On the other hand, it ought not to be forgotten that when Hiroshima and Nagasaki were vaporized by atomic explosions in the closing stages of the Second World War, there were victims of the blast who left their tragic outlines etched on the brick or concrete in front of which they had been standing when the nuclear blast struck them. There were also freakish "pillars" of concrete, stone or brick which had remained upright because a pathetic human victim had protected them from destruction by standing between them and the full force of the nuclear blast. Such grotesque pillars also bore the unmistakable profiles of the human bodies which had preserved them.

What was the *real* reason for telling the refugees from Sodom — including Lot's wife — not to look back? Could it possibly have been because the strange visitors who were about to set off the nuclear devices that destroyed Sodom and Gomorrah knew that staring into that flash would cause irreparable damage to the eyes?

When those grim facts are allied to the apparent inability of Lot's mysterious guests to blind the men of Sodom until they had dragged Lot to safety inside his house and slammed the door, plus their insistence that they could do nothing to the city until he and his family were safely away, it begins to sound far more likely that the enigmatic visitors were clandestine technocrats rather than mystical angels of the traditional religious type.

The biblical narrative concerning Lot's escape is interrupted at this point in the story to insert a short piece about Abraham's observation of the catastrophe from a distance.

The reader then learns that for some undisclosed reason — but one which was undoubtedly meaningful to him — Lot is now *afraid* to live in Zoar, and goes instead with his daughters to seek refuge in just such a cave in the mountains as he had previously avoided. Why was he now suddenly afraid of Zoar? Was that area becoming unhealthily radioactive? Had his mysterious visitors run a radiation check with their equivalent of a Geiger counter and advised him to get out of the town when they saw the readings?

There is a curious sequel to the story of Lot which is almost as bizarre as the events centred around the destruction of Sodom and Gomorrah: it relates back to the suggestions of genetic engineering touched on during our examination of the Eden narrative.

Suppose, however improbably, and just for the sake of pursuing the argument, that Lot's "angelic" visitors *were* genetic engineers from some technocratic culture: extraterrestrials or Atlantean survivors. Suppose also that one of the primary objectives of their engineering was to produce a *moral* species. Lot himself was evidently a Grade A success from their point of view — judging by the lengths to which he was prepared to go to uphold the sacred principles of protecting his guests from the hostile mob in Sodom. The engineers now wish to preserve his particular gene pool as their number one priority. Assuming that they have only limited equipment with them at this juncture — they may be a long way from their mother ship, or from some hypothetical, submerged headquarters — incestuous interbreeding of the desirable moral specimens is the surest way of preserving the successful Lot-type gene modification. But how can the engineers arrange that without contravening the specimens' strong anti-incest moral code?

In Genesis 19:30–38, the straightforward biblical account suggests that Lot's daughters made their father drunk, and then had sex with him without his having any knowledge — or subsequent recollection — of the event.

Shakespeare's comment on alcohol being the great equivocator as far as sexual activity is concerned seems relevant: he commented dryly that it enhances desire but inhibits performance. Incidentally, where did the girls get the wine from in that remote mountain cave?

If, on the other hand, the mysterious strangers had put them up to it, had played, perhaps, on their fears of childlessness — the ultimate humiliation for women of their era and culture — and had also supplied the "wine" (which could have been a formidable mixture of date-rape amnesiac, aphrodisiac, and performance enhancer) then the weird sexual episode involving Lot and his daughters in the cave becomes a little more credible.

The Genesis account makes the elder daughter the ancestress of the Moabites, which could be of considerable significance in connection with this ethical gene theory.

One of the finest and most admirable characters in the Old Testament is Ruth, who is a Moabitess, and therefore a remote descendant of Lot and his daughter. She leaves her own home and her own people to stand loyally by Naomi, her widowed mother-in-law, who has also suffered the loss of both her sons — one of whom was Ruth's husband.

Ruth is finally married again: this time to a wealthy and kind-hearted Israelite named Boaz. They had a son named Obed, who became the father of Jesse, whose son in turn became the great King David — father of Solomon by Bathsheba.

There are, of course, several less imaginative and speculative theories that can be put forward to account for the loss of Sodom and Gomorrah. In search of these more probable, geological explanations for the destruction of the vanished cities, the pioneering work of the American geologist, W.F. Lynch, is well worth examining. As early as 1848, he and his expedition

Curious rock formations around the Dead Sea.

hauled their boats over the southern Galilean hills to explore the mysterious waters beyond. Lynch was staggered to find that the surface of the Sea of Galilee lay over 200 metres below the surface of the Mediterranean, while the Dead Sea's surface was another 200 metres below that. When Lynch and his companions tried to swim in the Dead Sea to find out whether the ancient legends were true, they described their experience as being "almost as if the Sea was *rejecting* them." It was impossible to sink. This confirmed the story that during the great siege of A.D. 70 when Titus attacked Jerusalem, the Romans sentenced some prisoners to be chained together and thrown into the Dead Sea. To the amazement of the Roman executioners, the condemned men did not sink. They were dragged out and thrown in again several times — but they always floated. Finally, Titus — probably believing that the gods were intervening to save innocent lives — pardoned the prisoners and let them go.

Later geological expeditions attempting to unravel the mysteries of the Dead Sea bed discovered that it falls away at a very steep angle, more or less dividing the bed into two distinct zones. At one point it goes down as much as 400 metres: elsewhere it barely reaches twenty. The steep, dramatic descent of the River Jordan is also extremely unusual if not unique.

The Jordan Valley is part of a massive fracture in the crust of the earth, which includes strong evidence of prodigious volcanic activity in the past. It is more than likely that Sodom and Gomorrah were destroyed when the base of this gigantic geological fault fell still deeper into the magma beneath, causing traumatic earthquakes and volcanic eruptions.

Whatever the actual, historical cause of the destruction of Sodom and Gomorrah — natural or nuclear — it may safely be concluded that the judgemental conclusions drawn by the authors and redactors of Genesis were a very long way removed from the actual purposes of a loving and merciful God.

Christ was once asked about the people who had been killed when a tower collapsed and fell on them in Siloam. He assured his listeners that those unfortunate victims were neither better nor worse than anyone else: that God had certainly not singled them out because of anything they'd done wrong.

However else we may seek to explain human suffering, death, and destruction they are definitely no part of the Divine Plan of a loving God.

Chapter Thirteen

Do Miracles Happen?

Nothing can be decided about miracles without first defining the nature of the miraculous. Many attempts at definition have been made, but agreement is far from universal. A miracle is a phenomenon which cannot be explained within the observer's present frame of knowledge of cause and effect.

The word *miracle* is often misused. The re-awakening of natural life in the spring after the low activity levels of winter, for example, is often hailed as a miracle. The cyclic phenomena of courtship, mating, conception, birth, growth, and the attainment of maturity — in humanity as well as in nature — are sometimes hailed as miracles: but wonderful and exhilarating as they are, they are definitely *not* miraculous within our definition. Well understood, natural, scientific laws can be applied to explain them all. Rigorous research continually adds to our knowledge of them. It is the miracles which *defy* explanation within the parameters of our present knowledge which deserve the name — what might well be termed *Fortean Miracles*. Those are the ones that are truly interesting, exciting, mysterious, and worthwhile objects of further serious investigation.

Strange, intriguing, and enigmatic as alleged miracles are, they nevertheless succumb — as do lesser, mundane phenomena — to the human obsession for sorting things into categories, labelling them and placing them in pigeonholes. Even miracles, apparently, have their distinct types: there are miracles of resurrection, of mental, physical, and spiritual healing, of multiplying food, of making inanimate physical objects behave in ways which seem to be contrary to their nature, of controlling living creatures in the way that the lions were reportedly prevented from eating

Daniel, and of undertaking inexplicable journeys that seem to be made independently of all normal forms of transport.

Christ's own resurrection is not the only one recorded in the Bible. The evidence for the resurrection of Lazarus, the brother of Mary and Martha of Bethany, is laid out in graphic detail in the Chapter 11 of Saint John's Gospel. There are three possible conclusions to be drawn from that Gospel evidence. Firstly, the entire episode is a pathetic fiction from beginning to end, and that far from being miraculously resurrected Lazarus may never even have existed. It was only a cunning fabrication created by a gang of unscrupulous religious confidence tricksters, trouble-making preachers and writers called the Early Church, whose sole purpose in life was to tell this and similar irritating lies in order to annoy the respectable and worthy Jewish and Roman authorities and, consequently, to get themselves imprisoned, tortured, and executed as soon as possible.

The second possibility is that Jesus was an even more skilful and devious liar and confidence trickster than his dubious disciples, and that he and Lazarus secretly arranged the whole preposterous scheme between them. Lazarus was to lie there quietly spiced and wrapped in his nice, comfortable tomb with nothing to eat or drink for several days, and with a massive stone blocking the tomb entrance until he heard Jesus shout: "Lazarus, come forth!" At this juncture, as planned, Lazarus staggers out as best he can — impeded by his grave-clothes — and thus convinces everybody that Jesus really can work miracles. The whole thing, of course, was again planned simply to irritate the establishment and so motivate the High Priest, the Roman Governor and Herod the Tetrarch — together with all their guards, soldiers, and adherents — to get both Jesus and Lazarus out of the way (as per the treatment they had already meted out to silence John the Baptist) as soon as it could be done quietly, conveniently, and with a minimum of fuss.

Jesus raises Lazarus from the dead.

In the light of every shred of reputable historical evidence about the character and personality of Jesus, this explanation is statistically far less likely than the probability of recovering a crock of fairy gold from the end of the rainbow after capturing the leprechaun who owns it, or the theory that Mother Theresa was madam superior to a chain of Asian brothels which sold cocaine as a sideline.

Fortunately, there is a third option: astounding as it may seem, Jesus really *was* who he said he was; he genuinely *had* the miraculous powers that went with his unique role, and he truly brought Lazarus back from the dead — no trickery, no chicanery, no deception — just, pure, glorious, unadulterated *miracle*. As far as we're concerned, amazing as it is, that's the most logical and serious possibility.

In 2 Kings, Chapter 4, the details of the apparent miracle of resurrection performed by Elisha on the young son of the Shunammite woman who had generously befriended him are given in similar detail to the Lazarus account. In fact, so particular is the detail about Elisha recorded here that it is possible to deduce that although the boy is desperately ill, almost certainly from sunstroke, he may well have been in a coma rather than dead. The prophet's response to the boy's illness seems remarkably similar to modern mouth-to-mouth resuscitation techniques. This is a case in which the "miracle" may well be susceptible to scientific, medical explanation. The parameters of medical knowledge were narrower in Elisha's day than in ours, but with the benefit of hindsight it is possible to argue that perhaps this was a healing and restoration to health rather than a resurrection.

But what is to be made of the account in 2 Kings 13:20–21, where even Elisha's bones are credited with miraculous restorative powers? It was a turbulent period of Hebrew history, and roving warrior bands were

The risen Christ talks to two disciples on the road to Emmaus.

wreaking havoc on the Israelites. A burial party was taking the body of a friend or relative to his last resting place when they saw a hostile war-band coming towards them. There was no longer time to take their dead companion to his own tomb, but the funeral party was passing the tomb of Elisha when they sighted the enemy. In view of the emergency situation, they lowered their dead friend on top of the bones of Elisha. According to the biblical account, he revived and stood on his feet.

The implication of the passage is that there was some miraculous power in Elisha's mortal remains. Medieval pilgrims made their way to Canterbury to be healed by touching Becket's tomb, many centuries later. As with the Shunammite's son, however, there is no absolute guarantee that the man whom his friends were carrying was clinically dead. In time of war, a severe blow to the head followed by loss of consciousness and heavy bleeding would probably be enough to convince the man's comrades that he was dead.

Suddenly regaining consciousness to find himself being lowered on to Elisha's bones would have been more than enough of a trauma to get him back on his feet despite his injuries!

So much hinges on the veracity of Christ's own resurrection, of course, that along with the miracle of his incarnation it is one of the two great central supporting beams of history — and how the death-watch beetles and wood-worms have delighted in attacking it!

Theories abound that he wasn't really dead when he was taken down from the cross and laid in Joseph of Arimathea's tomb. The two "men in white" seen in the tomb on the resurrection morning were not angels but merely Essene healers from Qumran who had come to help him recover. The medical facts do not support this conjecture at all. There is evidence that a really severe Roman scourging of the kind that Jesus had suffered was usually enough by itself to save the executioner's time later on. His frequent heavy and painful falls on the agonizing journey to Calvary were clear evidence of his physical condition at that time. The final spear wound in his side was fatal in itself without merely serving as a primitive clinical test to ensure that death had already taken place. Except to the most recalcitrant opponent of the resurrection, the evidence is incontrovertible: Jesus was genuinely, clinically dead when he was taken down from the cross.

The next group of theories suggests that a crafty substitution had taken place. This belongs in the same garbage bin as the Jesus and Lazarus conspiracy theory. It is utterly opposed to all that we know of the man's character. Jesus who was more altruistic and unselfish than any other character in history, whose mental and spiritual strength and courage were

Jesus heals the paralytic.

unequalled, would *never* have allowed anyone else to be crucified so that he could make an ignominious escape. The centre of this theory is the hapless Simon of Cyrene who was compelled by the Romans to carry the cross after Christ had fallen. Upon that simple and straightforward incident, a remarkably cumbersome edifice of speculation has been built. Brutal and callous as they could be at their worst, the Romans had a primitive sense of fairness and justice. They would have been unwilling to crucify the wrong man. There was also the question of enlightened self-interest as far as the execution party was concerned. It would have been dangerous for them to execute the wrong man, when the authorities were so unswervingly set on killing Jesus. There is also the evidence of the preliminary suffering which Christ had endured, the crown of thorns had lacerated his head. The scourging had left deep cuts and weals all over his body. Either the man they were crucifying had these injuries or he did not. Mistaken identity was impossible. What of the vindictive enemies who stood around laughing at him as he died, those who mocked him and said: "He saved others, himself he cannot save"? They were so intent on his death that they could not have failed to see at once if the dying man on the cross had *not* been Jesus. Did his own mother fail to recognize him as she stood at the foot of the cross? Wouldn't *anyone* have spotted the difference and run to warn the Roman centurion in charge? The substitution theory fails.

There is also the tale that the Jewish authorities bribed the guards to say that the disciples had come along in the night and stolen Christ's

The Pool of Bethesda where Jesus healed another paralyzed man.

body while those same Roman soldiers were asleep. To this was added: "If you get into trouble over it, we'll square it for you with the Governor." Knowing the dire punishment for such a serious lapse of duty, no Roman soldier — however great the bribe — would have admitted falling asleep on duty. Supposing, however, that the High Priest's wild attempt to bribe the guards was true, the whole stolen body theory still falls fatally over the hurdle of the disciples' behaviour.

Their beloved leader had just been crucified. They themselves were currently in the gravest danger of meeting the same fate. To preach the truth about Jesus being the Messiah, the Son of God in a very special and unique sense, was to risk imprisonment and death. To dare to proclaim openly that he had been resurrected and that the corrupt authorities were responsible for his totally unjust death, was tantamount to committing suicide. If the disciples were *sure* of the truth about the resurrection, they would gladly have risked their lives proclaiming it. But who would be perverse and stupid enough to die for what they knew was a lie? Having taken the body out of the tomb and reburied it secretly elsewhere, who would then stand up fearlessly to oppose the murderous authorities by saying that Jesus had been miraculously resurrected? Courageous and committed men and women will die for what they believe to be true and worthwhile, but nobody risks death for what they know to be false. Whatever else may have happened to the body of Jesus, the disciples certainly did not steal it and hide it. They believed so firmly in the resurrection that they were willing to bet their lives on it.

A ninth-century illustration of Jesus walking on the water.

So then, Christ was truly dead when he was taken down. It was definitely the man himself, not Simon of Cyrene who had died in his place while Jesus escaped. The disciples did not steal the body and hide it. What really happened?

It would seem to have been a genuine miracle. Jesus was who he said he was and he actually rose from the dead. On that vast central miracle of his eternal life rests the certainty of our survival. Christ did not conquer death for himself alone — the whole point of his work is that the everlasting victory is there to be shared. In Christ, God reached out and became human. Through Christ humanity responds to God.

If miracles of resurrection are the most powerful of all, miracles of healing are not far behind them. From the earliest Old Testament prophets right up to the time of Jesus and the disciples — and into the ages beyond — numerous miracles of healing appear to have been performed. The prophet Elisha was a notable healer. One of his most famous cases was the one involving Naaman the Syrian captain and his leprosy. There are scholars who have put forward the theory that not all biblical skin diseases described as leprosy actually were leprosy as we know it today. Whatever Naaman suffered from it was some sort of chronic and debilitating skin disease, even if it was not leprosy itself. There was in his household a young Hebrew slave girl, who must have been well treated because she had the highest regard for Naaman and his wife. One day this little girl said conversationally to Naaman's wife that she wished they were in her homeland of Israel because there was a great prophet there — Elisha — who could undoubtedly cure Naaman's leprosy by the power of Yahweh, God of Israel. This was duly reported to Naaman, who, being a very high ranking officer and courtier, told his master, the Syrian king. He in turn wrote a letter to the king of Israel asking him to arrange for Naaman's leprosy to be cured.

The letter caused massive dismay. Entirely mistaking the honesty of the Syrian king's concern for his trusted and popular servant, Naaman, the king of Israel suspected that this request for healing was merely a pretext to declare war on Israel when no healing took place. The matter reached Elisha, who immediately declared that there was nothing to fear, and that with God's help he would cure the Syrian captain and demonstrate the power and glory of God in the process. Naaman duly arrives at the prophet's home, and is told to bathe seven times in the Jordan.

What follows is an object lesson in the dangers inherent in preconceived notions and prejudices. Naaman had expected an ostentatious flourish of healing paraphernalia from Elisha. As a patriotic Syrian he preferred his own rivers at home to the alien waters of the Jordan, and complained loudly. The account is also an object lesson in the true relationship between "masters" and "servants" who are real friends underneath the hierarchical roles which society imposes upon them. There was clear evidence of this earlier, when the young Hebrew slave girl showed genuine concern for Naaman, and sincerely wished that his leprosy could be cured. This time, as he is on the point of storming off disappointed and angry, the servants who are with him know him well enough to dare to reason with him. "If the prophet had asked you to do something difficult, you would have done it. Why not follow this simple advice about bathing in the Jordan?" Naaman is persuaded. He is a reasonable man as well as a good-hearted one. He follows Elisha's instructions, and is healed of his leprosy accordingly.

On a pragmatic level, might it be asked whether there were unusual but perfectly natural therapeutic properties in the Jordan water? Did it dissolve special salts and minerals from the rocks in the course of its journey to the Dead Sea? In that strange, deeply rifted geological district, were there sulphur derivatives from far below the earth's surface which had somehow percolated into the Jordan water?

There is no need to go back as far as the days of Naaman the Syrian to find reports of what look as if they might be remarkable, inexplicable healings. There are numerous astonishing reports from Canada, the U.S., and the U.K., concerning apparently miraculous gold teeth, or, at least, golden fillings. The Pioneer Church, a charismatic Christian organization, was founded as a new church by former postman, Gerald

Coates, a friend of Cliff Richard. Members of his group meeting in Norfolk in 1999 for a conference, reported receiving "miraculous" dental treatment. Other charismatic evangelic Christians in Burton-on-Trent in Staffordshire reported finding what they believed to be gold dust on their shoulders and hands.

Accounts of miracles of mental and spiritual healing also abound in the Bible. King Saul, David's unfortunate predecessor, had severe bouts of dangerous, homicidal insanity — more than once aimed at David himself. David, a talented musician and psalmist, would play to soothe the mentally ill king. This musical therapy seems to have been effective.

In the biblical account, Saul's insane behaviour is attributed to possession by an evil spirit, which raises the massive question of whether such entities actually have any objective existence. The theory ought not be lightly or casually dismissed. Solomon, deservedly noted for his vast wisdom and knowledge, was credited with having God-given power over them, and in many of the Solomonic legends he imprisoned them in various containers such as brazen bottles closed securely with his sacred seal. Jesus himself said that he had seen Lucifer fall as lightning from Heaven, and if anyone could speak authoritatively about that particular cosmic event, Jesus could. The Gospel records show that he and his disciples "cast out evil spirits" on numerous occasions. But what do those words really mean?

The complex — and frequently controversial — relationship between mind and brain is still only partially understood by the most advanced neurologists and psychiatrists today. Serious scientific psychical researchers often produce results which seem to suggest that *mind* — although undoubtedly in some respects, a manifestation, or projection of the *physical brain* — is capable of discrete, independent awareness and activity. If so-called "demon possession" implies some kind of traumatic personality change, where does that change actually take place? In the physical brain, or in the non-material, disembodied mind or spirit — if such entities can be proved to exist? Jesus addressed these "evil spirits" directly, as if they were individuals in their own right. He spoke not to the tormented, possessed individual, but to the entity that seemed to be in control of the victim. In the well known case of the Gadarene swine, where what purported to be numerous "evil spirits" were controlling the wild man who lived among the tombs, the supposed demonic entities actually asked Christ's permission to find alternative accommodation in the herd of pigs feeding nearby. It is, of course, easy enough to explain the fatal stampede of the hapless pigs by saying that the screams and shouts of the wild man terrified them so much that they rushed headlong, out of control, into the water.

However, whatever was wrong with the wild man had now been cured. He was calm, quiet, properly dressed, and in his right mind again. That transformation is far harder to explain — and it certainly cannot be explained *away*.

Personality, or character, can be defined as a style of response that recurs. The disturbing style of response which had previously been characteristic of the wild man from Gadara ceased to recur after Christ had healed him. Do we *always* behave as we do because we choose to, or are there internal and external forces that *propel* us in one direction or another — and sometimes in directions in which we very definitely do not wish to go? The most normal, calm, and rational people occasionally talk of *urges* or *compulsions* which tend to make them behave in particular ways. By contrast, the literature of psychiatry abounds with extreme and chronic cases of compulsion: the kleptomaniac who feels driven to steal; the pyromaniac who cannot, apparently, resist the temptation to set things on fire; satyromaniacs and nymphomaniacs whose prodigious sexual appetites cause them continual, severe, social, and personal difficulties. There are a great many additional weird and irrational behaviours towards which genuinely clinical psychiatric patients feel impelled. What are these driving forces? Some may well be bio-chemical and hormonal. Others may be the results of classic Freudian trauma during impressionable stages of early life. Some may be pathological — infection, inflammation, injury, or a neoplasm may be injuring the physical brain and making it respond oddly.

Jesus heals the lame man.

The old model of car and driver is still a useful one, although it falls a long way short of a full explanation. If the car and its computerized control panel are regarded as the physical body and brain, the detached driver who is controlling it, steering and planning the journey, represents the mind (or spirit), the will, the personality and the transcendent purpose of the individual. The car may behave incorrectly if the control panel is damaged — this represents illness or injury to the physical brain. The car may also behave incorrectly if a hijacker with a gun gets in beside the driver, sticks the gun into his ribs and shouts: "Drive where I tell you!" This would represent the phenomenon referred to as "possession." As a model, the car-and-driver scenario has severe limitations, but it clarifies the biblical idea of casting out evil spirits. Jesus, a disciple, or a modern exorcist, fulfils the role of psychic police officer, throws the hijacker out of the car and returns control to the rightful owner.

It is also possible to hypothesize about the brain "creating" various main and subsidiary personalities in the same way that authors and actors "create" their characters. We are all conscious of deliberately "putting on" different personas to suit different occasions. A tough and ruthless martial artist can — and will — kill if he has to while rescuing an innocent and helpless victim. That same lethally effective warrior will lie on the play-room carpet like a great woolly teddy bear and happily allow his children and their young friends at a birthday party to climb all over him. A priest does not conduct a wedding in the same mode that he uses for a funeral. A fatherly surgeon carving the Christmas turkey for his joyful and loving family is not wearing the same professional persona that he uses in the operating room while saving someone's life. This necessary kind of regular persona change is fully under our control. Are there other, more sinister, kinds? Robert Louis Stevenson's brilliantly revealing "The Strange Case of Dr. Jekyll and Mr. Hyde" written in 1886 more or less suggests that various good or bad personalities can subsist within the same individual like video tapes in a rack waiting to be played. What if there's a fault in the machine somewhere, and one tape refuses to come out again, or goes on rewinding and replaying itself against the owner's will and without his or her permission? Christ, a disciple, or a contemporary exorcist, then fulfils the role of the video repairer and removes the offending tape, putting the owner back in control of the equipment. A negative, subsidiary personality of that jammed-video type can be pretty "demonic" and destructive — even if it originated in the brain of the victim rather than in hell.

Whatever they are, and wherever they come from, these strange quasi-personalities which appear to be able to take over the normal functioning of a healthy mind and brain and produce disturbing, aberrant behaviour, can seemingly be "cast out," cured, or removed, by direct and powerful exorcism of the type which Christ himself used, by spiritual healing, by psychotherapy, or by medicine and brain surgery. In some extreme cases, their removal can probably be sheltered under the general umbrella of "miracle" as we have defined it here.

The next category can probably best be understood as miracles of multiplication. Christ's feeding of the five thousand comes readily to mind — but he was not the first to perform this type of miracle. A short passage in 2 Kings 4:1–7, records that Elisha saved the sons of a poor widow from being sold off as bondsmen to pay their late father's debts. Divine power, working through the prophet apparently multiplied the oil from a small vessel many times over. Those few millilitres of oil was all that she had of value. Miraculously, the oil continued to flow until she had filled every empty vessel which she had been able to borrow from her friends and neighbours. She then sold the oil — which raised sufficient funds to redeem her husband's debts and still leave enough extra cash for the widow and her sons to live on.

The details of this event as given in the biblical record are exact and convincing. It does not scan like a myth or fable, but as a careful account of a genuinely inexplicable happening.

Verses 42 to 44 of the same chapter tell how Elisha fed one hundred men with a few barley loaves which were again miraculously multiplied in much the same way as the widow's oil. Not only did the twenty small loaves provide enough bread to satisfy everyone, there was, just as Elisha had predicted, plenty of spare bread left over when they had all finished eating.

These miracles of multiplication are not totally unnatural, neither do they contradict human experience of agriculture in the material world. It is the *speed* of the multiplication that is changed. Growing olives from seed, planting out the additional olive trees so obtained, gathering the olives in due season, and extracting the oil from them is a perfectly natural process. If the number of olives needed to fill the widow's small jar in the first place had been planted and allowed to multiply naturally over the years, they would — given sufficient time — have been able to produce more than enough to fill all the vessels which she had been able to borrow. The miraculous element in the multiplication of food or drink is the foreshortening of the time taken for it to happen. As with the oil, so with the barley loaves. If the grain from which they were made had been sown and reaped for a season or two, there would easily have been enough bread made from it to feed one hundred men. The miracle consisted of the *immediacy* of the multiplication.

The corn and the olives did nothing that was against their basic nature — they simply did it much faster.

It is extremely easy for our human minds to become trapped within the phenomenon of *apparent time.* Shakespeare spotted its subjectivity when he asked for whom time stood still, for whom it walked, and for whom it ran. It is important to concentrate on that subjectivity. Time may not be anything as rigid or irreversible as we think it is. There are still many unanswered questions about the Philadelphia Experiment, for example. Did the warship *Eldridge* and its crew manage to vanish into another dimension of time and space in the 1940s? Did Einstein and Tesla have anything to do with it, or know anything about it? If extreme velocity can affect time, did something like that happen with the multiplication miracles? If time is not immutable, but is susceptible to significant variation when a body approaches the speed of light, what else can affect it?

Christ constantly emphasized the importance of *faith* when explaining the miraculous to his disciples. He taught that faith the size of one tiny grain of mustard seed can move mountains. He was not exaggerating. He was not joking. He was not using colourful, picturesque, Aramaic, linguistic imagery merely for the sake of bringing home an important point. He was explaining one of the most important, basic facts underlying the way that the universe works. Even after two thousand years of studying his teachings, that rudimentary truth which he taught about faith and its effectiveness is still not widely understood even today — nor is it consistently applied.

The problem is that faith's power is matched by its elusiveness. As a famous song lyric runs, we can only chase such abstract concepts as faith and love "across our dreams with nets of wonder." Paradoxically, once we understand the nature of faith, we are empowered to use it – but until we use it, we cannot begin to understand its nature. It is not a matter of wishing, of willing, of hoping, or of expecting: it is a strange process which comes closer to *knowing* and *accepting* than to anything else. In the matter of faith and miracle most of us are like carpenters' children who have strayed into our parents' workshop. We know that in their hands the plane and the lathe can create things of great beauty and utility: in our hands the results are less predictable — if we achieve any results at all.

An interesting alternative suggestion has been made in connection with Christ's feeding of the five thousand — the suggestion that it was a moral miracle rather than a physical one. The laws and customs of hospitality were such that if you had food with you in a situation such as that, it was your duty to share it with anyone nearby who did not have any. It is more than likely that people out on an excursion of that kind would have had the common sense to take an essential minimum of food and drink with them. No one was anxious in such a vast crowd to let his immediate neighbours know that he had food with him, in case they hadn't, and he was socially compelled to share it. When the innocent youngster produced what little food he had and brought it to the disciples to share, everyone felt rather ashamed and began to produce their own provisions. Thus it was, according to this theory, that with everyone sharing there was more than enough to go round. It's a nice idea, and it *might* conceivably be the right explanation, but the details in the Gospel account seem to indicate that a genuine miracle of multiplication took place.

If such multiplication miracles *do* occur — and there is reasonable evidence for them — they might be related to a highly localized zonal acceleration of time, which could, in itself, be related to the mysterious power called faith.

If miracles of multiplication, such as Christ's feeding of a crowd of several thousand with only a handful of loaves and fishes, are historical, paranormal, and extremely difficult to explain, what of the next category — those miracles which make inanimate, material objects react in ways that are contrary to what is generally understood about their properties and characteristic behaviour?

There are several such occasions in the Old Testament. An iron axe-head becomes accidentally detached and falls into the river. The man who was using it at the time calls out in dismay: "Alas, it was borrowed!" Iron implements were effective, rare, and by the standards of the day relatively expensive. It would be the equivalent of borrowing a friend's new car today and accidentally writing it off. Elisha hears the call, and throws a stick into the water. In the unforgettable phraseology of the King James Bible: "And the iron did swim." As the axe-head floated to the surface the grateful borrower retrieved it safely.

On another occasion, a cauldron of stewing food has accidentally had something toxic included among the ingredients. A desperate cry goes up from one of the diners who has just tasted it: "There is death in the pot!" Elisha throws a handful of wholesome, nutritious meal into the dangerous stew, and whatever toxins it may have contained are neutralized.

The use of both the stick which possessed the natural quality of buoyancy, and the meal-flour which was safe to eat, can be considered as examples of "sympathetic" magic. This type of spell characteristically employs something simple and natural which possesses the desired qualities and attempts to *transfer* them to the object which does not have them — in these two Old Testament examples, the buoyancy of the wood and the wholesomeness of the meal-flour are apparently transferred to the iron axe-head and the poisonous stew. Does sympathetic magic work? Its abstract principle is just as rational as a modern chemistry experiment in a school laboratory. A highly reactive metal will replace a less reactive one when added to a metal-and-sulphate compound, for example. Logically, as long as the "magician" knows how to work the procedure, qualities and properties may be able to be exchanged just as reactive chemicals can.

The Gospels record that Christ took command of the inanimate wind and water forces when he saved the disciples' lives by stilling the storm on Galilee. On another occasion it is recorded that he actually walked on water, and enabled Peter to do the same. Perhaps these miracles-of-control contain something broadly similar to the time-distortion-acceleration theory which might apply to multiplication miracles?

Another prime example of this kind of miracle is the record of Shadrach, Meshach, and Abednego walking unharmed through the fiery furnace, as recorded in Daniel, Chapter 3. What sort of control-miracle was that?

We dig ditches and canals to modify natural water courses. We build boats to cross oceans. We fly to the moon in spacecraft. A man cannot level a mountain with his bare hands, but he can invent and use machines and high explosives which will level the mountain at his command. Are the control miracles some strange type of *shortcuts*? It is perfectly normal and natural for a determined civil engineer and his crew to be able to control nature to some extent, to alter the contours of the landscape, to construct great dams, to change the courses of rivers, to hold back the sea, or to admit it. Does a control miracle somehow accelerate or even *omit* the intermediate engineering stage altogether and move directly from the engineer's will to his, or her, desired objective?

If inanimate nature can be coerced into functioning miraculously, would not the living creatures which comprise animate nature be even more susceptible to such miraculous control? If long periods of training and domestication can change an animal's behaviour over time, can that process not be shortened and accelerated to provide another type of control miracle? When Daniel, as recorded in Chapter 6, was not harmed by the lions, had a miracle of this type taken place?

Miraculous journeys form yet another significant category. Various prophets, saints and holy men have found themselves unable to account for the means by which they were transferred from one location to another. It is recorded in the second chapter of the 2 Kings that Elijah was taken from earth in a great whirlwind after he and his disciple, Elisha, were separated by a fiery chariot drawn by fiery horses. What did the faithful Elisha really see? Would a man of his era perhaps have described a space vehicle as a chariot of fire? Could the "whirlwind" have been some sort of tractor beam? Elisha took up Elijah's mantle — both literally and metaphorically — struck the Jordan with it and parted the waters according to the biblical record. Was it alien technology, magic, the power of faith, mind over matter, divine intervention (either directly or via intermediaries), or a combination of several such factors? There are no simple, clear-cut or facile answers: something very strange indeed seems to have happened to Elijah at the end of his earthly life, and Elisha, his successor, was credited with the possession of numerous paranormal powers.

The Acts records another type of paranormal journey where Philip, having just completed an adult baptism, is caught up "by the Spirit of the Lord" and apparently vanishes as far as his new convert is concerned. In the biblical account Philip turns up again at Azotus. This was the Hellenistic first century name for the ancient Philistine city of Ashdod, which was once part of the Philistine pentapolis. In Joshua 15:47, Ashdod is allocated to the Tribe of Judah, but along with its four co-cities of the pentapolis, it was never totally subdued by the triumphant invading Israelis. As recorded in 1 Samuel, Chapter 5, when the Ark of the Covenant was captured by the Philistines, it was taken to the temple of Dagon in Ashdod — with traumatic consequences for Dagon and the Philistines! Recent archaeological work has revealed evidence that the city was founded at least four thousand years ago — and may be even older.

Having arrived there, Philip lost no time in carrying on with his interrupted preaching tour. A miracle is a phenomenon which cannot be explained within the observer's present frame of knowledge of cause and effect.

There is much that still lies outside that vital framework, even today, when science is advancing exponentially. Miracles of every type remain among the most intriguing of all the Bible's mysteries.

Chapter Fourteen

The Mystery
of Joseph's Dream

If anyone needed a good spin doctor or PR adviser, Jacob and Joseph did. Patriarchal polygamy was a notorious generator of bitterness, rivalry, and jealousy. Joseph's famous "coat of many colours" was traditionally worn by the heir apparent. Not surprisingly, the ten older half-brothers were less than enthusiastic about Joseph's golden prospects. Jacob, their father, added insult to injury by his warm displays of affection towards his favourite son, displays which were not directed towards the ten older boys.

Against this tense and prickly background Joseph makes the mistake of telling his brothers the details of his dreams, as recorded in Genesis 37:5–11.

In the first of these dreams, Joseph saw his family in the harvest field with him, binding sheaves of corn together. His sheaf then stood upright and all the other sheaves bowed to it.

In the second dream, the sun, the moon, and eleven stars bowed to him as well.

The brothers' opportunity to level the score comes when Joseph is sent to visit them in Shechem where they are tending their father's flocks. They had already left by the time he got there, so he followed them to Dothan. As they watch him approaching, all except Reuben (Jacob's eldest son by Leah, and, therefore, the man with most cause for resentment) plan to kill him. Reuben intends to rescue Joseph and take him safely home to Jacob, but he fails when the Midianite and Ishmaelite slave-traders arrive. They buy the boy for twenty pieces of silver and take him to Egypt, where he is bought by Captain Potiphar.

Potiphar recognizes the boy's great ability and promotes him to be chief steward in charge of his household and estate. All goes well for Joseph until Potiphar's wife starts to fancy him. His own personal integrity allied to his gratitude and loyalty to Potiphar make him reject her advances. As soon as an opportunity arises, she accuses Joseph of attempted rape. Potiphar has him imprisoned in a jail where Pharaoh's prisoners are confined.

Just as Potiphar had recognized Joseph's great ability, so did the prison governor. As Potiphar had done, he put Joseph in charge. Under Joseph's aegis, all went well in the royal prison.

Pharaoh's butler and baker had both displeased him and were consequently committed to that same royal institution where Joseph was acting as a kind of administrative deputy governor.

The butler and baker each experienced a strange, symbolic dream while they were there. The butler saw a grape vine with three branches from which he gathered fruit, squeezed it into a cup and served it to Pharaoh. The baker dreamed that he had three baskets of baked food on his head and that birds had eaten the contents.

Joseph swiftly interpreted the symbolism of their dreams. The three vine branches in the butler's dream represented three days. After three days, Pharaoh would pardon the butler and restore him to his old job. The three baskets of the baker's dream also represented three days. After three days, said Joseph, the baker would be hanged and scavenger birds would eat his remains. This was a particularly bleak fate for an Egyptian, who believed that the better preserved his mortal remains were, the more enjoyable his spirit's experiences would be in heaven.

The three days duly passed. The butler was restored to royal favour, and the baker was hanged. Before he left the prison, the butler promised that he would tell Pharaoh what Joseph had done for him, and that Joseph, who was totally innocent of any offence, had been wrongfully imprisoned because of the lying accusation made by Potiphar's wife.

Being human, and fallible, however, the butler forgot.

Two full years passed before anything was done to help Joseph. This time it was Pharaoh himself who experienced strange, troubling dreams. In the first of these he saw seven fat, sleek, healthy cattle coming up out of the Nile. They were followed by seven thin, diseased cattle, which devoured the strong, healthy, vigorous ones. In the second dream, seven rich, ripe, healthy ears of corn came up from the river. They were followed by seven poor, thin, blasted ears of corn which "devoured" the good ones. (Quite how corn "devours" other corn poses something of a problem, but however it was done, it left a deep and lasting impression on Pharaoh!)

He summoned all the Egyptian wise men and magicians to interpret the dream for him: none of them could. The butler's dormant memory finally kicked in again. He told Pharaoh about Joseph, and Joseph was duly summoned to the palace. He made it clear to Pharaoh at the outset that he had no dream wisdom of his own; he could merely pass on what God revealed to him concerning the interpretation.

The meaning which Joseph passed on to Pharaoh was that the seven healthy cattle represented seven years of rich harvests and great abundance. The same meaning was attached to the seven full ears of good, wholesome corn. The emaciated cattle and thin, blemished corn symbolized seven years of crop failure and food shortage which would follow the seven plentiful years. These disastrously unproductive years would "devour" the benefits which the people had enjoyed during the prosperous years.

On learning of this, Pharaoh appointed Joseph as his second-in-command in Egypt with instructions to create and superintend grain storage facilities during the years of abundant harvests. It is interesting to note in passing that there is special significance in the cattle and ears of corn coming up out of the River Nile. It was during the "full Nile" flooding that the vitally fertile silt from the river was spread over the Egyptian fields. It was both literally and metaphorically true that Egypt's food came out of the river.

In due course, Joseph's brothers came to Egypt to buy grain because Canaan was also experiencing a severe famine during the same "lean years" which the dream had signified for Egypt. After a certain amount of understandable subterfuge, Joseph revealed his true identity to them, and there was a joyful reunion. As a result, the Israelites came to live in Egypt, in the area by the Nile delta known as the Land of Goshen.

Centuries passed. Joseph the Dreamer died. The dynasty of Pharaohs who had had good grounds to be grateful to him also died. The socio-

Ancient Egyptian cereal growing. Joseph administered their harvests skilfully and prevented famine.

137

Joseph greets his elderly father, Jacob, and welcomes his family to their new home in Egypt.

political climate of Egypt changed radically. The Israelites were physically robust and strong: their population was thriving and increasing fast. The Egyptians began to fear them — and that fear expressed itself in resentment and anger. From being the warmly welcomed guests of the great man who ranked second only to Pharaoh himself, they became exploited slaves, and remained so until Moses led them to freedom and nationhood.

Joseph's prophetic dreams, and his God-given ability to interpret and explain the dreams of others, raise the same fundamental questions for theologians and philosophers as are raised by other forms of what seems to be validated prophecy. The Joseph story also raises challenging questions about predestination and the validity of human freedom and autonomy. Joseph's dreams of sheaves bowing to him, and of receiving homage from the sun, moon, and stars, could certainly have been said to have come to fruition when his brothers paid their humble respects to him as a high ranking Egyptian administrator from whom they were hoping to buy life saving grain for their families.

What was the mysterious nexus between the dream and its fulfilment, between the symbolic promise of future greatness and its realization? Did the dream mean that once Destiny's promise had been made it would come true? Or was it just a tantalizing glimpse of what *might* come about?

The story of Joseph also provides a challenging riddle concerning the mysteries of purpose and predestination. It is all very well to argue — as a great many portentous Victorian clergy did with alacrity — that Joseph's adventures serve to illustrate God's controlling hand in the universe. When an honest, moral man like Joseph refused to yield to temptation, great good came from his virtue in the end, etc. But did those same pious simpletons argue with equal enthusiasm that their same "God of Providence" had deliberately designed things so that poor little Rachel (whom Jacob adored) died in agonized exhaustion when Benjamin was born? Did this same loving, caring, moral God of Destiny inspire Pharaoh to hang the baker and leave his corpse out for the carrion-eating birds?

The protagonists of providence and predestination cannot have it both ways. If they believe in a God who deliberately plans and carries out cruel and evil things, he *cannot* at the same time be good and should, therefore, be valiantly opposed and fought against by every means at our disposal — instead of being humbly obeyed and worshipped.

The inadequate theologian wrings his hands despairingly and murmurs feebly that we cannot understand the mysterious workings of Providence and so must bravely bear what we do not comprehend. If Providence does incomprehensible things we have every right to demand satisfactory answers. Is there a providential God running the show *or not?* When a happy African child skips innocently on to a land-mine, when a blissful young couple are celebrating their wedding in a bar and a mindless terrorist hurls a bomb through the window, when a drunken imbecile behind the wheel of a stolen car kills two young parents driving their children to a seaside holiday: *is Providence there?* Are we seriously expected to believe that some great future good that we cannot yet see will come out of all their pain and suffering, their bereavement and inconsolable grief?

There are no easy answers: but there have to be better answers than that.

Once again we are thrown back on the theory that love is the greatest joy and the greatest good which the universe can offer. Love can exist only

Joseph's father, Jacob, also experienced strange prophetic dreams. Was the gift inherited?

in conditions of perfect freedom. Nothing that can be bought, bribed, threatened, or coerced can be called love. If our suprapersonal God desires to give and receive the love of what he has created, then that creation has to be truly free. If we are truly free, irresponsible lunatics can drink and drive, fanatical terrorists can throw bombs indiscriminately, and profit-mad arms dealers can sell land-mines to cynical politicians for the feet of children to detonate. We are also free to love God and one another more than we love ourselves, and to give our lives in a good cause if called upon to make the ultimate sacrifice. Without the depths, there are no heights. Without darkness, there is no light. Without freedom, there is no love and no purpose in life. So we reject the false doctrines of predestination and providence. We decline the blandishments of destiny. We accept that we are the masters of our own fate: that, in Shakespeare's words, "the fault's not in our stars but in ourselves." But where does that decision leave dreams and their meanings?

The seventh chapter of the mysterious Book of Daniel contains a series of weird dreams, or, perhaps, semi-waking visions, which Daniel recorded. The terrifying beasts from the storm-lashed sea, who are conquered by the Ancient of Days and the Son of man, are open to many and varied interpretations. But like the dreams of Joseph, the butler, the baker, and Pharaoh himself, their interpretations are not necessarily what will come to pass unalterably.

It may be that in the dreaming, or semi-waking state, the minds of certain sensitive individuals are able to tune in to dimensions of possibility, alternative realities, or probability tracks. As far as our future is concerned all things are possible; nothing is impossible; some things are more probable than others. Life rolls forward on the precarious and eccentric wheels of "*if.*" We are not predestined. We are not the slaves of providence. We are God's own free men and women. He has given us genuine choice: it is our responsibility to use it in the right way. Through dreams, or any other medium of psychic communication, we may get advice, warnings, encouragement, additional data, or useful extra information — what we *don't* get is instruction.

Joseph is a prototype of all such dreamers. Perhaps, his greatest significance is to serve as a sign and a symbol for the rest of us. Dreams and their meanings are still a mystery — we cannot be certain what they are, nor how they work. We can, however, be confident that they do not rob of us our free will. We are the masters of our dreams — we must never allow them to master us.

Chapter Fifteen

The Mystery of Moses

Joseph invited his family as honoured guests to the Egypt which he virtually administered under Pharaoh during the seven grim famine years. Centuries passed. Times changed traumatically for the Hebrews. Their status declined from honoured guests to exploited slaves. But they were a tough and resilient race, and their population was thriving. The Egyptians began to feel afraid of them. There was a ruthless and brutal attempt to curb their numbers by killing all male Hebrew babies at birth.

It was during this savage time that Moses was born into the tribe of Levi, destined to become the special, Jewish priestly tribe. His mother hid him for as long as she could, and then decided to place her precious babe in a floating ark, or cradle, and leave him by the rushes at the edge of the Nile. His sister, Miriam, was sent to keep watch over the cradle to see what would happen.

Pharaoh's daughter and her maidservants spotted the ark and discovered the baby inside it. The Egyptian princess felt sorry for him, and at that critical moment, quick-witted Miriam ran up and asked whether the princess would like her to find a suitable Hebrew woman whom she could hire to serve as the baby's nurse. Moses's mother was duly appointed. As soon as he was old enough to leave home and fend for himself, his mother brought him to Pharaoh's daughter who raised him as an Egyptian prince.

Moses, therefore, was an unusual individual in that he shared two very distinct cultures: the Hebrews' tribal, patriarchal, Yahweh-centred monotheism suppressed by bondage and slave labour — and an Egyptian prince's polytheistic, luxurious, and privileged existence among palaces and gardens.

He was also an extremely powerful man physically, and tended not to suffer fools gladly. His great rescue mission, which took his Hebrew people out of slavery, as recorded in detail in the Book of Exodus, began with two brief episodes which clearly reveal that in hand to hand combat he was a warrior to be reckoned with.

In the first of these incidents, his fiery temper and direct approach to problem solving is apparent — a trait he shared with Alexander the Great who sliced through the incredibly complicated Gordian Knot. Moses encountered an Egyptian overseer, or task-master, ill-treating a Hebrew slave — and promptly kills the Egyptian.

The following day, he separated two quarrelling Hebrews, and asked the wrongdoer why he was attacking his brother. The man sarcastically asked Moses whether he was going to kill him as he had killed the Egyptian. Shrewdly guessing what Pharaoh's reaction would be once the story got out, Moses wisely decided on flight.

He reached the land of Midian, well clear of Pharaoh's jurisdiction, and sat down by a well. Seven girls, the daughters of Jethro (also known as Reuel) a local Midianite priest, came to water their father's flock at the well. The neighbouring shepherds, who also used the well, drove them back and took what should have been the girls' turn. Moses intervened and helped Jethro's daughters to water their sheep.

One man alone against a crowd of shepherds?

What sort of man was he? Tall, muscular, broad-shouldered, and carrying a lethal Egyptian sword at his belt; he was a man with an angry glint in his eyes and a strong, expressive face. He did not look like a soft target. The shepherds grumbled under their breath, but did as he said all the same. The girls thanked him and drove their flock home early.

Jethro was surprised to see them back so soon. Excitedly, they explained about the powerful Egyptian stranger who had sorted out the shepherds and then helped them to draw water for their sheep. Jethro was indignant: why hadn't they invited this excellent man home with them? Where was he now? They were sent back urgently to fetch him.

Moses duly joined Jethro's household, and married Zipporah, the eldest daughter, who subsequently bore him a son, Gershom. For a year or two, Moses kept Jethro's flock.

The first great, apparently supernatural mystery in Moses's long and eventful life is the mystery of the burning bush. The word *seneh* is used in the Bible only for that one *special* bush which Moses witnessed burning without its being burnt away. The Egyptian name for the species was *sunt,* and it almost certainly corresponds to our contemporary *acacia nilotica.* The other possibility is *crataegus aronia,* which naturalists have reported on Mount Sinai, but which is less common than *seneh.*

So intrigued is Moses by this strange phenomenon that he goes closer to examine it — and he hears a Voice calling his name from the bush. He removes his sandals on being told that he is on holy ground, and the Voice tells him that he is in the presence of God. Furthermore, Yahweh identifies himself as the ancestral God of the Hebrews, the God who called Abraham, Isaac, and Jacob to serve him. Moses instinctively covers his face because he is overawed by God's Presence and afraid to look at him.

If the Exodus record here in Chapter 3 is to be taken at face value, the Being who speaks to Moses from the burning bush, seems very different in power, personality and purpose from the Universal Father, the God of Infinite Love and Mercy, whom Christ reveals in the New Testament centuries later. Some theologians and biblical scholars ply us with various explanations that seem less than satisfactory: they explain that the Hebrews — including their great leader, Moses — were still a relatively primitive race at this time. They had to learn slowly. God had to teach them the basic alphabet of religious thought itself before they could read life's complex volumes of advanced morality and ethics. Some of what we learn in nursery school has to be unlearned before we can read science and philosophy at University.

Their alternative suggestion is that God never altered his approach — the people simply understood more as the years rolled on. It was not God that changed — it was their understanding and interpretation of him. To a primitive mind, a stroke victim has not suffered a blood clot in the brain, but rather an invisible superbeing, god or demon, has struck him down with a terrifying, invisible weapon. To the primitive mind, two hunters encounter a lion, which kills the first man but is itself killed by the second: the first man was the victim of a divine or demonic curse, but the second was blessed with divine protection. The first forgot his prayers, but the second said them dutifully night and morning.

The objective pragmatist would venture to suggest that the primitive mind is mistaken. The God of Love and Freedom does not desire the death of the hunter — nor, for that matter of the lion. Because we live in a universe in which cause and effect operate, it is the relative speed, strength, intelligence, and alertness of prey and predator which decide the issue of who lives and who dies.

An earthquake opens a huge chasm in a particular place at a particular time. Hundreds, perhaps thousands, disappear down it. That is no part of the plan of a loving and merciful God. That is not Divine Providence.

There were simple, natural, understandable, geological, economic, and demographic factors at work in the tragedy. Cause and effect were again operating impartially.

The other great problem about the message which the Voice delivered from the burning bush is the problem of trying to envisage a chess-playing God, who apparently delights to take on Pharaoh as an opponent in a punitive game of wits. Does the omnipotent and omniscient God of the Universe really have to do an escalating series of unpleasant things to Pharaoh in order to make him change his mind?

Then there's the even greater problem of "God hardened Pharaoh's heart" — apparently in order to make him refuse to do what God seemed to want him to do in the first place! Now, we not only have a bridge, chess, and psychological-mind-games playing God, but a whimsical and arbitrary one at that, one who can and does control which piece his opponent moves — or does not move — to any particular square!

Our God of Consistent and Unlimited Love, Power, Knowledge, and Mercy simply does not treat any of his creation like that. He never did and he never will. Infinite Kindness and Goodness do not act like scheming and devious criminal gang-leaders trying to outsmart their opponent for who gets control of the brothels and drug dealers on the East Side of the city.

If the Voice in the bush seems too *limited* to be God, and too *devious* to be God, *then who or what is it?*

Moses is astounded by the phenomenon of the burning bush. Drawn by Theo Fanthorpe.

Is there, perhaps, some disturbing similarity here with the Eden narrative, and with the destruction of Sodom and Gomorrah? We have already considered the possibility that the mysterious "angelic beings" who came to save Lot and his family behaved more like men with superior technology than like supernatural entities with unlimited "let-there-be" type magic at their disposal. They couldn't do anything to Sodom and Gomorrah until Lot and his family were clear. That sounds more as if they were activating the timer on a devastating nuclear device than performing a supernatural miracle of destruction.

Is it even *remotely* possible that we are dealing with extraterrestrial genetic engineers? Abraham, Isaac, Jacob, Joseph, sanctuary for generations in a friendly and hospitable Egypt: then it all begins to go wrong for their cherished genetic stock. Moses, that unusual man of two cultures, is ideally placed to extricate the Hebrews from slavery in Egypt and to get them established in their own free country, their Promised Land. He can't do it alone. The extraterrestrials — *if that's who they really are* — will use their superior technology to assist him.

Exodus, Chapter 4 gives details of the arguments and objections which Moses uses, and how the Voice from the burning bush overcomes them all. Moses is given "magical" (technological?) conjuring tricks — signs with which to impress Pharaoh and his courtiers. The rod can be turned into a serpent, and back into a rod again when you grab its tail. A healthy hand can be turned leprous, and healed instantaneously by the simple expedient of placing it inside one's robe in a Napoleonic gesture. The third sign is taking water from the Nile and pouring it out on the ground where it will turn to blood. These are all symbolic warnings to Pharaoh, foretastes of what to expect if he persists in defying Moses: the snake-rod is a sign of forthcoming plagues of living creatures — frogs and flies; the leprous hand is a warning of disease; the blood from the water is an omen of death.

When Moses goes on putting theoretical obstacles in the way, the Voice from the bush gets angry with him, as it does on subsequent occasions. Does that anthropopathic anger really sound like the behaviour of a God who is omnipotent, omniscient, and omnipresent, a God of perfect love and unlimited mercy?

Plague followed plague for the Egyptians, but the Israelites were unaffected by them. Was it extraterrestrial alien technology that reddened the Nile and killed the fish? Toxic dyes are simple enough to make and inject into a river. In ideal breeding conditions, with no fish-predators to eat their spawn and their tadpoles, frogs might well multiply alarmingly around the Nile. The plague of flies which followed the death of the frogs, would not be unexpected. Heaps of decaying amphibians under the hot North African sun would be a sumptuous feast for flies.

Each time there was a plague, or disaster, Pharaoh vacillated — first giving permission for the Israelites to leave, and then withdrawing it again as soon as the trouble had subsided. Finally came the death of the Egyptian first-born, from which the Israelites were exempt — an event on which the Passover ritual was founded. There is something here, again, that might just possibly be considered to have a *remote* connection with the destruction of Sodom and Gomorrah. The Israelites were instructed to mark the door-posts and lintels of their houses with blood. The Israeli houses were identified so that the "angel of death" would *pass over* them without taking any of their people. Why did they have to be marked if this widespread death is a genuinely supernatural miracle? However death was brought — magically or echnologically — whoever, or whatever, brought it needed to be able to *identify* the Hebrew houses, and to avoid them. This nation-wide tragedy was too much even for the despotic Pharaoh: the Israelites were able to leave at last.

The opening verses of the fourteenth chapter of the Book of Exodus are particularly interesting in connection with the subsequent disaster which destroyed the flower of the Egyptian army and their chariots in the "Red Sea." The original Hebrew words *yam suph* are better translated as "Sea of Reeds" than as "Red Sea." So where exactly was it? Most experts consider that it was a marshy lake, somewhere between the Gulf of Suez and the Mediterranean, very probably one of the Bitter Lakes near Baal-Zephon. These intriguing opening verses of Exodus, Chapter 14, tell how Moses was instructed by God — or whoever else was giving him his orders — to lead the Israelites to Pihahiroth, between Migdol and the sea and set up camp there close to the sea. Doesn't that sound as if Moses was being asked to set a trap for Pharaoh and the Egyptian charioteers? Did

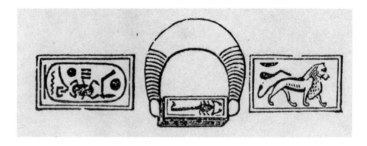

Some Egyptian treasures like those which Moses and the Israelites took with them at the Exodus.

whoever was directing Moses *need* to have the Egyptians in *exactly the right place* in order to drown them? Once again, it begins to sound rather more like technology than omniscient and omnipotent, divine intervention. When Moses stretched his rod across the sea, did some incredibly powerful mechanism spring into action and drive back the water? Once the Israelites were safely across the temporarily dry sea-bed, did *someone* switch off the power and allow the waters to swirl back to drown the Egyptians?

A universal God of love and mercy would surely have as much parental affection for the Egyptians as for the Hebrews, the Chinese, the Icelanders, or the Argentinians. He would no more deliberately lure one group of his children into a lethal trap as any other group. An extraterrestrial, genetic engineer, on the other hand, anxious to preserve his successful species, would use such technological weaponry as he had available to defend them from whoever, or whatever, was threatening his plans for their future. Such an engineer would quite happily set up a fatal water-trap for Pharaoh and his Egyptian charioteers.

It cannot be too strongly emphasized that this *suggestion* of the possible involvement of extraterrestrial genetic technologists in the Exodus in no way contradicts, precludes, or invalidates, the existence of God: on the contrary — it reveals him as vastly *greater*. He is then seen to be the Creator and Sustainer of millions of species, inhabiting billions of planets, spread across trillions of galaxies.

Who is to deny that by exercising their God-given freedom, just as we are free to exercise ours, older and more developed races are not playing key roles in the advancement of learning throughout the whole of this incalculably vast universe? Benign purposes can surely be achieved via benign intermediaries, just as evil comes from the misuse of their freedom by such powerful intermediaries. There is an old proverb to the effect that an evil mouse can do relatively little harm, whereas an evil elephant can do much more. An evil man or woman can do terrible damage, but an alien being with vast supernatural or technological powers, who has freely chosen to do evil, can create havoc and suffering almost beyond human imagining.

The next major mystery in the story of Moses is *why* Pharaoh changed his mind so dramatically and pursued the Israelites after allowing them to leave. It is helpful to recall that Moses was a man of two distinct cultures. His rank as an Egyptian prince gave him access to inner secrets of the Egyptian aristocracy, which was very much a priestly aristocracy. What if one of their greatest secrets, and a prime source of their power and knowledge, was something which had been salvaged from the destruction of

Atlantis, on the lines which Graham Hancock and other expert researchers like the Flem-Aths have suggested?

The Egyptians kept special treasures in sacred arks — similar in many respects to the Hebrews' Ark of the Covenant. It is even possible that rather than making the Ark, Moses had brought with him an Egyptian treasure ark, containing rare, ancient, and costly secrets: the so-called Emerald Tablets of Hermes Trismegistus, containing the "wisdom" of the Egyptian gods, perhaps. As Moses and the Israelites are setting up camp by Pihahiroth, Pharaoh discovers that this vital ancient treasure and power source is missing. He guesses at once that Moses has taken it. Nothing else now matters to Pharaoh. He has to recover it at all costs. Hence his insane deployment of chariots across a seabed which is liable to re-flood at any minute.

According to the biblical account, the mysterious *manna,* on which the Israelites were apparently sustained for some forty years, appeared on the ground each morning in the form of a small, white seed-like thing which looked rather like hoar frost. It did not occur on the Sabbath, so the Israelites gathered a double supply the day before. It also had to be gathered early, before the sun became hot enough to melt it. They were unable to store it, as it began to decay and become worm-infested if it was not eaten on the same day that it was gathered; the Sabbath manna proved an exception to this rule.

The Israelites would grind it and bake it before eating. It tasted of oil and honey, and was generally thought of by the Israelites as perfectly palatable and acceptable.

Various foods, condiments and medicines from the Eastern Mediterranean area and beyond are still described as "manna" today, but they do not bear much resemblance to the biblical manna described in: Exodus 16:14–36; Numbers 11:7–9; Deuteronomy 8:3, 16; Joshua 5:12; Psalm 78:24–25; and Wisdom 16:20–21. The biblical manna seems to have been accepted by the people as a direct and miraculous gift from God — not as a natural product.

The natural products occur only during limited seasons — normally from May to August — whereas the biblical manna was available all the year round. Natural manna is produced in relatively small quantities; the biblical manna must have arrived at the rate of *several hundred tons a day* if the numbers of Israelites are as great as recorded. Each person was allocated an *omer* of manna per day. This is approximately three one-pint measures, or about one-and-a half litres. An *omer* was the tenth part of an *ephah,* which has been estimated to have a capacity of about 18 litres. Working on these approximations, Dr. Smith's old, but nevertheless rigorous and scholarly, *Dictionary of the Bible* estimates a requirement of 6.75 million kilograms of manna each week to feed the whole Hebrew nation!

Natural manna can be kept for lengthy periods, just as spices and seasonings can, and certainly does not decay within a mere twenty-four hours. (Natural manna does not seem able to observe the Sabbath, either!) According to the account in Joshua, the supply of manna ceased suddenly; natural manna would be unlikely to do that.

The Arabian philosopher, scientist, and physician, Avicenna, was born in Bukhara, Iran, in 980 and died in Hamadan in 1037. One of the greatest and most influential Islamic philosopher-scientists of his time, Avicenna wrote the monumental *Kitab ash-shifa*, the "Book of Healing," which is a definitive medical encyclopedia. He also wrote one of the greatest books in the entire history of medicine: *The Canon of Medicine.* Avicenna had a phenomenal mind — he had memorized all of the Holy Koran before his tenth birthday, and his tremendous physical strength and equally strong constitution enabled him to work tirelessly by night as well as by day. At one time he was Vizier *and* Court Physician, and it was not until each day's administrative duties were completed that he was able to teach his medical students in the evenings. Those evenings were memorable occasions, full of highly enjoyable entertainment as well as deep learning. When the amazing Avicenna had an opinion about something, it was always worth hearing, and he certainly had views on manna: "Manna is a dew which falls on stones or bushes, becomes thick like honey, and can be hardened so as to be like grains of corn."

The substance which is now called manna in the Arabian deserts is collected during June from the *tamarix gallica*, or tarfa, the tamarisk shrub. An expert named Burckhardt described it as falling from the thorns on to the sticks and leaves with which the ground below the bushes is covered. He noted that it had to be collected early in the day, or it would melt in the sun later on. Some local users clean it and boil it, strain it through cloth and store it inside leather. Treated like this, it can be stored successfully for several years. It was customary for those who had stored it in this way, to spread it on unleavened bread like honey or butter, but it was not customary to make it into cakes and eat it alone. The problem with trying to identify the biblical manna with tamarisk is that the tamarisk manna is only available in any quantity when there is more rain than usual. In dry years it practically disappears.

Another expert named Ehrenberg believed that the tamarisk secretions were caused by a minute insect, *coccus manniparus*, which made innumerable small punctures in the tamarisk bush.

Two early travellers, Rauwolf and Gmelin, both thought that the manna they came across in the Middle East resembled coriander seeds, and Gmelin noted in particular how white it was.

In Ispahan, the local people gather the leaves of a shrub which they call "the sweet thorn" and thresh them with sticks, almost as early farmers threshed corn. The grains of manna which are released by this treatment are collected in large sieves.

Niebuhr was at Mardin in Mesopotamia, when he described what his hosts referred to as manna lying like coarse flour or meal on the leaves of a tree which they called *ballôt, afs,* or *as.* It looked to Niebuhr like a species of oak, but he wasn't sure. The Mardinese harvest it in July and August, and the supply is positively correlated with the season's rainfall. It is often collected before sunrise and gathered on a cloth. When taken in this way it is very white and pure, and looks almost like powdery snow. When it is left on the leaves to be collected later, it melts and thickens in the strong sunlight. The coated leaves are then gathered and placed into boiling water. This causes the manna to float to the surface like thick oil. The people of Mardin refer to this as *manna essema,* the manna of Heaven, or the manna of Paradise.

While making further explorations in the Jordan valley, Burckhardt discovered another gum-like form of manna on the leaves of the *gharab* or *salyx babylonica.* This grows to about the same size as an olive tree. The *gharab* manna is sweet when first gathered, but quickly becomes sharp and acidic in flavour. Two other shrubs which are strong candidates for the role of scriptural manna are the *alhagi maurorum* and the *alhagi desertorum* which are both found in Syria. None of them matches the biblical manna profile perfectly.

Etymologically, the word manna seems to have come from the root *man-hu,* meaning: "What's this?" When the Israelites first saw it, it seems that they had no idea what it was. The Hebrew word *man* is simply the neuter interrogative pronoun: "What?" If it had been only the ordinary, edible exudation of some familiar local shrub, wouldn't some of the Israelites have known what it was?

If this mysterious edible *something* was not familiar to them, and if it behaved in decidedly unnatural ways at times, just as the biblical account records, could it have been another example of alien technology? When we consider the special vitamin and mineral rich supplements that are included in astronauts' diets, and the concentrated health foods that are available to help dieters lose weight without missing out on any essential nutrition, it is germane to wonder if there is any similarity between these products and the mysterious white powder which fed the Israelites during their forty-year sojourn in the wilderness? Did the Voice from the bush (whoever he *really* was) *manufacture* the manna the Israelites needed by using technological means? Various modern food manufacturing techniques for creating powdered milk, or augmented milk substitutes, tend to have white, or light-coloured, powder as an end product. Was manna made on the genetic engineers' orbiting mother ship and delivered each morning for the Israelites to gather?

The arduous and extended gathering process itself could also be significant. Collecting small granules of the white, powdery food, cleaning it, preparing it — perhaps grinding and baking it as well — were not quick or easy jobs. One of the great problems facing the leaders of a large group of loosely organized people, such as the Israelites were when they first left Egypt, *is to keep them occupied.* Shrewd leaders knew that trouble and discontentment were most likely to arise when such groups were under-employed. When malcontents have time to lounge around airing their grievances in leisurely conversations, they tend to attract followers.

Over the centuries, the organizers of the armed services devised thousands of irritating and trivial ways to fill a soldier's time: polishing boots and buttons, whitening webbing, and laying gear out for inspection in minutely prescribed ways. Was the elaborate daily gathering of manna a subtle way of keeping the Israelites gainfully employed and out of mischief? That sounds more like the devious thinking of a crafty, technocratic, genetic engineer than a perfect thought from the infinite mind of a loving God.

An ancient Egyptian statue which would have been familiar to Moses.

151

Mysteries of the Bible

The account of the giving of the law on Mount Sinai is one of the best known episodes in the Bible. The Ten Commandments are among the best known and least kept laws in the world. The first three are directly concerned with humanity's response to God: he is to be first and foremost with no rivals; idols and graven images are forbidden as objects of worship; God's Name is not to be taken in vain. The fourth concerns observation of the Sabbath Day. The remaining six are concerned with social behaviour and inter-personal relationships: the care of elderly parents; the forbidding of murder, adultery, theft, lying, and covetousness.

It is interesting to note that many of these superb moral teachings are also found in ancient Egypt. *The Confession of the Righteous Soul* in *The Book of the Dead* contains the lines:

I have not slain men ... I have not made others miserable ... I have not made the beginning of the day hard and difficult for those who worked for me ... I have not made others hungry ... I have not made others weep ... I have loved my wife and done all I could to make her happy ... I was like a walking stick for my father: I came and went as he commanded me ... I have never stolen from anyone, especially from the dead ... I honoured the old ... I gave my staff to an old man who needed one ... I have never complained about a slave to the master who is set over him ... I have treated those I know as fairly as those whom I do not know ... I have not told lies nor uttered falsehoods ... I have given bread to those who were hungry, drink to those who were thirsty, clothes to those who had none and a ferry boat to those who had no means of crossing the water.

It may, perhaps, be asked whether any of these commendable ancient Egyptian ethics might have been in the mind of Moses when he passed on the Sinai Law to the Israelites. If Moses had, in fact, taken some rare, precious, and powerful things from Egypt, did they include *The Book of the Dead* complete with all its ethical teachings? There are some even stranger reports about the Ten Commandments which also deserve consideration.

In 1995, reports came through alleging that an archaeological expedition to Jabal al Lawz in Saudi Arabia had been led by a Professor Jan van Hessing from Holland, accompanied by an Israeli expert named Isadore Ginsberg, together with Alger Johnston, an English linguistic consultant. They were said to have discovered caves on Jabal al Lawz, (sometimes spelled Jabal al Laws) in which they had found an ancient gopher wood box. When this box was opened it was said to have contained fragments of inscribed stone, which were believed by some members of the expedition to have been the original stone tablets of the Sinai Law. It was also reported that a *further set* of somewhat different — but not contradictory — commandments, was discovered concealed in a glazed niche in the cave wall. These new commandments contained ideas about health-giving herbal remedies that prolonged life; ecological instructions to keep the earth pure and undefiled; commandments to share and help the poor, to refrain from selfishness and greed, to treat women and children with gentleness, honour, and respect, to invoke the power of prayer for healing, to be humble — *because there were countless other worlds in God's keeping, and some of his creatures who dwelt there were much greater and holier than terrestrial humanity.* This is such an immense and revolutionary claim, that we would want to see the originals for ourselves, to have them independently, scientifically dated, and to interview the actual finders, before venturing an opinion.

That Jabal al Lawz is the biblical Mount Sinai, however, is a sensible argument and one which deserves to be taken seriously. In his fascinating and challenging book *The Gold of Exodus,* Howard Blum makes a good case for locating Mount Sinai at the southern tip of the Sinai Peninsula, just inside the borders of Saudi Arabia. Adventurers Larry Williams and Bob Cornuke — a pair of real-life Indiana Jones types — made their way there in the 1980s and believed that they had found the route which Moses and the Israelites took across the seabed. They also believed that they had discovered the pillars and boundary stones which Moses erected, and the altar which Aaron used for the notorious worship of the golden calf. They certainly seem to have found some very strange artefacts there — including ancient and mysterious carvings of cattle.

Tough, adventurous, and outgoing, Bob Cornuke is president of the BASE Institute, who have their own web site at http:/www. baseinstitute.org/bob-cornuke.html. (BASE stands for Bible Archaeology, Search and Exploration.) Bob — a former SWAT team member — has dived in the Red Sea in the hope of discovering traces of Pharaoh's lost chariots, been arrested by the Saudi authorities on charges of spying, escaped from jail, and beaten his pursuers to the border. One of the most remarkable of the discoveries which Cornuke and Williams made on Jabal al Lawz was its strangely seared and blackened summit, which seemed to them to confirm the biblical references to the fire on top of Mount Sinai. It is undoubtedly an interesting speculation, and a number of reputable Bible scholars accept the possibility that Jabal al Lawz really is the same Mount Sinai where Moses received the Ten Commandments.

The final mystery of Moses is the report of his reappearance with Elijah on the Mount of Transfiguration, when these two outstanding figures of the Old Testament — one representing the sacred Law and the other representing the prophets — were said to have been in conversation with Jesus. Undoubtedly, the innermost group of Christ's disciples, Peter, James, and John, gave the best report that human observers could give of an event that was beyond human understanding. There on that mountain top something extremely strange took place. The mystery of the Shechinah Glory reasserted itself: Jesus, Moses, and Elijah were glowing with its inexplicable power.

The mystery of who and what Moses really was, and who guided and helped him, is one of the most challenging in the Bible. Whether it was God himself, or some extraterrestrial intermediary, who spoke to Moses from the burning bush, something dramatic changed Moses's life forever — and with it, the history of the world.

Chapter Sixteen

The Secret of Samson's Strength

The mystery of Samson begins with the account of his miraculous conception and birth as recorded in the Book of Judges, Chapter 13. Manoah, Samson's father, was a Danite living in Zorah during a low point in Hebrew history when they were subject to the Philistines.

As was the case with Hannah, the mother of the prophet Samuel, Manoah's wife had no children. The account in Judges records that an angel appeared to her and told her that she would bear a son and that he would become a great leader, one of the judges of Israel, who would begin the process of delivering his people from Philistine domination.

Broadly speaking, early Hebrew history can be divided into a series of distinct epochs: the founding of the nation by Abraham and the ensuing patriarchal period under Isaac and Jacob; the move to Joseph's Egypt and the slow decline into subjection and slavery during the nation's residence in Goshen; the Exodus and wandering under the leadership of Moses; the conquest and settlement of Canaan led by Joshua; the period of the judges, when great leaders like Samson arose from time to time to defeat neighbouring enemies; the united monarchy of Saul, David and Solomon; the division of the kingdom when Jeroboam led the ten northern tribes away; captivity and exile in Babylon; the return and rebuilding led by Ezra and Nehemiah; the arrival of the Seleucids and the nation's problems with the insane despot, Antiochus Epiphanes; the successful fight for freedom led by Judas Maccabeus; the Roman occupation and the dawn of the Christian era.

Samson was one of the great leaders who arose as they were needed during the turbulent period of the judges: between Joshua's conquest of Canaan and the establishment of the united monarchy under Saul. When the strange being (whom Manoah's wife believed to be an angel) first appeared and gave her the news about her forthcoming pregnancy, Manoah was not with her. She was told to refrain from alcohol, and to be especially careful to observe all the strict Hebrew dietary laws. On no account must she eat anything regarded as "unclean." The child was never to have his hair cut, and was to be raised as a Nazirite. This term is based on the Hebrew word *nazar,* which means to abstain from certain things, or to dedicate oneself to something such as the service of God or a personal, political, or religious cause.

The Nazirites can best be described, therefore, as a fanatically ascetic early Jewish religious sect whose observances included total abstinence from alcohol and leaving their hair uncut. At the start of the movement, being a Nazirite was something which was undertaken for life: certainly this was the case during Manoah's time. In later epochs, however, it was possible to become a Nazirite for a limited period only, undertaking to keep the strange vows for only three or, perhaps, seven years. When the time was up, the Nazirite would make a special offering to God, and resume a normal, sensible lifestyle again.

The primitive Nazirites, of Samson's era and earlier, were similar in some ways to the fanatical men who joined the "Schools of the Prophets." They practised mysticism, asceticism, and frequently went off into bouts of ecstasy and wild religious enthusiasm — giving contemporary observers the impression that these "prophets" might well be possessed by something paranormal.

Nazirites were also associated with the sacred warrior tradition — an ancient ideal that was not exclusive to Israel and went back for millennia. It

Pagan gods from the days of Samson.

reached its peak with the development of the magnificently courageous and indomitable Templars from 1119 to 1307. It was based on the belief that warriors were in a special religious state while on duty or engaged in combat.

A related idea can be identified among the Norse Berserkers, who were ecstatic religious warriors dedicated to their Viking god, Odin. The original Berserkers dressed in wolf or bear skins, and travelled in wild, uncontrollable gangs who — despite their *religious* aspirations — were notorious for rape and murder. They were employed as body guards by Norse kings and war lords, and were also used as highly effective, first-impact troops in battle. When in their berserk, or "possessed," battle fury, they were thought to be invulnerable, and certainly they themselves *believed* that they were.

Cú Chulainn, the famous early Irish warrior, was also a type of berserker. He was reputed to be the strongest and fiercest of the Red Hand Knights, the great heroes who fought for King Conor of the Ulaids of north-east Ireland, two thousand years ago. Just as in the case of Samson, and several similar warrior heroes — biblical and otherwise — there was something decidedly *strange* about Cú Chulainn's birth. Were his singular gifts also the result of genetic engineering experiments?

His mother was Dechtire, the sister of King Conor, but his father was the Irish god, known as Lug, or Lugh, of the Long Arm. Cú Chulainn was bigger and stronger than the average man of his time, and in addition — which again sounds rather like a genetic engineering experiment — he was said to have seven fingers on each hand and seven toes on each foot. He also had seven pupils in each eye. His tremendous feats were comparable to those of the Greek heroes Herakles (Hercules) and Achilles, and, as already noted, he *also* had the awesome characteristics of the best type of Scandinavian Berserker. When only seventeen years old, for example, Cú Chulainn successfully defended the whole of the land of the Uliads against the formidable warriors of Queen Maeve of Connaught. Sadly, just as Samson was deceived by the treacherous Philistines over the matter of the lion and honey riddle — and far more gravely by Delilah — so the mighty Cú Chulainn was tricked into an unfair fight and killed before reaching his thirtieth birthday.

When Manoah's wife reported the "angelic" visit and message to her husband, he prayed that the strange being would return so that he could hear the instructions as well. The unusual visitor duly came back while Manoah's wife was sitting in the field. She ran immediately to fetch Manoah so that he could speak to the mysterious being. He asked what he and his wife were to do, and the instructions regarding alcohol and diet were repeated.

Manoah, in the best traditions of Middle Eastern hospitality, tries to persuade the stranger to have a meal with them, but their paranormal visitor declines all food and drink. Manoah next asks for the stranger's name, explaining that he will then be able to honour him when his prophecy about the miraculous conception comes to pass. Again the visitor declines: his name, he says, is secret, and he will not divulge it to Manoah.

It was widely believed in early times that to know someone's name was to acquire a degree of power over them. The folk story of Rumpelstiltskin illustrates this principle clearly.

As their guest will not eat with them despite all their entreaties and persuasion, Manoah offers a burnt offering as a sacrifice. While he and his wife look on, their mysterious companion *ascends in the flame.*

If this is a straightforward, factual record of what Manoah and his wife witnessed, what does it mean? The first possibility is that their visitor was some type of genuinely paranormal being, that he was literally an angel and was simply exercising some of his magical, angelic powers. A second possibility, however remote, is that he was one more highly significant piece in the jigsaw of the genetic engineering theory. It is curious, to say the least, that so many of the remarkably gifted charismatic characters in the Bible are recorded as having been born following unusual conceptions. The prophet Samuel is another prime example.

If Samson's mother was given abnormal genetic material, if Samson was not, in fact, the *biological* son of Manoah, what exactly was in that particular bundle of genes? Did the fierce, impulsive and immensely powerful Samson possibly have the rare XYY structure, allegedly — and very controversially — making him in some senses potentially hyper-male? Or had he been given some other dynamic, genetic cocktail — perhaps of alien origin — which would be rendered even more hazardous if he ever drank alcohol? The old saying that alcohol "inhibits the inhibitions" has a hard core of common sense in it.

Is it remotely possible that the rare XYY ingredient — which informed medical opinion now regards as totally innocuous in any case — or some *different* form of genetic interference could, perhaps, have contributed something to the berserk strength which enabled Samson to rip up a lion with his bare hands?

Could being an XYY man — or being the product of some totally different, artificially implanted, genetic program — also have accounted for Samson's extra-strong sex drive: a perfectly good and positive thing in itself, but a factor which ultimately contributed to his downfall?

The Secret of Samson's Strength

The pioneering Italian criminologist, Cesare Lombroso (1835 – 1909), was a scientist whose theories were based on Darwinian evolution. Lombroso investigated the physical characteristics of persistent criminals and came to the conclusion that there was a connection between criminal behaviour and atavism: he wondered whether recidivists were actually reversions to a more primitive human type, whose genes still existed in the general pool.

Other early studies investigated the possible correlation of somatyping and criminality. Some researchers believed that they had found a link between mesomorphs (those with the muscular, athletic build of Samson and Hercules) and criminal behaviour. They thought that endomorphs with soft, plump, rounded bodies, and ectomorphs with long, slim torsos, were less likely to indulge in socially deviant behaviour.

Such theories have now been almost entirely abandoned, but there are still a few criminologists who wonder whether there *might* just be an extremely tenuous link between the XYY super-male chromosome and an increased risk of criminality. Although some early studies investigated the incidence of XYY men among convicted prisoners, it is essential to emphasize as strongly as possible that an overwhelming majority of XYY men lead exemplary, socially acceptable lives, and that recent expert research from Yale University Medical School concluded: "the boys with XYY Karyotype have shown no aggressive or delinquent tendencies."

In view of the Philistine ascendancy in Canaan during Samson's time, and the resentment the Israelites felt towards them, it was practically unheard of for marriages to take place between the two races.

On a visit to Timnath, however, Samson meets a Philistine girl with whom he becomes infatuated, and tells his parents to get her for him as a wife.

What seems to be an editorial aside at this point in the biblical narrative (Judges 14:5) suggests that this was all part of a divine plan to create an incident with the Philistines. Yet again, we encounter the same curious anomaly as we did in Exodus: the idea of God apparently acting like a subtle and devious games player instead of the all-powerful and all-loving Master of Universe which we firmly believe him to be. There is also the far more serious philosophical and theological contradiction between the true nature of our Universal God of Love, Mercy, and Justice and the deliberate instigation of a chain of events involving Samson and the Philistines, events that are calculated to culminate in death, suffering, and intense misery.

Samson revisits the carcass of the young lion which he killed only to discover that wild bees have already rested in it and produced honey there. It is another small indicator of Samson's physical toughness that he scoops out the honey unhesitatingly, regardless of the bees, eats some himself and then takes the rest home to his parents.

The unexpected presence of the bees inside the dead lion gives him an idea for a riddle, which he poses to thirty Philistine guests at his lengthy wedding feast: "Out of the eater came forth meat, and out of the strong came forth sweetness." There is a wager between Samson and the thirty Philistine relatives and friends of the bride's family: if they guess his riddle, they each get a change of raiment and a sheet of cloth. If they fail to guess it, they each give clothing and a cloth to Samson.

This riddling game goes back into the mists of antiquity. There was, for example, the riddle of the Sphinx: "What goes first on four legs, then on two, and finally on three?" Very few were able to work out that it was a human being, crawling on four legs as a baby, walking on two during the fit, healthy, active adult years, and finally depending upon a walking stick, or staff, for support in old age.

A lion of the type Samson killed with his bare hands, and in which the bees made honey.

The late Professor J.R.R. Tolkien, a world authority on ancient languages and half-forgotten cultures, introduced the riddling game into *"The Hobbit."* His hobbit hero, Bilbo, and the lethally possessive, carnivorous Gollum are playing for Bilbo's safe conduct to freedom against his imminent appearance on Gollum's supper menu. What is especially noteworthy in Tolkien's narrative is that even a dyed-in-the-wool villain like Gollum (who is practically devoid of any redeeming features) should feel duty bound to honour the outcome of the riddle-game.

As far as the Philistine wedding guests were concerned, the riddling game was sacrosanct, but the end justified the means when it came to unscrupulous methods of obtaining the answer.

Samson's new bride-to-be is given a gangland-style offer she doesn't feel able to refuse: if she does not provide them with the answer, they will burn her and her father along with their house. At this point, with the unfair advantage of hindsight which is the historian's privilege, it is tempting to ask why the girl did not have the sense to confide in Samson regarding their threats. Here was a man who could kill a lion with his bare hands. Thirty normal men would not have been able to match him. Compared to the deeds that are recorded of him later, despatching only thirty opponents would have been less exacting for Samson than a pleasant afternoon's stroll over the hills. The girl's wrong reaction and incorrect decision provide one of the great "ifs" of history, an "if" that could perhaps have changed the destiny of the Jewish and Philistine nations. What *if* that terrified little bride had trusted Samson with her life as committedly as Rahab the Jericho harlot had trusted the two Hebrew spies? What *if* Samson had then faced down the Philistine guests, and threatened them in turn with gruesome reprisals such as they had never dreamed possible in their worst nightmares should any harm came within 161 kilometres of his new bride and her family? Samson was no idle utterer of hollow threats. There was no empty bluster about him. The Philistine guests would have been left in no doubt that if they started trouble, Samson would undoubtedly finish it — *and them.*

But the girl made an understandable human mistake because of the pressure she was under. In terror for her own life and her father's, she worked desperately on Samson to get the answer from him to try to placate the aggressive demands of the surly Philistine wedding guests.

Now, it is Samson who makes a major error of judgement. Did his enormous, raw, animal strength and ferocity camouflage an unsuspected lack of tenacity and a fatal weakness of *will*, a weakness which his later, horrendous experience as a blind prisoner finally overcame?

When a blackmail attempt was made on the iron-willed duke of Wellington, he simply snarled back: "Publish and be damned!" Couldn't Samson have said something equivalent to that when the girl continued trying to wear him down with her desperate tears, pleadings, cajolings, and emotional blackmail?

Tragically, Samson gave in and told her the answer; she in turn caved in, betrayed her new husband, and told the bullying Philistine wedding guests, who must have looked insufferably smug and self-satisfied as they repeated it to Samson.

Was Samson's volatile response to their treachery a further indicator of his possible XYY make up, or of some other abnormally high androgen-based, aggressive genetic characteristics? He makes a bitterly sardonic reply to the jubilant Philistines: "If you had not ploughed with my heifer, you would not have guessed my riddle."

But in that raw culture, the old riddling law still imposed its implacable demands upon Samson, and even though they had won by foul play — by his standards — the Philistines must still be given their winnings. Samson's method of obtaining the thirty garments with which to pay his gambling debt was direct and ruthless.

In Chapter 14:19, his dramatic change of mood is piously attributed to "the Spirit of the Lord" taking him over. Again, it is helpful to have recourse to the concept of editorial interpretation based on the norms and mores of the period. The simple historical narrative simply means that Samson became furiously angry — anger which was totally justified and understandable in the circumstances — and consequently raced down to the Philistine city of Ashkelon bent on mayhem and murder.

Archaeological research has indicated that Ashkelon was certainly inhabited in 2000 B.C. — and probably earlier than that. Egyptian records from 1900 B.C. make reference to it. There were five great cities like Ashkelon which made up the Philistine Pentapolis during the period of the Judges, and the united Jewish monarchy. The famous ancient Egyptian *Amarna Letters* dating from 1400 B.C. also make reference to it.

Samson descended on Ashkelon like a hurricane. He killed the first thirty male Philistines he encountered, stripped their clothes from the corpses, took anything else they had of value, and stormed back to the wedding party to pay off his riddle debts.

In the meantime, assuming that after her betrayal of his secret riddle the treacherous bride would now be rejected by her lethally angry husband, her father had passed her over to the man who had acted as Samson's best man at the wedding.

In due course, Samson's anger subsided. Wishing now to be reconciled to his bride and to forgive her treachery, he took a young goat as a peace offering to her father and headed for the bridal bedroom. Her deeply embarrassed father explained apologetically that she had now been disposed of elsewhere. There was a younger sister, however, who was much more attractive, wouldn't Samson like her instead?

If Samson had been angry before, his fury now went off the scale entirely. He decided to destroy the Philistine crops. As Francis Drake would send fire ships in amongst the Spanish Armada's galleons three thousand years later, Samson sent terrified foxes in amongst the Philistine corn harvest with firebrands tied between their tails. From Samson's point of view, the results were very satisfactory. From the Philistines' point of view they were a major agricultural disaster. Word spread faster than the devastating, crop-destroying flames that this was all the fault of the man from Timnath and his daughter. Far too afraid of Samson to try to wreak their vengeance on him, the Philistine farmers vented their spleen on Samson's erstwhile wife and father-in-law Both were burnt to death.

The old law of an eye for an eye and a tooth for a tooth, is often misconstrued as commending vengeance. It doesn't. In its day it was a singularly civilized law, designed to *prevent* just that kind of morbid escalation which now embroiled both the Philistines and the Hebrews. Written and understood in full it really means: "Take *no more* than an eye for an eye. Take *no more* than a tooth for a tooth." Samson killed thirty men because the Philistines had cheated him. When his bride was given away to another man, he destroyed most of the Philistines' corn harvest. The Philistines' reprisal was to burn the bride and her father. Then Samson *really* went to work on them: there was a truly memorable slaughter. The Bible does not give numbers, but he probably killed several hundred Philistines during these punitive raids on them.

What is the truth about the episode at Ramath-lehi?

The Israelites at this time were subject to the Philistines, more or less as they had once been subject to the Egyptians. Because of Samson's raids on the Philistines and the number of Philistine corpses that had resulted, they demanded that the Jewish elders hand Samson over to them. In order to save his people, Samson agreed to be handed over. Once in Philistine hands, however, he seized an ass's jawbone and set upon his captors with characteristic, berserk fury. Numbers are uncertain, but upwards of one thousand Philistine warriors probably died at Samson's hand that day.

What was this fearsome ass's jawbone that he used as a weapon? Was it simply and literally the jawbone of a dead ass? Bone is a surprisingly tough material, and the jawbone of an equine species would be about the size of a hand-axe, or tomahawk — a good, effective, close-combat weapon. The teeth, if several were still in place, would be coated with dental enamel which is extremely hard. They would give the improvised weapon a formidable cutting edge, which might help to penetrate armour or helmet in the hands of a really furious and determined axe-man. But was the weapon really *something else* which merely resembled the size and shape of an ass's jawbone? Chapter 15:5, says simply that he *found* it. In those days, bullocks, horses, and donkeys were used everywhere, and the sight of their skeletons would not be thought unusual.

To the effective and experienced martial artist with plenty of imagination and initiative, anything and everything can be improvised as a potential weapon. There are Bible scholars who suggest that *"The Jawbone of an Ass"* was a colloquial military term used by the Philistines and Canaanites of that era to indicate a relatively short, hand-held, close-combat weapon — something between an axe and a mace. The broad, weighted end was equipped with short, sharp iron spikes which protruded rather like teeth. The tapered end was fashioned to fit the user's hand comfortably. It might also have been designed to deliver a swift, stabbing, backhand blow as well as a sweeping, skull-smashing frontal one. A downward swing to dispose of an opponent in front of the user could then easily be augmented and carried through to stab an attacker approaching from behind.

When all his Philistine enemies had been slaughtered, or had the good sense to run for their lives from the berserk murder-machine that Samson had become at Ramath-lehi that day, he flung his "ass's jawbone" away. His next problem was desperate thirst. He had put so much energy into that amazing one-man battle against the Philistines, which must have lasted several hours, that he was now on the verge of severe clinical dehydration.

Water was provided — apparently miraculously — in the very curious phrasing of the old Authorized King James Version: "But God clave an hollow place that was in the *jaw*, and there came water thereout." What *jaw* is the Bible referring to at this point? Is it the jawbone of the ass, the super-weapon, which Samson has so recently flung away? Is it from the retrieved jawbone that he obtains water? Does "and he cast away the jawbone out of his hand" at the end of the long fight, mean that he flung it some distance away, or that he simply dropped it on the ground nearby, in the place where he now stood exhausted? If that's what the phrase "cast away" really implies, then he could very easily have retrieved it again.

Suppose that it was no ordinary ass's jawbone in the literal sense of being part of a normal equine skull, lying in the vicinity by chance, but was an artefact of some description *brought to him just when he needed it most.* Was it a timely gift from the genetic engineering technologists who were looking after him, and monitoring his progress? Was it also capable of producing water when water was desperately needed? Having drunk the miraculous fluid from the "hollow place that was in the jaw" Samson revives at remarkable speed. Could ordinary water have done that to him? Was it something stimulating and nutritious, specially vitaminized and mineralized for just such an occasion?

The Secret of Samson's Strength

The next twenty years of Samson's life remain something of an enigma. We have no knowledge of what he did during that period except that he "judged Israel in the days of the Philistines twenty years."

It has been suggested by some students of classical antiquity, myth, and legend, that the adventures of Hercules (Greek Herakles) and the adventures of Samson are so similar that they may actually refer to the same hero. The Philistines and Phoenicians were maritime peoples, as were the Greeks. The stories of the amazing Danite warrior who had slaughtered hundreds of his enemies in single combat would certainly have reached Athens via these Sea People.

The ancient Egyptians record two major wars against the Sea People. The first of these took place in the fifth year of the reign of Pharaoh Merneptah, circa 1236 until 1223 B.C. The second occurred during the rule of Rameses III, circa 1198 until 1166 B.C. The Egyptian records include references to the Philistines under the name of the Peleset, who probably originated in Crete. They seem to have been the only tribe of what the Egyptians called Sea People who actually settled permanently in Palestine.

The Phoenicians, on the other hand, arrived in the area circa 3000 B.C. and established their main cities of Tyre and Sidon. They were merchants, traders, and colonizers on a massive scale. Their great city of Carthage became an important sea-going and mercantile centre until its exhausting wars against Rome brought about its final destruction. The Phoenicians were an artistic and cultured people, and highly literate. Although they also used cuneiform, they had their own distinctive alphabet as well. They excelled in the making of glass, and their goldsmiths and metal smiths were second to none in the ancient world. As carvers of both wood and ivory, they had few rivals.

Was it the Philistines, the Phoenicians, or both, who carried the stories of Samson's prowess to the Graeco-Roman world, where he became confused with Hercules?

Both men were enormously strong and fierce in battle — yet both were easily deceived and defeated by women. Samson slew the lion which gave him the inspiration for the fateful riddle, and Hercules killed the dreaded Nemean lion. Herodotus tells a very odd story of Hercules being held captive in Egypt and led about — almost as Samson was when he was finally tricked by Delilah and captured by the Philistines. The Egyptians were planning to offer Hercules as a sacrifice to Jupiter, but once he reaches their altar and the ceremonies began, he exerted his prodigious strength and killed them all. This seems remarkably similar to Samson's destruction of the Philistine temple.

An even stranger parallel can be found in a passage from the works of Lycophron of Chalcis, a Greek poet and scholar who flourished in the third century B.C. He worked in the great library at Alexandria round about 280 B.C. and is generally believed to have written a very obscure, academic work known as the *Alexandra*. This purports to be a commentary on the strange prophecies of Cassandra, but there are a great many other cryptic messages hidden within it. One of the strangest of these is Lycophron's comment on Hercules being swallowed by a sea-monster and emerging again after three days *having lost all his hair*. At first glance this seems to be a curious amalgamation of the stories of Samson and Jonah.

Publius Ovidius Naso, better known simply as Ovid, was an outstandingly good Latin poet. He was born in 43 B.C. and lived until A.D. 17, eventually dying in exile (the milder form, known as relegation, which did not involve confiscation of property or loss of citizenship) in Tomis in Romania, where he had been sent having offended Augustus Caesar. Ovid's most famous works are *Metamorphoses* and *Fasti*. In this latter compilation, section 54 refers to a Roman circus custom of tying a lighted torch between the tails of two foxes in memory of the damage done to the harvest by a fox which had burning hay and straw tied to it. Bochart, a scholarly commentator on Ovid's work suggests that this circus practice came about as the result of information which the Romans had heard from the Phoenicians: part of the story of Samson.

Theologically, the redactor who worked the old stories of the judges into the book as we have it today, had two basic messages he wished to convey. He seems to have wanted to say that when the Israelites obeyed the will of Yahweh and followed his holy laws all went well with the nation, and their enemies were defeated or held in check. When the Israelites neglected Yahweh and his commandments, their enemies were successful and oppressed them. This editor's slant on the story of Samson lay strongly in this direction: according to his version of the narrative, as long as Samson keeps his Nazirite vows, he is successful against his — and Yahweh's — enemies, the Dagon-worshipping Philistines. When Samson errs — almost invariably because of a non-Hebrew woman — he becomes weak and ineffective.

The *symbol* of this religious vow-keeping — of which the editor of Judges naturally approves — is Samson's long, Nazirite hair. Delilah prises the vital secret of his super-human strength from him, arranges for his hair to be cut while he sleeps, and then betrays him to his enemies: he is lost.

There are a few, high-ranking martial arts Grand Masters — especially in the Far East — of whom it is said that they can kill with the mere touch of a finger. There is *allegedly* a strange psychic force, a mysterious spiritual energy, under their control, which enables them to focus their mental powers in a way which is somehow supraphysical — but which nevertheless produces an energy that has a devastating effect in the physical world. Was Samson's superhuman strength of that type? Did he need to concentrate his mental and spiritual powers — knowingly or unknowingly, consciously or unconsciously — in order to make it available? Was it anger that triggered his particular type of muscular magic? Was it his belief that Yahweh was supplying his power? If there was this important psychological element within him that enabled the power to flow — or which in the wrong circumstances inhibited it — does that go some way towards explaining why he was unable to use it once his Nazirite hair had been cut? If the power flowed at least to some extent from his belief in it, if it was at least partly triggered by his faith in his Nazirite vows as a means of connecting him with Yahweh, then the loss of his hair could possibly have convinced him that his strength had gone.

After he had been blinded and humiliated by the Philistines, and sentenced to hard labour in their prison, his hair began to grow again. During those long, heavily-chained months of grinding labour and Philistine mockery, Samson's other great ally — his uncontrollable, Berserker's temper — was also slowly building up an awesome head of psychological steam inside his mind. If he really *was* an XYY man, and *if* a very small percentage of such men *occasionally* have strengths, qualities, and a relentless, implacable, driving force and energy which most normal XY men lack, what was that onerous and protracted Philistine prison experience doing to Samson's mind, spirit and will? Was it the antidote to his former lack of will power and tenacity that had allowed a succession of Philistine women to get the better of him?

His smouldering anger finally reached its optimum level. Tides of androgen and adrenaline were surging through his huge, prison-toughened body. His hair had grown again. He could feel it falling across his empty eye sockets.

It was the day of the great Philistine festival in honour of their god, Dagan, also rendered as Dagon. Samson reached the two great pillars which were the main support of the entire temple, prayed fervently to Yahweh that his paranormal strength might return — *and it did!*

The temple shuddered, rocked, and crashed to the ground. Thousands of Philistines died in the rubble. Avenged and contented, Samson died triumphantly with his enemies.

167

Who, or what, was this strange old pagan deity known as Dagan, or Dagon, whose temple Samson destroyed? Many experts would describe him as the god of crop fertility worshipped by the ancient Semitic tribes of the west. The word *dagan* in Ugaritic and Hebrew simply meant "grain," "cereals" or "corn." Dagon, second only to the supreme god, El, was allegedly the inventor of the plough, and the father of Baal, another Palestinian god of agriculture and fertility. But if Dagon is regarded as an agricultural god of grain by several authorities, he is believed by others to be a *fish-god.*

The Pergamum Museum in Berlin contains an interesting carved stone washing bowl, or laver, from ancient Assyria. The priests who are cut into its sides appear to be either part-fish, part-human, or to be wearing elaborate fish-skin costumes over their other robes. The head of the fish is apparently fitted over the head of the priest, who is carved in an attitude of sprinkling water over the worshippers. In Strong's Hebrew Dictionary, Dagon is defined as a Philistine deity and a fish-god.

The pagan mother goddess Cybele, also identified with Agdistis, Rhea, Gaia, and Ops, was the wife of Chronos and mother of Zeus.

Co-author Lionel's recent prize-winning poem entitled "Gaia" sums up her characteristics in an updated Christian context:

I am Gaia.
It was Lovelock who found me again:
My brother, the soldier, showed him where I was hiding.

Sagacious James Lovelock,
Whose thoughtful eyes turned from the distant red world
And saw me here in green beside him.

Above him, around him, below him:
Enfolding and supporting him.

Inseparably discrete, my myriad unity
Coils in the oceans' depths,
Leaps with the chamois to her highest crag
And photosynthesises in the leaf.

I am the hunter and his prey, priestess and sacrifice,
Virus and cell,
The root insatiable that drinks her own life's blood:
Evolving spiral and revolving wheel.

Mine is the strength that lifts each feathered wing;
Mine are the hooves and pads that beat earth's drum.
Mine are the streamlined scales that wend the waves
To comb the krill and plankton of my hair:

So each to other gives and all is one
Because the one is all.

And if the part can think, and ask,
And reason out some answer for itself,
Find love's completion in some other part,
Can I not do the same?
Is to be all less than to be part?

Electron, atom, molecule and cell;
Tissue and organ, sinew, muscle, mind;
Tiger and eagle, cedar, pine and oak:
Each one is part of me, yet each remains its own true self.

And colder than denial by closest kin
Is the denial of your own right hand.

Yet I am not alone, although unrecognised by my own flesh,
For He is a greater far Who made both sum and parts.

I am but Gaia: He is God.

Byron, in *Childe Harold*, uses Cybele as a poetic image when describing the city of Venice: *"A ruler of the waters and their powers."*

She was held in great awe and highly regarded by the Romans. When Hannibal invaded Italy in 204 B.C., they believed that he would be defeated if Cybele was brought to Rome along with a small meteorite which had become her sacred symbol. Her later identification with Ceres, the goddess of agriculture, links her again with the Philistine Dagon, who seems also to be a dual purpose deity — like the forerunner of the modern civil service combination of agriculture and fisheries for administrative purposes!

Dagon is sometimes depicted with a hat that looks remarkably like the head of a huge fish with its mouth open, and it has even been suggested that a Christian bishop's mitre has unwittingly been based on that same, ancient, giant fish-head design!

Whether agricultural, maritime, or a bit of both, Dagon and his temple were brought crashing to the ground in ruin by Samson's last great, triumphant act of revenge. If Dagon was more closely associated with the grain harvest than with the harvest of the sea, Samson's attack on the ripe Philistine corn fields with his fire-foxes years before, would have been particularly offensive to the priests and worshippers of Dagon. It was their god of the grain whom Samson was insulting by destroying the crop. Perhaps it seemed especially fitting to them to have the blinded Samson mocked and humiliated during their Dagon festival.

After the passage of some three millennia, the story of Samson had a profound effect on the outstanding seventeenth century English poet, John Milton, who was also blind. Through Milton's own suffering, his empathy with, and appreciation of Samson enabled him to create one of the most powerful poems of all time, *Samson Agonistes*. Largely because of his own grim life experiences, Milton saw "patience and heroic martyrdom" as the greatest of life's successes. As the poet gets inside Samson's mind *"eyeless in Gaza at the mill with slaves"* he moves the great Danite hero's thoughts from self-pitying misery and disgrace to humility and fresh spiritual strength as he finally renews his personal relationship with Yahweh. Milton himself seems to have undergone a similar mental pilgrimage in which he passed from political and social crusading to a personal faith.

Samson might just *possibly* have been the hapless victim of extraterrestrial genetic engineers, but, whoever he *really* was, the mayhem and murder, destruction and carnage of both Philistines and Israelites which surrounded him were as far from the will and purpose of a loving, universal God as the east is from the west. It was only the unfortunate theological interpretation superimposed upon the Samson story by the well-meaning — but totally mistaken — redactor of the Book of Judges that misjudged the God of Universal Love and Mercy so tragically.

As with the mystery of Samson, the doors of all the biblical enigmas and mysteries can be opened with four great keys: interpretation, imagination, investigation, and toleration.

Chapter Seventeen

The Secret of Samuel

Just as there were unusual circumstances surrounding the birth and upbringing of Moses and Samson, so a similar birth mystery is attached to Samuel — the last of the judges — who anointed Saul to be the first king of Israel, and founder of the united Hebrew monarchy.

Samuel's apparent earthly father was a man named Elkanah, an Ephrathite from Ramathaim-zophim on or near Mount Ephraim. He had two wives: Hannah, who was childless, and Peninnah, who had given birth to several of Elkanah's children. The social climate being what it was in the Israelite culture of that period, Peninnah was jubilant about her fertility while Hannah was deeply distressed because she didn't seem able to have children.

Peninnah laughed triumphantly at Hannah, mocked and humiliated her — which added considerably to her unhappiness.

At this time, Shiloh was the central sanctuary of the Israelite confederacy. Their holy Tabernacle and the Ark of the Covenant were both kept there. The Shiloh sanctuary priest during this period was a man named Eli. It was the custom for Elkanah to take his family to Shiloh every year to join in the worship and sacrifice to Yahweh. This was an occasion when special gifts of food would be distributed to wives and families. Elkanah treated Peninnah and her sons and daughters fairly and generously, but he was *especially* generous to Hannah, and did his best to comfort her over the problem of her childlessness.

When the Samuel narrative opens on the latest of these annual religious visits, Hannah is praying fervently but soundlessly, and making a vow that if Yahweh will grant her desperate prayer for a son, she will dedicate him to God's service for life as a Nazirite. Eli mistook her silent but urgently moving lips for drunkenness, and reprimanded her for having had too much wine in the holy place. Hannah explained the situation, and Eli in turn prayed that her petition would be granted. Sure enough, Hannah conceived, and gave birth to a son whom she named Samuel, meaning "he who was asked of God." She did not go up to Shiloh again until the boy was old enough to be left as a priestly apprentice with Eli. As soon as Samuel was old enough to fend for himself in Eli's care, Hannah and Elkanah took him to Shiloh with a generous gift of cattle, flour, and wine for Eli and the sanctuary. She explained that this was the son for whom she had prayed so fervently when she and Eli had last met, and that in due fulfilment of her vow, she had now brought the boy to Shiloh to be a life-long servant of Yahweh.

As the years passed, Hannah had three more sons and two daughters, and every year she and Elkanah visited Samuel at Shiloh and brought him a new coat as he grew up.

Meanwhile, Eli was having serious problems with his own adult sons, Hophni and Phinehas. They were abusing their privileged position as sons of the sanctuary priest. They and their servants intimidated the worshippers who came to Shiloh and demanded from them the choicest cuts of the meat which they had brought as sacrifices to Yahweh. As if this sacrilegious theft and exploitation of the worshippers' offerings was not bad enough, they also demanded sex from the women who had come to the door of the Tabernacle to pray and worship. This was probably because the worship of the neighbouring Canaanite fertility gods, Baal and his consort Ashtoreth, involved the kind of sexual activities normally associated with primitive fertility cults of that type.

Hophni and Phinehas, sons of Eli, were probably influenced by the eroticism of pagan fertility cults.

One night, while Samuel was asleep not far from the Ark of the Covenant, he was convinced that he heard a voice calling his name. Eli was elderly and only partially sighted by this time and heavily dependent upon Samuel. Helpfully, the boy went through to see what the old priest needed.

"I didn't call you," said Eli, sounding perhaps just a little puzzled. "Go and lie down again."A few minutes later the mysterious voice called Samuel's name again. This time he was convinced that Eli was calling him, and once more went over to see what help he could give the old priest.

Eli had some difficulty in persuading Samuel that he had not called him. He may have wondered whether the boy was experiencing a vivid recurring dream. That idea would have made him thoughtful. Dreams were believed to be meaningful portents, warnings, guidance as to important future decisions — or messages from God.

Samuel heard the call yet again, and went as before to see what Eli needed. By now both of them were growing seriously bewildered. Was Samuel wondering whether Eli's age was beginning to affect his mental abilities? Had the old priest called him and then forgotten what he had intended to ask for? Was Eli wondering whether an excitable boy was imagining things, or was Samuel developing a mischievous sense of humour, perhaps?

As various possibilities went through the old priest's mind, it finally occurred to him that God might be calling the boy. *If so, what for?* Eli's life was clouded by the bad behaviour of his sons: their greed, their arrogance, and their immorality. Very probably he felt guilty and dissatisfied with himself for failing to control them as a father was expected to do in that culture. There was no question about his ability to exercise such control had he really wished to. Hophni and Phinehas were extremely unpopular with the people, and their father's priestly authority was massive. He had only to issue the necessary orders to any group of visiting worshippers and his disobedient sons would be swiftly overpowered to await his judgement and sentence. Eli undoubtedly still had the *power* to assert his authority over his two recalcitrant sons; what he lacked was the *motivation* and *will.* He had pleaded and remonstrated with them, but they had scornfully ignored him. Was Eli now wondering whether God's message to Samuel was in some way connected with the disobedience of Hophni and Phinehas?

With the likelihood of the Voice Samuel had heard being a direct call from Yahweh now uppermost in the old priest's mind, he tells the boy that if the call is repeated he is to answer: "Speak, Lord, for thy servant heareth."

The biblical narrative in the 1 Samuel 3:10, records that not only did Samuel hear the Voice on this occasion, but "the Lord came and *stood.*"

The Old Testament contains a number of episodes, such as Moses's experience beside the burning bush, when Yahweh himself, or one of his angelic messengers, actually *appears*. In Chapter 3:31, there is a record of at least one further divine appearance to Samuel.

As Eli had feared, the message did concern divine retribution for the evil behaviour of Hophni and Phinehas and for his own abject failure to check it. The house of Eli is to suffer in perpetuity. No offering or sacrifice will ever neutralize the evil that has been perpetrated.

Overawed by what he has heard, young Samuel lies quietly thinking things over until sunrise.

Part of his regular duties as Eli's servant is to open the doors of the Shiloh sanctuary each morning. He gets up and does this as usual — very much afraid to tell Eli the contents of the divine message. It is only when — suspecting the worst — Eli insists on hearing the *whole* message that Samuel gives him the bad news. In that culture at that time, if there was a belief in an afterlife at all it was, at best, Sheol, a place of shadowy half-life. Posterity was, therefore, infinitely more important. To die leaving a large, thriving, flourishing family and a goodly number of happy and prosperous descendants was to die fulfilled and contented. To be told that your family was eternally blighted was a worse sentence than death.

Yet, to his credit, bitterly unhappy and disappointed as he was at the news, Eli remained stoical and philosophical.

"It is the Lord," he said, "let him do what seemeth him good."

To the priestly editors, redactors, and compilers of the two books of Samuel, this piously resigned submission to fate, circumstances, or what was perceived to be the "will of God" seemed — incredibly — to be virtuous. To the courageous and independent modern mind, it's the exact opposite.

Start with the *sine qua non* that God must be infinite Goodness, Love, and Mercy. His perfect will for all his children is that they should grow up to be free, blissfully happy, and to inherit eternal and abundant life with him. Resignation to, and acceptance of, anything *less* than that ideal is indicative of weakness and ineptitude rather than holiness and piety.

The mind of the redactor and the mind of God appear to be poles apart once more.

It cannot be over emphasized that in any serious and objective theological consideration of biblical mysteries, what the Bible *says* God did is in fact only what the writer or editor of that particular passage *thought* God said or did. That biblical writer's *opinion* is worth neither more nor less than yours, ours, or anybody else's.

When, for example, there was a defeat or a victory, a triumph or a disaster, a tragic death or a miraculous recovery, the biblical writers, editors, and redactors merely interpreted those events in the light of their own particular religious and moral paradigms. If they began, as most of them did, with the assumption that *every* event was ordained by God for some special purpose, then they were often hard put to it to explain why evil often flourished, while goodness and innocence suffered.

What other possible rational explanations might there be for the Voice which Samuel heard as he lay near the Ark of the Covenant in the sanctuary at Shiloh that night?

The boy had a distinctive and arguably traumatic and deprived childhood. His desperately fraught and anxious mother, Hannah, had committed him to a life of religious servitude irrespective of whether he wanted such a rigorous vocation or not. He had been raised by a pious and kindly, but rather ineffectual, old man, and so, presumably, had enjoyed none of the normal fun and games of a family childhood playing with brothers, sisters, cousins, and friends.

Work, albeit largely of a religious, ritualistic, and ceremonial nature, had been his constant companion since Hannah had delivered him to the sanctuary at Shiloh. Had those unenviable childhood experiences damaged him in any way? Was the Voice a purely self-generated psychological phenomenon, a seemingly externalized product of a sensitive and intelligent young mind under intolerable pressure?

Was the Ark of the Covenant involved in some way? If it was an advanced technological artefact rather than a holy and supernatural object, was it a sophisticated communication device? Having established aural contact with Samuel, was it then able to produce a hologram, a mysterious-looking, illuminated figure, which young Samuel assumed was God? If we have recourse yet again to the notion of intervention by technocratic alien intelligences, who were concerned with improving human specimens genetically, the draconian condemnation of Hophni and Phinehas makes sense.

It is also possible to consider the likelihood of the previously infertile Hannah being brought into their genetic engineering experiment. It was all too evident that Hophni and Phinehas were dismal failures if the genetic modifications had been intended to improve ethical and moral behaviour. Why not bring in new blood?

There is, of course, the simple and straightforward possibility that the scriptural record in the two books of Samuel is literally and historically true, but this runs head-on into the problem of the character and nature of God.

To exact unending and merciless vengeance on Eli's descendants for moral failures for which *nothing can ever atone* simply cannot be reconciled with a God of love, or even with a God of fairness and justice. Unless, of course, a modification is considered: the *call* to Samuel may well have been a genuine divine call to his vocation as priest, prophet, and judge of Israel. What may *not* have come from God at all, but from the depths of Samuel's tormented young mind was a burning resentment of Hophni and Phinehas. If they were as unpleasant to him as they were to the visitors who came to worship at Shiloh, he would have had good grounds for loathing them. Could the *call* have been from God, and the *curse* from Samuel's subconscious?

There are other mysteries connected with Samuel. According to the biblical account of his life after the failure of Hophni and Phinehas and the loss of the Ark of the Covenant to the Philistines, Samuel became the judge, priest, and prophet of Israel. He was the inspiration behind a great Israelite victory over the Philistines at Ebenezer, who were then quiescent throughout the long remaining years of Samuel's rule as a judge over Israel in the traditional, semi-formal way.

When the elders asked Samuel to anoint a king for them, like those in the small neighbouring kingdoms, the old prophet's answer was at first one of indignation and refusal.

Yahweh, however, revealed Saul, son of Kish, to Samuel as the man whom he was to anoint as king of Israel. Samuel duly complied with Yahweh's instructions, and Saul became the first monarch of the united Jewish kingdom. He decisively defeated the Ammonites and the Amalekites, but infuriated Samuel first by performing a sacrifice himself instead of waiting for Samuel to arrive, and secondly by taking plunder and prisoners — especially King Agag — from the defeated Amalekites when Samuel had specifically ordered him to destroy everybody and everything pertaining to Amalek.

Samuel then faded into comparative obscurity in the sanctuary at Naioth. After his death, his ghost was summoned by the Witch of Endor to talk to Saul and the message the king received was a cheerless one.

The problem with the biblical accounts of Samuel's life and activities is their apparent radical contradiction. In one version, he seems to be a national figure, appointing, and dismissing kings. He is not only a religious leader as both a prophet and priest, but a war leader — or war inspirer — and law officer.

Close examination by textual scholars and historians suggests that an attempt has been made to combine two or three different early versions of the Samuel story. It is possible to distinguish what such experts refer to as a pro-monarchic source and an anti-monarchic source. The pro-monarchic passages are found in 1 Samuel 9:1–10, and in Chapter 16. The anti-monarchic source is visible in 1 Samuel 8 and 10:17–27. In the pro-monarchic account, Samuel seems to be only a small-scale village seer. The coming of the monarchy is entirely in accord with Yahweh's will, and Samuel is only there to explain the action — like a Greek chorus in one of Euripides' plays. The anointing, in this version, is not followed by any record of an official accession. It goes straight on to Saul's destruction of the Ammonites. In yet another apparently interwoven text, Saul rises to power and prominence by the simple expedient of being as bloody, bold, and resolute as Shakespeare's Macbeth. Was the Samuel narrative just a colourful intrusion into the historical account of the rise and fall of Saul?

The anti-monarchic version gives most of the power and pre-eminence to Samuel, with Saul as a bashful young man more or less selected like a lottery winner! One of the major problems here is that if Samuel's victory over the Philistines was as decisive as it was made out to be, why did Saul and his successor, David, have such protracted trouble with them?

How can these strange contradictions be reconciled?

What if Samuel was emerging at this time as a leader of one of the first bands of "sons of the prophets" — the young and excitable religious fanatics who roamed the country giving displays of religious ecstasy? Such a position would have given him the sort of power base that would have made his support valuable to Saul. The conflict between the pro-monarchical and anti-monarchical strains in the books of Samuel can then be seen as a reflection of the ambivalence that the ultra-conservative, fundamentalist "sons of the prophets" felt towards the rising monarchy. It contradicted their traditional preference for the old system of charismatic judges, raised up, as they believed, as and when God wanted them, and the more effective administrative and military advantages of strong kingship in a dangerous Philistine-dominated age.

A split between Saul and Samuel then becomes historically probable, and may go some way towards explaining the apparent anomalies in the narrative.

Chapter Eighteen

The Secret
of David's Sling

The martial arts mystery of David's victory over Goliath hinges on weapon-skill, tactics, and strategy, without in any way detracting from David's religious faith. To assume, as the biblical editors do, that God deliberately intervened to bring about Goliath's spectacular downfall, is to interpret God's will as narrowly nationalistic rather than impartially universal. God was undoubtedly Goliath's Creator and Sustainer as well as young David's. There was as wide a place in the love and mercy of God for the arrogant and boastful Philistine champion as there was for the dauntless Hebrew shepherd boy.

It can be argued that Goliath's aggressive arrogance brought him down as surely as the stone did. He was also, evidently, fatally inexperienced against a slingsman. Had he lived at a different time and place, and seen the Roman gladiatorial contests between a slingsman and a heavily armoured swordsman, he would have known which side to bet on. It was all a question of range and effectiveness. At anything up to forty metres a powerfully delivered sling stone would be almost as effective as an eighteenth century black-powder, musket or pistol ball. A stone weighing between 50 and 100 grams impacting at up to 300 kilometres an hour would deliver a lethal impact unless stopped by thick leather or metal armour.

Robin Hood's Sherwood archers with their great yew bows and heavy cloth-yard shafts enjoyed similar tactical advantages over the slow-moving Norman men-at-arms in their chainmail. The famous Mongolian bowmen were just as lethal. Such an iron-tipped arrow as Hood's men or the Khan's men used could penetrate several inches of oak when a strong arm drew the bow.

David's youthfulness and small size were also deceptive. Goliath looked disdainfully on what he must have regarded as a mere boy. He totally failed to realize that in his mid-teens David's reactions and stamina would be at their peak. Of course, the boy had only about a third of Goliath's vast muscular capacity: but this was a no-holds-barred fight to the death, not an Olympic weight-lifting competition. Had David been stupid enough to try to tackle Goliath at close quarters, he would have been killed by Goliath's first blow, or crushed to death in those immense arms.

David had no such intentions. Here was a dangerous and versatile young fighting machine with a brain that matched his courage, skill, and agility. He had already killed lions and bears in defence of his flock. That had required considerable fighting *intelligence* as well as all his other talents.

He selected his sling-stones with great care, and went out to weigh up the situation. The man was heavily armoured, but his size made him ponderously slow. That was a great advantage for David. The giant would be unlikely to get his shield up in time. In all probability, David circled Goliath carefully — glancing up at the position of the sun to make sure it was at his back when he took aim. The sun in Goliath's eyes would prevent him from tracking the flight of the fatal stone and intercepting it with his shield. David also looked for the best target areas — any unprotected vulnerable spots? Goliath's *forehead* was ideal. The helmet did not come down far at the front: it was meant to stop a sword stroke from the side, or an axe blow descending from above — not that many axemen would have been tall enough to bring a blade *down* on Goliath! David decided to go for the forehead. He fitted the first stone into the snug little leather pouch on the

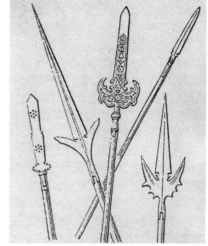

Ancient spears similar to the one Goliath would have used.

faithful sling, wound the retainer cord around his hand and gripped the release end deftly between finger and thumb. It spiralled slowly at first. David's keen young eyes never left Goliath's forehead. The distance between them was closing. Goliath raised his spear. David smiled grimly to himself. The thing was like a weaver's beam. It looked formidable, but it posed little or no threat to an agile opponent. Goliath's throwing arm and body posture would signal its release long before it left his hand, and it was far too heavy and awkward to be an accurate missile. It would also have a very limited range. They were perhaps 15 metres apart when the whistling sling reached its maximum velocity and David released the stone. It flew like the Angel of Death, impacting just below Goliath's helmet with a satisfying thud that cracked the bone, and concussed the brain beneath. The momentum sent him crashing backwards.

David was on him in seconds. As Goliath lay inert, David wrenched the giant's own sword from its sheath and severed his head with it.

As soon as the Philistines saw that their champion was dead they fled in blind panic. The jubilant Israelites pursued them relentlessly, littering the ground for miles around with dead and dying Philistines who lay where they fell. David took the dead giant's head as a trophy to King Saul.

The contest between David and Goliath had been an intellectual, psychological contest as much as a physical one. The first vital input had been David's faith, confidence, and courage. He was a realistic hero, not an imaginative or fanciful one.

He had weighed the situation up carefully before getting involved in a life-or-death adventure against the enormous Philistine champion.

Ancient Egyptian slingsmen were not as good as David.

David evaluated his speed, agility and skill as a slingsman against Goliath's size and strength. David had seen clearly that the blow his sling could deliver was potentially lethal. He had also carefully worked out that he had a definitive advantage as far as weapon *range* was concerned. Unless things went devastatingly wrong, David had *all* the significant advantages, and he used them well.

Goliath had psychological and physical *disadvantages* which accompanied him to the fatal field as morbidly as coffin bearers. He had had long years of military experience and especially single-combat experience, but a shepherd's sling was not a normal weapon of war. Goliath had never fought a slingsman before, or if he had, that opponent had not handled the lethal cords as effectively as David could. Perhaps, once or twice Goliath *had* met ineffectual slingsmen, men lacking David's *accuracy*, who had wasted their stones on Goliath's shield and armour, prior to feeling the business end of his gigantic spear.

Was this why he was so contemptuous when he saw that David intended to fight him with only a sling and a few stones? Perhaps Goliath regarded such ineffectual slings as he had seen before, as mere toys to send unwelcome dogs skipping on their way. He mistook what was a singularly lethal weapon *in David's hands* for a toy: it was a mistake that had fatal consequences for the giant.

His next great problem was his arrogance and misplaced self-confidence. His long history of successful battles had made him careless. A fighter learns more from defeat than from victory — *provided he survives the defeat!* Goliath had stood toe-to-toe with mature swordsmen and axe-men almost as big and strong as he was. He had traded many a hail of blows with such formidable warriors and inevitably beaten them. David was less than half the size of most of the men Goliath had destroyed during his long military career. The giant decided that this small, inexperienced boy carrying only a dog-scattering toy was nothing to worry about at all. Goliath felt so confident of the outcome that he promised to feed David's remains to the local carrion birds as soon as their contest had reached its inevitable conclusion.

Goliath was relying on his state-of-the-art armour and weaponry. No mere stone could penetrate it, and this foolish boy had no blade that Goliath could see. It never occurred to the doomed giant from Gath that David's speed and agility were superior to Goliath's strength and size.

So he lumbered confidently to his death at the hands of the fierce young Jewish shepherd-boy: slain by the secret of David's deadly sling.

Chapter Nineteen

Did Ezekiel See a Spaceship?

The book of the prophet Ezekiel is one of the strangest and most mysterious in the entire Bible. It begins with a very detailed account of the time and place of Ezekiel's *visions* of God. A great deal hinges on our understanding of the precise meaning of the word which is translated *vision* in the Authorized King James Version. There is one sense in which it can be construed to mean a purely subjective, mental, or spiritual experience that is not apparently generated by the external physical environment. It may, however, also refer to a phenomenon that is audible or visible — albeit to differing degrees — *by more than one human witness:* Saint Paul's experience on the Damascus Road, for example. Elijah's parting words to Elisha may also fit into this category.

The Second Book of Kings 2:9–13, records the episode. Elijah is "taken up to Heaven" in what is described as "a chariot of fire and horses of fire." Elisha's request for "a double portion of Elijah's spirit" is to be granted *subject to his being able to see Elijah's actual departure in this blazing chariot.* He did see it, and consequently the biblical chronicle of the rest of Elisha's earthly life is filled with miraculous episodes that seem to provide evidence that a significant share of Elijah's remarkable paranormal powers had indeed been handed on to Elisha.

What strange, objective reality actually separated Elisha from his mentor at that critical moment? Did the *vision* of the fiery horses drawing the blazing chariot *camouflage* something from another dimension? Was that colourful description of the aircraft, space vehicle, or interdimensional ship, which called to collect Elijah, as close as a man of that period could get to describing what he really saw in the shimmering air above him?

The third type of biblical "vision" has a substantial physical reality behind it. What the writer describes in these cases is entirely objective and is as accessible to examining, weighing, and measuring as is any other material phenomenon.

Which type of vision was the writer of Ezekiel referring to in Chapter 1:1? Possibly an external, physical reality?

Verse 4 contains some rather interesting indicators, although they cannot be regarded as definitive or conclusive: "And I looked, and, behold, a whirlwind came out of the north, a great cloud, and a fire infolding itself, and a brightness was about it, and out of the midst thereof as the colour of amber, out of the midst of the fire."

It is the significant clause "*and I looked*" that suggests that the writer of Ezekiel was describing an objective, material reality rather than a subjective, mental experience. The fact that he gave it *direction* and a *point of origin* may also be relevant. The different elements of this strange phenomenon also fit together *consistently*, which may again be more indicative of a genuine external reality than of some imaginative internal imagery. The writer goes to great lengths to describe the colours, and the different intensities of light which he can see radiating from the object.

Verses 5 to 14 describe what the writer cautiously referred to as being *the likeness* of living creatures. It's significant that he was careful not to call them living creatures *as such*. These four strange objects emerged from the dazzling brightness of the vehicle — if that's what it was — which Ezekiel had variously described as a whirlwind, a cloud, and an infolding fire in verse 4. He said that they *resembled* men. Does he mean only their general humanoid size and shape, the positioning of a head-like structure at the top, and limbs branching out from a central trunk?

Did Ezekiel encounter extraterrestrial genetic engineers?
Drawn by Theo Fanthorpe.

Did Ezekiel See a Spaceship?

These humanoid features may be a useful descriptive *foundation,* but there are some startling modifications to consider. As Ezekiel looks closer, each "head" carries four distinct "faces." We suggest that what he is trying to describe is probably a metallic cuboid with four distinct panels of sensors set into it: *Ezekiel's "creatures"* are either robots, or servo-mechanisms.

The four joined wings, perhaps serving a similar purpose to the skirt of a hovercraft, and brought into play when the craft landed, could also have been brought into play as containers or deflectors. Were they meant to keep fierce heat or radiation away from vulnerable terrestrials like Ezekiel, or to protect the ship's landing gear from anything injurious that might be lurking on a planet's surface?

Verse 7 records Ezekiel's observation of the robots' feet: "Their feet were straight feet; and the sole of their feet was like the sole of a calf's foot; and they sparkled like the colour of burnished brass."

In the reign of James I, "straight" could also have the meaning of "narrow," as well as "not curved" or "not angled." If it was meant in this passage in that seventeenth century sense of "narrow," what sort of bases did these robot landers have, and what purpose did they serve? Were tough, narrow "feet" like tripod leg-ends designed so that they could get a sharp grip on alien surfaces, just as the studs in a hiker's boots enable the walker to get a firm, sharp grip on rugged mountain tracks? There would seem to be little doubt that they "sparkled like the colour of burnished brass" *because they were made of metal.*

Ezekiel now carries out a more detailed examination of the strange, joined wings which he has noticed so distinctly on the "creatures." Under each wing is something which looks like a human hand, but there are *four* such "hands" — one under each wing. Are these hand-like appendages some kind of robotic grapples of the type used in radiation laboratories today? Are they adjustable retaining hooks for the wings, so that those wing-like shields or skirts can be adjusted remotely by whoever, or *whatever,* is controlling the vehicle — always allowing that it really *is* a vehicle?

What *are* these very mysterious "faces" and the equally mysterious "wings"?

Ezekiel now concerns himself with the peculiarities of the *movement* of this inexplicable object.

In verse 9 he records: "they turned not when they went; they went every one straight forward."

Imagine a wheel that is made up of a series of very short, cylindrical rollers, assembled so that they lie end to end around the circumference of the large wheel. The controller of a vehicle equipped with such wheels

185

could make it go in one direction by using the rotation of the large wheel in the normal way. He or she could also make it move at an angle of 90° to the direction of the rotation of the large wheel simply by bringing the rollers into play. Ezekiel's clear description of the movement he observed seems to suggest that the unique design of the wheels must have been something along these lines.

The four "faces" and the abnormal movements of the "creatures" as described in verses 10 to 12 provide valuable clues as to the true nature of the construction. Each "creature" is identical. The "faces" described as resembling the faces of a man, a lion, an ox, and an eagle are located in similar positions relative to one another on all four of the "creatures." This tends to sound like four identical lander-robots rather than four living beings. The controls are so laid out on each identical lander-robot that those which look like a human face are always in the same place relative to the other three. The human face and the leonine face are on the left; the bovine and aquiline faces are on the other side.

Verse 13 takes the investigation a stage further: the lander-robots were glowing like burning coal. They were bright, like lamps. This radiant, flaming glow illuminating the lander-robots was itself moving and fluctuating, as though the power was being varied — as it frequently has to be during sophisticated landing and docking procedures. Something inside the mechanism was also flashing brightly and very suddenly, which made Ezekiel describe it as lightning.

The likelihood that Ezekiel was looking at a machine — and very probably at a spacecraft or an inter-dimensional vessel — is significantly increased when he goes on to describe four wheels that appear close to each of the four-faced robot-landers. All four are beryl coloured and exactly identical. Ezekiel then goes on to explain that there were *wheels within wheels.*

This is a particularly interesting personal reference as far as the authors are concerned. We were investigating a spiritualist church in Norwich way back in the 1950s where a very effective and accurate female medium was addressing the congregation. She turned suddenly to co-author Lionel and said: "I have a message for you. Someone from the other side is showing me the sign of *wheels within wheels* — and the wheels are locked. But they will be freed and you'll make progress again."

It so happened that his high school teaching career was not going anywhere as far as we could see at that time, and the symbol of locked wheels seemed to symbolize it all too appositely. We told the medium that we thought this was the meaning of the symbol which she said she'd seen in the air over Lionel's head. She again reassured us that the wheels would be released and the career would eventually open up. She was right — he finished his teaching career a few years later as the Headmaster (Principal) of a tough Group 10 urban high school with over a thousand students aged from eleven to eighteen years, a school which he ran with great success for over ten years. The teaching career wheels which the medium saw in her vision certainly unlocked themselves and moved positively for him. After all those years with Lionel in that top high school post, we decided to leave teaching and launch into our writing, lecturing, radio, and TV work full time.

When we got back from that spiritualist meeting nearly half a century ago, we chatted to Lionel's mother about the medium's strange message. She expressed mild surprise and considerable interest. Her mother (Lionel's grandmother) Phoebe Garbutt, had died a few years before and — unknown to either of us until Lionel's mother told us about it that night — Phoebe's favourite aphorism had always been "wheels within wheels."

Had *she* sent us that cryptic message of encouragement via the medium that night? Certainly, she had always been deeply religious, and Ezekiel's strange prophecies would have been very familiar to her.

Verses 17 to 21 are again finely detailed and make it abundantly clear, that — whatever they really are — those enigmatic "wheels with wheels" are attached to the robot-landers and move with them.

It is this close, accurate observation of the ship's movements, and the relative functioning of its different components, which enhance the possibility that this "vision" which Ezekiel recorded was not merely something going on inside his head, but something real and external which he was looking at and describing objectively and as thoroughly as an expert ornithologist examines and describes a rare bird.

Ezekiel then moves on from a description of the wheels to a description of some mysterious "rings" — possibly the perimeters, or circumferences, of another part of this strange structure he is examining so minutely. He describes these rings as very high and "full of eyes." Could those "eyes" have been the lenses of the ship's observation units? Laser weapon caps? Navigational sensors?

Most intriguing of all is the description of a "firmament," or dome, above the heads of the quadruple-faced "creatures." Is this the pilot's cockpit? Ezekiel describes it as the colour of the "terrible crystal." What can be *terrible* about the colour of a crystal? Would the word be better translated as "awesome" or "majestic"? The "wings" — the screens or shields — linking the four robot-landers are now straight and pointing towards one another. Is the ship preparing to leave again — or to settle down and complete her landing sequence? Are her mighty engines doing something different?

Ezekiel hears what he describes as the "noise of their wings" and compares it to the roar of a huge torrent of water, or a vast crowd shouting. He hears a voice speaking over the tumult. He sees dazzling rainbow lights, and, through all this, he sees what he describes as *a human figure inside the cockpit.*

When the voice from the ship speaks to Ezekiel clearly and distinctly — in a language he can understand — it addresses him as *Son of man.*

The instructions which Ezekiel receives from the being, or beings, controlling the ship are not the instructions which would really be expected from a God of love and mercy. They are, however, very much like the instructions a trainer would give to intelligent creatures who were able to understand his words, when he was trying to improve their behaviour for their own benefit.

The message which Ezekiel is to take to the Israelites is that those who sin will die. Those whose behaviour improves will live. Those who once behaved acceptably, but who have returned to sinful behaviour again, will also die. The voice from the ship is also insistent that Ezekiel's warning role in all this is a vitally important one. Even if the being in the ship is only an extraterrestrial, genetic engineer, this technocrat who seeks to improve human morality is himself, or herself, an ethical being. There can be no mistaking the draconian *severity* behind the technocrat's morality, but there seems to be fairness and justice there as well. If people disobey the moral laws, they will die: but hey will not die until they have been duly warned and have had an opportunity to reform themselves and comply.

What type of vision did Saul of Tarsus see on the Damascus road?

Did Ezekiel See a Spaceship?

This rather unexpected "Son of man" form of address is almost like the stereotyped "Greetings, earthman" or "Hello, humanoid" from old science fiction B-movies. When Christ refers to himself as the Son of man during his earthly incarnation, is he carefully and deliberately making use of that ancient phrase from Ezekiel's writings to identify himself absolutely with our terrestrial human race? Is he, perhaps, using it to make clear to any extraterrestrial technocrats and visiting genetic engineers that *someone* infinitely higher in the cosmic hierarchy than they are, is now directly concerning himself with humanity and its tragic problems *by becoming part of it himself?*

Is it possible to suggest a celestial scenario in which mysterious technologists from afar either *created* the human race on this planet, or *interfered* with earlier, simpler anthropoids who were doing reasonably well here until the extraterrestrials turned up and modified them?

Ezekiel is continually transported from location to location. More than once he describes the rushing sound of the UFO and the noise made by its wings and wheels. Chapter 3:13, is a typical example of this.

No less remarkable than Ezekiel's encounter with the apparent UFO, which he described in such compelling detail, is his journey (*in* the UFO again, perhaps?) to a valley full of dry bones (Chapter 37). Whoever, or whatever, is directing Ezekiel at this point gives him a conducted tour all around these dry bones so that he gets a good, detailed look at them. If this is purely a mental experience, it's a very minutely described one, and the narrator refers again to his moving from place to place so that he is able to study the valley and its contents thoroughly. He comments especially on the dryness of the bones which he finds there.

This is parallel to a certain extent with Elijah's duel against the priests of Baal on Mount Carmel. The nature of the conflict is that both sides are calling upon their God to light their sacrifice by sending miraculous fire from Heaven. The prophet deliberately sets out to make the task more difficult — and thus to display Yahweh's absolute power more dramatically. Elijah soaks the wood under his sacrifice with several barrels of water. When the fire from Heaven duly arrives and burns up Elijah's sacrifice, even the water in the trench around the wood is consumed as well. For a dry sacrificial fuel heap to be ignited spontaneously might just possibly have been an accident: for a soaking wet one to catch fire by accident, the statistical probability is a lot less than 0.0001.

Just as with Elijah's saturated altar fire, so it was with Ezekiel's dry bones in the valley. The men who were presumably killed in battle there are a very long way from being fresh corpses which look as if they have

189

only fallen asleep. They are not even relatively recent, complete skeletons; they're *very dead*, and *very dry*, scattered bones.

As Ezekiel watches, however, these singularly unpromising components begin to join together to re-form unified skeletons. Shortly afterwards, these re-assembled skeletons are clothed with flesh and sinews once more. They are complete human beings again now — but still not alive.

It was a common element of Hebrew belief that life was a sort of vital breath which distinguished the dead from the living. This vital breath now enters the corpses and their resurrection is complete. Coleridge describes something very similar when the dead sailors are reactivated by the angelic band, so that their dead limbs can work the ship again and get the Ancient Mariner safely back to port. In Ezekiel's mysterious valley of dry bones, a whole host stands up together, miraculously alive once more in that sinister valley of death.

The text goes on to explain the *symbolism* of the event. These dry bones in the valley represent the whole nation of Israel, now at a very low ebb in captivity and exile by the Chebar River. The message behind the miracle is plain enough: if Yahweh has the power to restore and resurrect dry bones from a long-forgotten battlefield, he can also restore the exiled Hebrew nation to its former glories.

Many critics and Bible commentators — especially those who lived before DNA and genetic engineering were properly understood — have dismissed the valley of dry bones as nothing more than a colourful myth, a dream with a meaning, like the ones Joseph could interpret so well. But just because it can be shown to have as good and relevant a meaning as any purely fictional fable, or parable, which never sets out to be historical truth as well, the account of the multiple resurrections in the valley does not have to be *only* illustrative fiction. If the power directing Ezekiel *was* our hypothetical, extraterrestrial, genetic manipulators in their UFO, then restoring a valley full of interesting old DNA — no matter how dry — would have presented them with a very trivial problem.

The question of whom and what Ezekiel *really* encountered remains unresolved to this day, but if his accurately detailed descriptions are taken into account as fully as they deserve to be, then the UFO and genetic/DNA revival theories merit at least an honourable mention in history's despatches.

Chapter Twenty

Miraculous Survivals:
Daniel in the Lions' Den, Shadrach, Meshach, and Abednego in the Furnace

The mysterious Book of Daniel begins with similar dating detail to the Book of Ezekiel. The reader is told that Daniel's captivity began in the reign of King Jehoiakim of Judah and his defeat by King Nebuchadnezzar of Babylon. (This powerful monarch was actually Nebuchadrezzar II, son of Nabopolassar who founded their dynasty.) Ashpenaz, one of Nebuchadrezzar's senior officers, is given charge of Daniel and three other young Hebrew captives: Hananiah, Mishael, and Azariah. Daniel's name is changed to Belteshazzar. His three young companions are renamed as Shadrach, Meshach, and Abednego respectively.

The first section of Chapter 1 of the Book of Daniel deals with Hebrew dietary requirements and records how the four young Israelites turned down the exotic foods sent to them from Nebuchadrezzar's own table. They much preferred an altogether simpler, plainer diet that complied with their Hebrew religious food laws. When the king sends for them, he finds that their general health and appearance are significantly better than those of their peers who have been eating regularly from the exotic contents of the royal table.

The four young Hebrews are also far wiser and more intelligent — ten times so, according to the Book of Daniel — than their peers, and, consequently, the king selects them as his counsellors and companions.

Just as dreams featured so prominently in the story of Joseph's rise to power in Egypt, so dreams play a prominent role again in the story of Daniel.

In the second year of Nebuchadrezzar's reign he was troubled by strange dreams. Accordingly he sent for the Chaldean magicians, astrologers, and sorcerers to interpret the dream for him. There was, however, a major problem. Nebuchadrezzar recalled being troubled by the dream, but he had forgotten — or, at least, he *pretended* that he had forgotten in order to test the paranormal gifts of the would-be interpreters — the exact contents of the disturbing dream. The magicians were all confident that they could interpret it once they knew what it was, but this did not satisfy Nebuchadrezzar. Either they could tell him what he had dreamt or they were charlatans and, as such, would die.

The magicians protested vehemently that what the king was asking was far beyond the reach of any mortal mind. Only a god, they exclaimed, could solve that kind of a problem. No king or emperor since the dawn of time had ever asked his wise men to solve a problem as difficult as that. Nebuchadrezzar became furiously angry when they argued in this way. In one sense, he was offended by their implication that he was being unreasonable by demanding something that no wise man could be expected to solve. In another sense he was angry with them for attempting — as he saw it — to deceive him with some carefully pre-prepared, ambiguous answer. He sent out a decree that the magicians, sorcerers, and soothsayers should all be executed. The king's officers went out to comply with his commands.

Daniel became involved at this stage. It is interesting to note that when the royal messengers and soldiers went out to deal with the magicians they included Daniel in that category. Earlier verses indicate clearly enough that Daniel and the other three young Jews were regarded as superior in *wisdom* to the Chaldean wise men, sorcerers, and magicians; but were they also regarded as being superior in *magic*? Moses, at the Exodus, was reported to be able to defeat the Egyptian magicians in their own field of expertise. Was there some ancient strain of powerful Hebrew "magic" (unless "magic" is just superior technology, after all?) that enabled both Moses and Daniel to overcome the Egyptian and Chaldean wonder workers?

Ruins from the great days of the Assyrian-Babylonian Empires of Daniel's time.

192

Daniel speaks with Arioch, the officer who has been sent to destroy the Babylonian magicians and wise men. Arioch explains the situation to Daniel, who requests Nebuchadrezzar to grant him a little time so that he can solve the problem. Daniel consults his three young Hebrew friends, Shadrach, Meshach, and Abednego, and they pray that God will reveal the mystery of Nebuchadrezzar's hidden dream to them. Their prayers are answered and the mystery is made clear to Daniel. He then contacts Arioch and asks him to arrange an audience for him with Nebuchadrezzar. During that audience, Daniel tells the king what he dreamt and what it means.

The strange dream consisted of a huge and terrifying statue, or image. The head was gold, the chest and arms were silver, the trunk and upper legs were brass. The lower legs were iron, and the feet were iron mixed with clay. A small stone — cut from the quarry without human hands — struck the vulnerable and brittle feet of this huge image so that it crashed to the ground and shattered. When Daniel interpreted the dream for Nebuchadrezzar, he told the king that he and his powerful Babylonian kingdom were the golden head of the great image. The other metals represented different kingdoms which would come after his. Finally, the small stone, cut without hands, represented the last kingdom, a Divine Kingdom, that would endure forever. Was Daniel talking about that same "Kingdom of Heaven on Earth" which was at the core of so much that Christ himself taught during his incarnation?

Assyrian-Babylonian gods like Ishtar were more familiar to Nebuchadrezzar than Daniel's God of holiness and justice.

193

As recorded in the biblical account, Nebuchadrezzar's response to Daniel's description of the exact contents of the strange dream featuring the conglomerate metal image, together with his *interpretation* of it, was to reward him with many costly gifts and a job with optimum responsibility and authority over the whole of Babylonia. Daniel, in turn, requested the deputizing of his three companions to actually run the affairs of state, while he himself "sat in the gate of the King" — a richly descriptive aphorism suggesting that he was to have the king's ear and be the major influence as far as Nebuchadrezzar was concerned.

Whatever the historical exaggerations and deviations of the Daniel narrative may be, there are portions of it that are vibrant with totally credible psychological and sociological truth. For all the fairness and generosity displayed by Nebuchadrezzar himself, there are deep, dark undercurrents of bitter resentment and jealousy motivating many of the Babylonian officers and courtiers. There is nothing like a little success for someone else to activate such feelings: a rival's great success — like Daniel's — will bring them rapidly to the boil. Just as Joseph's elder brothers detested him, so an odious group of Babylonian anti-Semites loathed Daniel and his three very able young friends.

Chapter 3 describes Nebuchadrezzar's creation of the vast golden image which he sets up in the Plain of Dura, and which everyone is supposed to worship — *or else!* There is some cause to wonder whether advice other than Daniel's was at the back of that little scheme. Daniel may well have been at the king's gate, but someone else had crept into the royal woodshed!

The Master of Ceremonies at the golden image's dedication ceremony had rather more persuasive sanctions at his disposal than the irritable hissing whispers of today's fanatical church ritualists. These are the control freaks who want everyone else in the congregation to be silent, or to sit, stand, kneel, or genuflect in conformity with the compulsive ritualist's own quaint little ideas about what's appropriate. Fair enough on a military parade ground, perhaps, where Regimental Sergeant Major's can exercise their inflated egos, but definitely *not* the way God's family should be ordered to behave in what should be their loving Father's informally friendly and warmly welcoming House. When you feel happily at home in a place, isn't it natural to want to *talk* to the loving brothers and sisters who also enjoy being there?

Nebuchadrezzar's Master of Ceremonies was empowered to throw dissenters into a furnace — "to encourage the others!" Needless to say, the devout and fearless young Jews have no intention of worshipping any kind of idol or image, no matter how opulently it has been adorned, and no

Shadrach, Meshach, and Abednego unharmed in the furnace.
Drawn by Theo Fanthorpe.

matter what the consequences. They are Yahweh's men to the grave and beyond. The anti-Semitic Babylonian informers duly bleated their complaints against Shadrach, Meshach, and Abednego to Nebuchadrezzar. His anger knows no bounds. He orders the furnace to be made seven times hotter than usual. The toughest of the Babylonian hard-men are ordered to bind the three defiant Hebrews and hurl them into the superheated heart of the terrifying furnace. So great is the heat — even by the entrance — that the guards themselves are overcome by it. Shadrach, Meshach, and Abednego appear to be totally impervious to it. From a suitably safe distance Nebuchadrezzar is watching in blank amazement. He sees *four* men walking imperturbably through the flames as though they are strolling through green pastures. The form of the fourth man, in Nebuchadrezzar's words, was like *the Son of God.* What was it about this strange and mightily powerful being that filled Nebuchadrezzar with so much awe and respect?

It is not easy to overawe a monarch who smashed a superior Egyptian force at the Battle of Carchemish, who captured the almost impregnable city of Jerusalem in 597 B.C., and who rebuilt, fortified, and expanded the city of Babylon with a grandeur that rivalled any city of the period. This is the man who became the hero of Verdi's opera *Nabucco.* This is the man whom many reputable and thoughtful historians have compared to Napoleon. When such a man is overawed and astonished, it is worth looking very carefully and thoughtfully at the *cause* of his astonishment.

195

To give Nebuchadrezzar his due, when he is angry — he punishes savagely, often fatally; when he is favourably impressed — he rewards generously. He is quixotic and extravagant with both praise and blame, and, enjoying the power that he has, the rewards and punishments that he hands out are on the grand scale. Now that he has seen the power of the Protector of these fearless Hebrews, he responds swiftly. Never mind worshipping the huge golden image on the plain of Dura: that has already shrunk into microscopic insignificance in Nebuchadrezzar's agile mind.

The hero of *Wind in the Willows,* the amazing Toad of Toad Hall, is rather like a fictional microcosm of Nebuchadrezzar. It would be rather interesting to ask whether Kenneth Grahame, who wrote the original, or A.A. Milne, who wrote the stage version, had had Nebuchadrezzar in mind when rounding out the marvellous character of the lovably ebullient but mercurial Toad.

Far from throwing the worshippers of Yahweh into the furnace for disobeying his orders regarding the huge golden image of Dura, Nebuchadrezzar is now proclaiming that anyone daring to utter a word against their God will be turned into sushi and his house used as a sewage repository.

Taking the biblical record at face value as far as the miraculous survival of Shadrach, Meshach, and Abednego in the furnace is concerned, how could it have been achieved? The first and clearest answer is simple divine intervention, but this raises the old insurmountable problem. Why them? Why not other good people as well? Granted that they were good and courageous men, granted also that they were men of faith as well as bravery — so were hundreds of thousands, indeed *millions,* of others, who died in

Daniel survives miraculously in the lions' den. Drawn by Theo Fanthorpe.

the Nazi hell-camps, and at the hands of insane tyrants and despots for millennia before that. If good and courageous people, martyrs who were willing to die for their beliefs, were *always* saved from furnaces, arenas, prisons, torture chambers, and concentration camps by divine intervention, then the message to the rest of us would be clear and consistent — *but it's not*. The sickest and most evil sadists and mass murderers get away with their atrocities for years: women, children, the elderly, the helpless, and the innocent fall victim to them with terrible regularity.

It's all very well to argue that human freedom of thought would be eroded, and our vital autonomy corrupted, if goodness was always swiftly rewarded and evil ostentatiously and unmistakably punished in this material world. If evil thoughts, words, and actions always brought disaster in their wake, while goodness led just as surely to immediate prosperity and happiness, there would not really be any freedom left. As a piece of cool, academic, abstract, theoretical, theological philosophy, it works well enough: in a desperate world full of injustice, crippling wounds, disabling diseases, agonizing pain, sudden death and inconsolable grief — seemingly ladled out impartially on the guilty and the innocent alike — it never seems to satisfy those gaunt, white-hot question marks which sear the soul.

If Shadrach, Meshach, and Abednego *were* delivered by direct and deliberate divine intervention, why does it not happen more often?

But what if the fourth man in the furnace was not an angel, or a benign deity at all? What if he or she was the pilot of a UFO like the one that seems to have visited Ezekiel? The huge moral interrogation mark melts away in the fiery furnace of common sense. With all his technology, and with all his

Daniel's tomb, near Susa.

good intentions, the UFO pilot couldn't save *everyone*. Just suppose, yet again, that we *are* dealing with extraterrestrial technocrats, and that — like us — they are basically benign, on the side of the angels, even though not quite angels themselves. Our UFO pilot — especially if he's from the same team as the one who met Ezekiel — seems to be at home in a hot, glowing environment. Maybe his technology has long since passed the cumbersome spacesuit stage and developed personal force fields which are more convenient as well as being more effective. Perhaps the parameters of such protective fields can be expanded to include three or four other beings. That would be a sensible piece of rescue design. A colleague is down on a dangerous alien planet. His or her force field has failed, or is on the point of failing. The rescuer zooms down and simply expands the protection perimeter of her field to encompass the astronaut in trouble; then the two of them go back to the pod together. It's only an electronic extension of the helicopter winch-rescue, or the scubadiver taking surplus air to a trapped companion. The biblical record is detailed on the fact that the hair and clothing of the three heroes are not scorched. Only something like an advanced force field could achieve that.

The beauty of the benign-astronaut-rescuer-theory is that it avoids the moral dilemma of why divine intervention doesn't always rescue the innocent and the deserving. We have absolutely no doubt that the justice of a loving, caring, and all powerful God is such that those who have suffered so desperately here will be more than compensated in the world to come. One of the greatest delights of Paradise will be to see children from Africa and Kosovo who lost their limbs to shells and land-mines bounding over meadows and fields — or their glorious, heavenly equivalents — with the joy of newborn lambs. There is no moral or theological problem once we take the eternal dimension of divine recompense and compensation into our calculations — it is the damnable injustice and suffering of the innocent and helpless on this gritty old earth of ours *here and now* which is so hard to take, and so much harder to explain.

If we allow a little mileage for the benign alien force-field theory, that same mileage also takes us over the problem of Daniel unharmed in the lions' den. A hypothetical force field that will keep out a temperature capable of melting bronze would be more than a match for a pride of lions — no matter how hungry or bad-tempered they were!

Chapter Twenty-one

The Mystery
of the Maccabees

One of the greatest *ifs* of history is: what might have happened *if* Alexander the Great had not died at such a tragically young age? How far would his enlightened and liberalizing empire eventually have extended: all over Europe? Asia? Africa? Would his fearless Greek sailors have crossed the Atlantic and brought the Americas in as well? Could the octogenarian Alexander have ended as a just and kindly Emperor of the World and brought in a true Golden Age?

He died young. His dream died with him. The Alexandrian Empire fell apart. One or two dangerous little pieces of its wreckage continued to float about in the form of the Seleucids, who ruled Syria. A particularly nasty specimen named Antiochus IV was top man there from 175–164 B.C.

Styling himself Antiochus Epiphanes (the God-man), he was better known to his contemporaries as Antiochus Epimanes (the mad-man). He was the third son of Antiochus III (another vain Seleucid) who modestly encouraged his subjects to refer to him as "The Great." Despite this self-styled greatness, he was well beaten by the Romans, and had to leave his son, the future Antiochus IV, in Rome as a hostage from 189 until 175 B.C. It was during these years in Rome that Antiochus acquired a taste for Greek and Roman culture, and so came eventually to his Seleucid kingdom as an enthusiastic Hellenizer.

Having news of an intended Egyptian invasion, Antiochus forestalled it by defeating the Egyptian army near Mount Kasion, en route to Pelusium, and then by advancing to conquer all of Egypt with the exception of the great city of Alexandria itself. As the Egyptian Ptolemy VI was Antiochus's nephew, he used that as a convenient excuse to appoint himself as Ptolemy's guardian and so give a quasi-legitimacy to his occupation of Egypt.

Shortly afterwards the Romans intervened on behalf of the Egyptian royal family, and Antiochus found himself negotiating with Popillius — a singularly tough, no-nonsense Roman ambassador. Antiochus was told to get out of Egypt and Cyprus — or else. The wily Seleucid asked for time to think. Like the forerunner of some tough, Midwestern American in a Mark Twain story, Popillius used his walking stick to draw a circle in the sand around Antiochus. "You tell me 'Yes' or 'No' before you leave the circle," gritted Popillius — and meant it. Antiochus prudently took the "Yes" option and left with his life and most of his own original kingdom still intact.

Safely home again, Antiochus went busily to work on his dream of Hellenizing his realm. He sent a generous contribution to the Temple of Zeus in Athens, and to the Greek theatre. He built numerous Greek quarters in cities such as Antioch on the Orontes, and named these special suburbs Epiphania as tributes to himself. Even the great old Persian city of Ecbatana was renamed Epiphania and duly Hellenized.

These persistent Hellenizing efforts brought Antiochus into head-on confrontation with the Jews. During the Seleucid period, it was possible to distinguish two main Jewish groups. There was a Reform Party which supported Hellenization, and there was a rock hard traditional religious group, known as the Hasideans (The Holy Ones). After a number of vicissitudes, Antiochus decided to take Jerusalem and establish a Hellenistic culture there by brute force.

The Jerusalem Greeks, with their allies and associates, came together as a sort of Antiochan Community. Just as with Nebuchadrezzar, Daniel, Shadrach, Meshach, and Abednego, failure to conform was punishable by death. Worshipping Yahweh, or performing Hebrew ceremonies, incurred an automatic death penalty as far as the Antiochans of Jerusalem were concerned. The last two straws for the Hasideans came when a statue of Zeus — and his altar — went up in the Hebrew temple; and an image of Antiochus was also placed there, along with orders to make offerings to it as you went past.

The Maccabees were a Jewish priestly family, descended from Mattathias. Judas, his son, was the most powerful and prominent of them. He had four brothers: John, Simon, Eleazar, and Jonathan. Simon's son, John Hyrcanus, was also a notable member of this outstanding family, who were all superb examples of the fine old warrior-priest tradition. The word *Maccabee* is an honourable title which was bestowed on the family in view of their courage, daring, and determination. It can be translated from the Hebrew in a variety of ways: *hammer, hammerer, destroyer, breaker,* and *extinguisher.* The idea of "Hammer" in the same sense that it was applied to Edward I, the English king who reigned from 1272 until 1307 and was regarded as the "Hammer of the Scots," is probably the most appropriate meaning. There were several other ways in which the qualities of the Maccabees resembled Edward's: like them, he was an accomplished fighting man who thoroughly enjoyed both war and politics; his prowess in the Crusades gave a certain religious flavour to his military achievements; he was also as tough and inflexible as the strongest and best of the Maccabees.

The Kingdom of Judah, with its great capital city, Jerusalem, was situated between Syria to the north and Egypt to the south. The Ptolemies were the power in Egypt, just as the Seleucids were the power in Syria. Judah had been an Egyptian province for years before the troublesome Antiochus came along.

Part of Antiochus's dark designs included integrating his empire with its mixed races and cultures by forcing one form of religion on them all. He had no understanding of Judaism at all. He found it annoying, exclusive, nonconformist (from *his* Hellenistic point of view), and something of an irritation. With his strong Hellenistic sympathies, Antiochus was doing all he could to spread Greek religion and culture as widely as possible. In theory, he said he wanted a "progressive" and "liberal" world where humanity could be free to develop and enquire into the universe — provided always that this much vaunted "freedom" and "spirit of enquiry" complied strictly with the views of Antiochus! He was a perfect example of the timeless truth that no one is quite so intolerant of other people's views as a politically correct progressive liberal!

The pious Hasideans who followed the Maccabees regarded the Hellenizing Seleucids with profound and justifiable suspicion. They looked with deep disfavour at Antiochus's attempts to persuade the local Canaanites that he was in reality their ancient fertility god, Baal. The Hasideans regarded the ancient Canaanite deities as mere personifications

Head of Antiochus IV on a coin. He was the insane Seleucid tyrant who fought against the Maccabees.

201

of human failings like lust, envy, greed, and anger. They saw the mission of Israel — God's chosen people — as a great missionary endeavour. Their task was to spread the revealed religion of Yahweh, which included justice, love, and mercy. Their Judaism was a complete way of life to them — just as Hellenism was a complete way of life to the Antiochans. A battle to the death between such contradictory concepts was as inevitable as the later clash between imperial Rome and mercantile Carthage.

It was only after Antiochus had placed the pagan statues and altars in the temple at Jerusalem, that the Hasideans were roused to battle fury. Judas Maccabeus led them in one successful guerrilla battle after another, defeating the Seleucid generals again and again. By 164 B.C., Judas had recaptured the temple, torn down the pagan statues and destroyed their shrines and altars. The temple was reconsecrated to Yahweh forthwith. This exceptional Maccabean strength and courage held an independent Jewish State together for the best part of a century.

Just how bewilderingly brilliant those Israeli victories were can best be understood by considering the military statistics. At Daphne, near Antioch, in 166 B.C., Antiochus had mustered almost fifty thousand infantrymen, and close on ten thousand cavalry. They were backed up by three hundred elephants in full battle armour — like the ones Hannibal used against the Romans at the Battle of Zama, when the brilliant Scipio Africanus defeated the wily Carthaginian by a whisker.

The secret of David's victory over Goliath, the lumbering Philistine giant, was his skill as a slingsman and his youthful speed and agility. What was the secret of the Maccabees? They were convinced beyond any shadow of doubt that they were right and that God was on their side against those whom they considered to be blasphemous pagan Hellenizers and idolaters. The Maccabees also had great military skill, zeal, courage, and determination. But did they have anything else as well? Were they in possession of strange secret weapons? Where was the Ark all this time? If it had gone to Sheba with Solomon's son, had it been brought back in time of direst need to win great battles against the Seleucids? Did the Maccabees have access to the same hazardous, secret powers which had brought terrible plagues on the Egyptians before the Exodus? Did they know *how* the Israelites had walked safely across the bed of the Red Sea, just before the Egyptians had been drowned in it? If anyone knew the deepest secrets hidden within the temple, the pious Hasidean followers of the Maccabees did. Was that why there was such outrage and anxiety when the statue of Zeus was erected within its sacred precincts? Did the Hasideans fear that strange workmen in the temple might accidentally stumble upon some secret door behind which lay treasures worth infinitely more than gold? Was that why the despised Seleucids had to be driven out at whatever cost?

Could this have been an ironic reversal of our earlier theory that Pharaoh changed his mind and hazarded his chariots across the Red Sea because Moses and the Israelites had taken with them the most valuable artefact in Egypt? What if that artefact — or part of it — or something just as ancient, powerful, and valuable, had lain for centuries concealed and unsuspected in the temple, its whereabouts known only to the Maccabees and their trusted Hasidean followers?

How else could a small band of guerrilla fighters such as the Maccabees and their men have overcome an enemy able to put six thousand men and three hundred armoured elephants into the field?

Courage is essential. Determination and stamina are great assets in war. Being convinced that you fight in a *righteous cause* and that God is with you and your soldiers is another huge plus factor. Granted that the Maccabees had all these things, it still seems highly likely that they had something else as well.

Precisely what it was, how it was used, and in which of their frequent battles against the Seleucids it was of maximum effect, is something for the thoughtful reader to speculate upon. But there is one more tantalizing clue in the Book of Proverbs. It refers to a poor man who saved a beleaguered city from the enemy by using some strange secret weapon, which he had either devised or discovered, and then went unrewarded when the enemy was defeated and danger was passed. The rich rulers of the unappreciative city treated him as badly as the ungrateful Mayor of Hamlin treated the Pied Piper once the rats had gone. Was the strange weapon in Proverbs connected in any way with the mystery of the Maccabees' victory against overwhelming odds?

Chapter Twenty-two

Will the World End?

The darker, weirder side of our human nature is fascinated by grim forebodings of death, doom, and disaster. It probably goes back to our Neanderthal and Cro-Magnon ancestors, hiding in caves and shinning up trees to avoid the long-toothed, sharp-clawed, lynx-eyed predators who waited for them at every turn. Bows, arrows, clubs, spears, muscle, and courage levelled the odds a little. Firebrands and pits lined with sharpened stakes also swung the balance our way. Yet from those earliest days, fear of a sudden end for the individual, the family, or the whole tribe was part of daily life: it seeped into the subconscious. It emerged in a score of primitive religions which also encompassed earthquakes, volcanoes, forest fires, floods, storms, and lightning bolts. There was also the problem of sudden death from no visible, external cause. Even cavemen — despite healthy diets and plenty of exercise — had strokes and coronaries. These inexplicable deaths, our ancestors reasoned, were caused by evil spirits, offended gods, mischievous demons, or the curses of witches and wizards.

If a man could die, and a tribe could die, why not an entire world? If flood or fire could sweep away a village, could the same things on a grand scale sweep away the whole earth? The first cave-dwellers thought that it probably could, and so the tale was woven into their religious myths and legends.

It is a psychological truism that misery loves company. Knowing that you're going to be hanged or beheaded at dawn isn't quite as bad if you can spend your last night in the raucous company of a dozen other condemned pirates, rebels or highwaymen. So in a crazy, inverted way, end-of-the-world mythology became strangely comforting. Death is not something to which any normally cheerful being looks forward: but the end doesn't seem quite so miserable if we're *all* going to hell *together* in the same big bucket — which is the burden of most end-of-the-world prophecy.

Wherever end-of-the-world prophecy came from originally, it has no place in a religious and philosophical paradigm based on a God of infinite love and mercy combined with absolute power and wisdom. Only a petulant child with inadequate supervision smashes its own toys — let alone anyone else's. To imagine an omnipotent and omniscient Creator and Sustainer destroying his great creation and every living, thinking, feeling being within it, plumbs the depths of blasphemy. It is no use clinging to end-of-the-world horror stories and attempting to justify them by protesting that our feeble little human minds cannot hope to understand God: of course we can't — but we can distinguish creation from destruction, love from hate, mercy from savagery, and sustenance from neglect. Even something like a slug with a single figure IQ knows the difference between being offered a juicy lettuce leaf, and being crushed under the gardener's boots. There is an infinitely great *quantitative* difference between God's power to understand the universe and ours — but whether you're the slug or the gardener food is food and being crushed is being crushed. There is no *qualitative* difference between the unlimited divine conception of love, and the limited human conception of it. What we know as joy, God also knows as joy. What we know as suffering, God also knows as suffering. A God of love and mercy does not kill and destroy his people or their universe. The two things are absolutely and definitively incompatible; purple cannot be green, up cannot be down, and right cannot be wrong — all at the same time. Either God is love or he is not. If he is love, he is not going to terminate us all with wars, plagues, storms, and earthquakes. If he is not love, then he is not the God whom Jesus his Son, revealed so clearly.

Most eschatology — writing about the end-of-the-world — was produced by persecuted people during hard times. The nation was occupied by harsh invaders and atrocities were part of daily life. It became comforting to think that all this would end one day; the cruel persecutors would go somewhere really warm with diabolical daily torture and humiliation as a non-optional extra, and all the nice guys who were suffering here would go somewhere pleasant where they could sit in ease and comfort to watch all the bad guys being put through the hoop. When life is pretty hellish anyway, the end of the world seems like a good idea, and great comfort can be derived from forecasting exactly when it's all going to happen — preferably sooner rather than later.

Co-author Lionel Fanthorpe in the house of Nostradamus who prophesied the end-of-the-world.

How are those of us who are starting on the third millennium to understand the two thousand year old Book of Revelation and what seem at first glance to be the awesome prophecies it contains?

In the first place it is not really possible to understand Revelation out of context, and its context lies fairly and squarely among the so-called apocalyptic literature which reached its zenith during the two centuries on either side of the birth of Christ.

The word apocalypse itself means "disclosure," "revealing," or "unveiling." By that standard, a book such as Revelation is a book which by its very nature sets out to expose and exhibit secrets which were formerly concealed. It is characteristic of apocalyptic literature, then, to take little or no interest in history, or in the here and the now of the contemporary world in which the author's own life experience is set. The apocalyptic writer sets out to reveal things which he, or she, believes belong in the future.

Co-author Lionel recently presented a one-hour U.K. Channel 4 TV documentary on "The Real Nostradamus" whose story is featured in depth in one of our earlier Hounslow titles: *"The World's Greatest Unsolved Mysteries."* There is a sense in which Nostradamus, like the writer of Revelation, is very clearly an apocalyptic writer: he is setting out to uncover what he believes to be some of the strange mysteries hidden in the amorphous mists of the future — whatever "the future" turns out to be once one of Einstein's successors is able to produce a satisfactory explanation for the nature of the time phenomenon itself.

We recorded many TV interviews for that program — not only with academic linguists and historians who were experts on Nostradamus — but with contemporary seers and astrologers who practised the same methods. Scryer Rosie Malone, for example, actually demonstrated her uncanny mirror-reading technique for us on the program, and we deliberately recorded the date on which the images appeared in her mirror. It was May 18, 1999. The mirror showed her a grim picture of a Balkans hospital hit by a bomb. Dead and injured children were being carried out of the shattered building. It was a harrowing scene of blood and destruction. On May 20, 1999, about thirty-six hours after Rosie saw it in her scrying mirror, the same scene was on all the TV newscasts. A Balkan hospital had been hit, and several children were among the dead and injured. Had the scrying mirror really shown Rosie what was about to happen? Could it have been only coincidence? Once again, as with the prophecies of Nostradamus, how much of a *real* glimpse of a *real* future was revealed?

That thorny old question prickles the enquiring mind yet again. If the future is cut, dried, and inevitable, what's the point of living? If we are only passive railway wagons being shunted along the lines of destiny by the locomotive of fate, there's nothing left for us to do: we have no ambition; we have no freedom of choice; we have no control over our lives — and no particular reason for living them.

We grasp at possible alternative hypotheses. What if the physicists and science fiction writes *are* on the right track when they speculate about the "wheels of if" and probability paths through the space-time continuum? If every decision we make at every passing moment has an

Co-author Lionel Fanthorpe at the tomb of Nostradamus in Salon, Provence, France.

Plaque on the wall of the house of Nostradamus.

effect on our future, then depending upon which decisions we make, which trains we catch, which jobs we apply for, which personal relations we start and which we drop — so our future will follow a different path. If all the paths we *didn't take* still exist somewhere in an infinite cosmic limbo, are they what the seers sometimes glimpse when their visions *don't* come to pass? Do the scrying mirrors and candle-lit water bowls reflect the mysterious might-have-been, as well as the what-will-probably be? And neither the seer nor the subject knows which visions will come to pass *because the subject has not yet decided which path to take.*

It's all tied up with God's hazardous but essential gift to us of that real freedom without which love — the greatest thing in the universe — cannot exist.

So the prophecies of Nostradamus (as well as the prophecies of Revelation and the other apocalyptic literature dating from the two critical centuries before and after Christ's birth) are not indications of what *has* to be, but only warnings of what *may* come to pass unless we all do everything we can to increase humanity's tolerance and willingness to compromise.

If, as we saw in the chapter on the Maccabees, Antiochus IV had not been such an arrogant, bigoted fool, he might never have triggered the war against the formidable Maccabees and their fearless Hasidean followers. Any gifted seer or psychic scryer might still have forecast such a war as the Maccabees fought against the hated Hellenizers, but if Antiochus had realized that putting an image of Zeus in the temple at Jerusalem was tantamount to putting a kilogram of sodium in his bathwater, their grim guerrilla war of attrition which destroyed him, could, perhaps, have been avoided.

Apocalyptic literature, in a beautiful description of it used by the late Professor Herbert T. Andrews of London University, "strives to open a window through which it is possible to look into the realities of the unseen world. "

What, if any, is the relationship between apocalyptic literature and prophecy as such? Prophecy opened the door through which apocalyptic literature entered God's Library. Prophets were preachers, men who carried and proclaimed what they sincerely believed were important moral and ethical messages from God. When, and if, their messages were recorded in written form as well was largely secondary, and almost incidental.

Co-author Lionel Fanthorpe with an astrolabe of the kind Nostradamus used.

When David arranged the death of Uriah the Hittite in order to save his wife, the beautiful Bathsheba (to whom the passionate warrior-king had already lost his heart), it was Nathan in the role of both priest and prophet, who dared to challenge and rebuke the powerful monarch. He tells David a fable about a poor man who owned just one ewe lamb, a treasured family pet which was given titbits from its master's table. A rich man in the same city had large flocks and herds (David had a healthy sexual appetite, numerous glamorous wives, and several nubile concubines as well). In Nathan's fable the rich man needed a lamb to slaughter as a guest had arrived and needed a meal under the old Hebrew laws of hospitality.

The selfish rich man in Nathan's story steals the poor man's pet ewe and kills it for the table. David is furious at this greed and injustice. "That man shall surely die!" he roars in a burst of righteous indignation. Fearlessly Nathan looks David straight in the eye: "Thou art the man, O King!"

David suddenly recognizes the magnitude of his sin in committing adultery with Bathsheba. Even her overwhelming beauty and enthusiastic compliance cannot excuse or justify the wrong that David has done to his loyal soldier, Uriah. He is overcome with bitter remorse and regret. It is greatly to David's credit that he *accepts* Nathan's admonition and his own guilt. Very few Middle Eastern despots in 1000 B.C. would have taken that comment as nobly as David did. If Nathan had made that same devastating challenge to almost any other king, his head would have been on the royal battlements and his entrails — still warm and twitching — on the royal garbage heap. But, however wrong David had been over the irresistible Bathsheba, he was still David. Deep down, he was residually moral. At heart — whatever his powerful male hormones had led him into — he was still Yahweh's man, and *Nathan knew that.* His life depended on the accuracy of his judgement of David, and his judgement had not failed him.

Nathan was a prophet — first, last, and always — not an apocalyptic writer. Prophets in Nathan's tradition were concerned with here-and-now morality of the David and Bathsheba kind. Apocalyptists have given up completely on the here and now. They wait for the Divine Theatre Owner to ring down the curtain, finish the run and put on a whole new play.

Almost five hundred years drifted past between the age of the last great prophet and the dawn of the first apocalyptist. With this in mind, it is possible to suggest *why* the apocalyptists took such a downbeat view of things. The basic message of the prophets had always been: "When Israel obeys God's laws, we'll prosper as a nation. When we disobey, we shall be defeated." In order to try to prove the validity of this totally fallacious hypothesis, various priestly editors and redactors worked over the holy texts until every king of Israel, or Judah, who had had an unfortunate reign was automatically written off as having "done wrong in the sight of the Lord." When the various Hebrew monarchs and their reigns are analyzed, this judgemental priestly view is patently untenable. Good kings lost battles, territories, and their lives. Bad kings reigned for an interminable period and died happily of over indulgence. It made no kind of moral sense, and trying to lay the blame for the multiple disasters at Yahweh's door was perilously close to the worst kind of blasphemy. God isn't like that; God does not do that.

From the apocalyptists' point of view, it was worse than trying to square the circle; not altogether surprisingly, they gave up and tried a whole new tack. With five additional centuries to analyze, half a millennium after the last prophet had written his message, the apocalyptists saw how badly God's chosen people had fared during those five centuries in terms of relative political, military, and economic success — with the sole exception of the all too brief glory of the Maccabees.

The redactorial priestly formula was threadbare. In temporal terms, the apocalyptists could say: "It will all have to end and begin again. There will have to be a fresh start. The program has crashed: re-boot the computer!"

In order to understand the Book of Revelation — even partially — we need to examine the situation in which it was written. Once it is understood and locked firmly into its historical context, all the eschatological bric-a-brac can be sent cheerfully to the next garage sale. Revelation was written solely as morale-raising encouragement for desperate early Christians who were continually being persecuted, vilified, ridiculed, tortured, martyred, and attacked from all points of the compass. A repeated theme is the rich reward that faithful martyrs will receive in Heaven.

Isolated on Patmos, the writer of Revelation has three clear beliefs to fill his long, lonely hours of exile. First, he shared with most Christians of the first century, the certainty that Christ was coming back to earth in power, glory, and judgement *very soon*. Today was possible. Tomorrow was probable. Next week was a cast-iron certainty. Second, he believed — as all good apocalyptists did — that God would burst into history like an avenging dragon. The sinners would meet dire and terrible punishment. The righteous would be richly rewarded. Peace and justice would be enforced under God's irresistible power: then Christ would reign in glory. His third firm belief was in some sort of judgement process. Antichrist, the leader of evil, would be cast down and a kingdom of jubilant saints would replace him.

All one can say without sounding unduly cynical is: "It hasn't happened *yet*." No doubt people have said that almost immediately before losing a war, falling off a cliff, being engulfed in a flood of boiling lava or drowned by a one hundred foot tidal wave! But it hasn't happened yet, and, furthermore we're confident that it's not going to happen.

Expecting that it will, living in mind-bending awe of it, losing healthy ambition, being unwilling or unable to plan your next venture because of an irrational fear that the world's going to end before you can complete it, is about as much help in life as a serious hangover combined with a powerful dose of typhoid fever.

The best thing to do with the end-of-the-world theories is to forget about them. The most any of us have to bet with is our lives, and we unhesitatingly wager ours on our God of Love and Mercy. He is a bringer of joy beyond human imagining; he is not a harbinger of terror and suffering. There is no more to fear from God than from the visit of a much-loved parent, carer, or guardian, whose only thoughts towards us are love, protection, and companionship. If he ever does appear suddenly in this earth he has made, it will be as the Personification of Peace, Joy, and Love.

It is no part of God's plan that this beautiful, green world of ours will end with either a bang or a whimper. He will develop and improve it, as he develops and improves us. He will enrich it and enhance it. The more we are able to work environmentally as the watchers and guardians of God's creation, the better life will be for us and for all the myriad other life forms with whom we have the privilege of sharing the planet. There is nothing that men and women of goodwill cannot improve. There is no good thing that we cannot accomplish together — with God's enthusiastic encouragement and approval.

We want to bring the world of greed to an end.

We need to bring the world of selfishness to an end.

We strive to bring the world of cruelty, suffering, and death to an end.

Goodness never ends.

Love never ends.

The abundant, eternal, and joyful life which is God's plan for us all never ends.

Chapter Twenty-three

Did Jesus Teach Reincarnation?

In the Book of Malachi 4:5, there's an intriguing prophecy that Elijah will return before "the great and terrible day of the Lord." This could be understood by some readers to mean that Elijah will come to act as herald for the Messiah — as John the Baptist did for Jesus — or that Elijah will return just in time to do some more good work shortly before the end-of-the-world. Malachi is not particularly clear or precise on that point.

As Jesus descends from the Mount of Transfiguration with Peter, James, and John, they ask him about Malachi's prophecy: will Elijah return before the Messiah comes?

Meanwhile, John the Baptist (the front-runner for the returned Elijah's post) has already been beheaded on Herod's orders because of Salome's mother's bitter hatred of him. Jesus then explains to the puzzled disciples that Elijah has *already* returned — and been killed! The reference to John the Baptist is now unmistakable. Of all the great religious heroes of the Old Testament, it was undoubtedly Elijah — or Amos — who bore the closest resemblance to John the Baptist in New Testament times. All three men were rugged, powerful, untamed, outdoor types. They shared a simple, forceful version of the faith. Not one of them was prepared to compromise. But it was Elijah, not Amos, who featured in Malachi's prophecy — so it was Elijah who was being compared with John the Baptist. Both of them were as ruthless and direct as the Hasidean Maccabees.

When Elisha asked for a double portion of the departing Elijah's spirit, it was a truly potent human spirit that he hungered for.

To the perceptive, clear-thinking Jesus, the similarity between the two men was undeniable. John was certainly the same *type* of man as Elijah, but was Jesus implying that he was *the same person as Elijah?*

Does Christ's resurrection rule out the possibility of reincarnation?
Drawn by Theo Fanthorpe.

Some traditional Christians are concerned and unhappy about the whole concept of reincarnation, but why should they be? There is no real contradiction between the central idea of a loving God and his possible choice of an alternative method of perfecting some members of his creation over more than one lifetime, is there?

It's reminiscent of the old Victorian dispute between Darwin's Theory of Evolution and Direct Creationism. Does it matter one iota whether God made us instantaneously, or over hundreds of millions of years of gradual evolutionary change? He's still God; he's still our loving Creator and caring Sustainer. God the Ultimate Magician says: "Let there be" and it appears. God the Ultimate Craftsman first designs a sophisticated instrument called Evolution and then says: "Let us make."

As long as our parents love us and want us, it doesn't matter a damn whether they got us from a womb, a test-tube, an adoption agency, a refugee camp, or an alien UFO. We could have been carved from wood and brought to life like Pinocchio in the folk tale, and it wouldn't matter at all. It is being here, being alive, being conscious, being capable of giving and receiving love that counts.

The same argument holds firm for reincarnation. How many lifetimes would Nero, Caligula, or Hitler need to reach perfection? Couldn't Saint Francis or Mother Teresa do it in one? We suspect that most of us would probably fall somewhere between those two extremes!

And couldn't a sophisticated theory of reincarnation also accommodate those searching questions about animal souls? The dog, the cat, the budgie, the hamster, the rabbit, the pony that someone truly loves — is there more than we sometimes dare to imagine in their expressive, and meaningful eyes? Does the exceptionally faithful and intelligent dog make it a stage up the ladder and come back as a human being next time? Does the domineering, wilful, aggressive, and unsympathetic human being need to learn certain vital lessons next time around as a cow in a dairy? *We don't know* — but the idea is not ridiculous, and it has its own kind of morality to defend it.

It's essential to remember when considering any of Christ's words that he spoke the colourful Aramaic of a first century Palestinian Jew. It's a language full of imagery and hyperbole. It's a religious language rather than a scientific one. In Aramaic, camels go through the eyes of needles, Peter is a rock and James and John are the Sons of Thunder. In Aramaic, Jesus, whom we unhesitatingly believe to be the Son of God in a very special, unique sense, chooses to refer to himself on occasion as the Son of man — with all the deep shades of Ezekiel's strange adventures attached to that mysterious phrase. So when Jesus tells his questioner in Aramaic *"Elijah has already come,"* and when it is clear from the context that he means John the Baptist, are we to understand that Jesus is expressing a sublime idea in a language which can be confusingly ambiguous for us in translation? Did Jesus mean only that the *similarity* between the characters of John and Elijah is so great that John can be understood as a *type* of Elijah?

When John himself was asked who and what he was, he stringently denied that he was Elijah. What was going on inside that brave and intelligent head which the imbecilic Herod severed at the whim of a petulant dancing girl and her evil mother? Do we recall who we were in a previous life? Not very often, apparently — but when it does happen, the results can be dramatic. There are several quite impressive cases recorded in the literature — especially in Asia — where the infant reincarnee has recognized middle-aged men as the sons she brought up and loved dearly *in her previous life.*

Just because John had no recollection of his previous life as Elijah, does not mean that he might not have been Elijah.

There is then, of course, the other stumbling block of Elijah's exemption from death. If we accept the story of the "fiery chariot" which was associated with his final ascent in a whirlwind, did he die subsequently? Or has he remained alive the whole time without passing through the gates of death like the vast majority of those who have gone before us? We also have to remember that both he and Moses were actually on the Mount of Transfiguration with Jesus, Peter, James, and John. How can the living, deathless Elijah be in two places at once? If his spirit is, or was, in John the Baptist, then who exactly is talking with Jesus and Moses on the mountain? However, as John the Baptist has already been judicially murdered by the repugnant Herod, has the Elijah spirit, which was John's during his earthly life and mission, now gone back to that Divine Realm of Light and Joy where it belongs?

Another point to consider is the idea of a spirit as *powerful* as Elijah's being shared out or *apportioned* in some strange way. What if men like Elijah are so full of spiritual power and energy that they have more than enough for themselves and some to spare? Whatever fell on Elisha obviously left enough of itself with the ascending Elijah for him still to be abundantly himself in the heavenly sphere. When Jesus said that John the Baptist was — in a special sense — Elijah, did he mean that John had an extra portion of Elijah's spirit in him in much the same way that Elisha had? If that was what Christ meant, then the whole question of reincarnation, in so far as it concerns John the Baptist and Elijah, can be safely placed on one side.

If reincarnation happens, does it also go some way to refuting the anti-God argument of those materialists who point to the vast ages of cosmic and geological history and say: "How can there be a purposeful Mind behind all this waste?" If reincarnation goes hand-in-hand with evolution, there is no waste. *There never was any waste.* When the first microscopic speck of primordial life came together as a bio-chemical sequence that could make its own little pattern reappear, did something *more* than physical repetition come into being at the same time? Was there a mysterious, surviving *entity* that moved on to occupy he next tiny body? Was that reincarnated entity living inside an adventurous pterodactyl who died when he crashed into a Jurassic ocean millions of years later? Did that same immortal, reincarnating soul-spark develop into a sabre-toothed tiger? Then, perhaps, a mammoth that froze instantaneously in Siberia? A horse in a Roman cavalry squadron? A Chaldean farmer? A Carthaginian potter? A medieval painter? An Italian sculptor? A gifted and caring American physician?

If reincarnation *does* happen, wouldn't it be the finest school of life, and the ultimate university? How can any of us hope to learn even 1 percent of 1 percent of what we need to know about this immeasurable cosmos in one lightning flash of a human lifespan? But if we've been around since we were specks of protoplasm floating in primeval soup, and if we're still going to be around when genetic engineering, cybernetics, cryogenics, and cloning have raised our lifespans to millions of years, there may be hope of progressing a little way beyond the kindergarten!

But if we can't *consciously recall* these things, how do they help our development from aeon to aeon and from simple organisms to more complex and intelligent ones? A great deal of interesting work has already been done with hypno-regression, and it's a field that's well worth further study.

But we don't have to be consciously aware of something for it to be safely there in our minds and doing its job effectively. While you're writing an e-mail, walking your dog, or watching an adventure video, a great many processes are going in the vast labyrinth of your subconscious mind to control blood pressure, heart beat, breathing, digestion and so on. We can all "sleep on a problem" — let the subconscious work on it through the night — and come up with a solution in the morning which the conscious mind had previously failed to find.

Don't let any long-faced, timidly disapproving, Christian traditionalists persuade you that reincarnation is somehow anti-Christian: *take it from us that it isn't.* When you strike up an instant and meaningful friendship, or a great love-at-first-sight personal relationship in this life, the explanation may well be that you and your partner knew each other long ago — and liked what you knew.

God is Love, and Love is the most permanent thing there is.

If anything at all of our previous life experiences occasionally lingers in our *conscious* memories — or manages to slip in there from time to time — you can bet that it will be love.

Chapter Twenty-four

The Secret of the Dead Sea Scrolls

Any serious investigator of the Scrolls and their strange secrets would do well to begin with the mystery of the true identity of Saint James, described in the Bible as the *brother* of Jesus, and credited with the authorship of the New Testament Epistle which bears his name.

Top Dead Sea Scroll experts like Robert Eisenman and Michael Wise suggest that there were *two* very different new religious organizations growing up in the middle years of the first century A.D. The Christianity of Jerusalem and Palestine was a religion of patriots and nationalists like the Zealots — people who were similar to what the Maccabees and Hasideans had once been. This organization relied on apocalyptic ideas and tended to distance itself as far as it could from those who were not Jews. It might — judging by the contents of James's Epistle — almost have been called *Jamesianity*. The other form of Christianity — the overseas version — could have been labelled *Paulianity* to distinguish it from the Palestinian, or Jamesian, type. The overseas, Pauline, version was enthusiastically and inclusively evangelical, pacifist, patient, enduring and largely inclined towards antinomianism — the idea that complying with moral law and ethics was rather less important than faith in the matter of salvation via Christ, who is believed by antinomians to have transcended the old moral law and wiped out all sin by his sacrificial and atoning death on the cross.

Early writers like Eusebius and later reformers like Martin Luther were unhappy to find James's Epistle in the Canon of Scripture at all; given a deciding vote, both would happily have omitted it!

When we use the term Qumran (actually just the *location* where the scrolls were found) as a convenient piece of shorthand to indicate the scrolls themselves and the gist of their contents, as well as a description of the religious community who were responsible for creating and concealing them, we can say that the Epistle of James is full of Qumranisms. It could just as easily have been written by a member of the mysterious Messianic community at Qumran as by the Christian brother of Jesus of Nazareth.

In what sense *is* James the brother of Jesus? There are some shades of meaning in which the Greek word *adelphoi* means brethren in the broad, inclusive, non-biological terminology of a preacher who addresses his church congregation as "My very dear brothers and sisters," or in which modern jazz musicians call one another "soul-brothers."

But there are more general usages in which it means what it says in terms of simple family relationships, where brothers and sisters literally have the same parents. Several theorists have put forward possible explanations. Hegesippus who lived in the second century A.D. suggested that Joseph the carpenter, husband of Mary the Virgin, was brother to Alphaeus whose wife was also called Mary. This Alphaeus was the father of four sons, one of whom grew up to become Saint James, author of the controversial Epistle. Alphaeus and Mary also had several daughters. The Hegesippian theory makes Jesus and James first cousins, so that *adelphoi* is used to mean close relatives rather than siblings.

The Origenistic or Epiphanian Hypothesis credits Joseph with being a widower when he married Mary the Virgin, and makes James Joseph's son by this former, deceased wife. This makes James a notional half-brother to Jesus, in so far as Joseph was also Jesus's "father," but in the sense of being his mother's husband and Jesus's guardian and protector during his infancy and boyhood. The Hieronymian theory was the one that was warmly advocated by Jerome who lived during the fourth century A.D. This thesis has Mary the wife of Clopas, mother of the Saint James who wrote the Epistle, as a sister to Mary the Virgin. Jesus and James are then cousins on their mothers' side. The final, Helvidian theory, which is the one we favour, comes from a book which Helvidius wrote around the year A.D. 380. He believed that James, Joses, Simon, Jude, and some sisters were born in the normal way to Mary the Mother of Jesus and were fathered by her husband, Joseph the carpenter from Nazareth. Matthew 1:24–25, gives massive historical support to this Helvidian theory. Matthew writes: "and took unto him [Joseph the carpenter] his wife: and knew her not till she had brought forth her firstborn son: and he called his name Jesus." That pivotal word *till* seems to leave little room for doubt: from Mary's immaculate conception until Jesus was born, there was no sexual relationship between her and her husband Joseph. Afterwards — until Joseph predeceased Mary — they enjoyed a perfectly normal, happy, and sexually fulfilled marriage which led to the birth of James and their other sons and daughters. So as far as their friends and neighbours knew, James *was* the brother of Jesus.

As close study of James's Epistle clearly reveals, he believed in the importance of *action* rather than in abstract *faith* — that same faith which was central to the lives of the antinomian Paulinists. James actually ridicules the idea of faith as an instrument of salvation. In Chapter 2:14, he writes: "What doth it profit, my brethren, though a man say he hath faith, and have not works? Can faith save him?"

James's answer to his own rhetorical question was that it most certainly could not. He makes the point even more clearly in verses 17 and 18 of the same chapter: "Faith, if it hath not works, is dead ... show me thy faith without thy works ... and I will show thee my faith by my works."

He argues his case even more strongly in verses 24 and 25 of this same chapter: "Ye see then how that by works a man is justified, and not by faith only.... Likewise was not Rahab the harlot justified by works, when she had received the messengers and sent them out another way?"

Whatever was going on in Qumran could fairly be categorized as Zealotism, Messianism, or Essenism — and it was a very different strand of religious thought and behaviour from what Paul was spreading across the known world of his day. There was also a strong *Retreatist-Elitist* atmosphere permeating the Qumran community. They had taken Isaiah 40:3, in a very direct and literal sense: "The voice of him that crieth in the wilderness, 'Prepare ye the way of the Lord, make straight in the desert a highway for our God.'"

This had encouraged the people of Qumran to "separate" themselves from what they considered to be the spiritual and moral pollution of the ordinary, happy, common-sense life of the normal world. This general tendency towards "separation" and "exclusiveness" is characteristic of many religious cults and sects, as it is of those who choose incomprehensibly to live in monasteries and nunneries even today, and of others who feel an irrational compulsion to go off on frequent religious "retreats."

John the Baptist, who acted as the herald and fore-runner of Jesus, is described in Matthew 3:3, as: "he that was spoken of by the prophet Isaiah, saying: The voice of one crying in the wilderness, 'Prepare ye the way of the Lord, make his paths straight.'"

This is such a clear Qumranism that it seems to establish a definite link between John the Baptist and the scroll-making community, or between them and the author of the Gospel attributed to Matthew — or, most probably, between *both*. John, the wilderness-dwelling hermit, who dressed, spoke, and lived like the wildest of the Old Testament prophets, had all the hallmarks of the Qumran community.

Another characteristic feature of the Qumranites was their great affinity for organizing camps in wildernesses and deserts where they believed that they were preparing themselves to be reinforced by bands of angels who would join them in the battle of Armageddon to wipe out the hated Roman occupiers — and everything else in the world which the Qumranites regarded as evil.

This particular Qumranian attitude provides useful clues to their real motivation, and the suspicion that their "ascetic holiness" was largely camouflage for the kind of militaristic, "holy-war" Puritanism that characterized Cromwell in England and the early New England colonists of the U.S.A. The deadly, self-righteous arrogance which leads such groups to believe that they and they alone are right is all too frequently the starting point from that they set out to convert (or destroy!) the rest of humanity. Such sinister religious insanity is the spawning ground for atrocities like the Salem witch-hunts, the Holy Inquisition and the arbitrary torture and burning of those classified as heretics.

It is because of this hazardous attitude among the Qumranites, that some of the most interesting of their scrolls are the ones which contain their visionary, messianic material.

The Dead Sea Scroll texts are very carefully numbered to facilitate quick access and identification: 1Q, for example, means that the scroll concerned came from cave number one. 2Q indicates that it came from the second cave and so on. The letters after the Q identify the document itself. D represents the Damascus Document, for example — so 4QD

Scrolls from the caves in the Qumran area. What strange secrets do they hold? Drawn by Theo Fanthorpe.

refers to the Damascus Document from the fourth cave; 4Q560 from that same cave is a formula which is supposed to be effective against evil spirits when used as an amulet, and so on. In 4Q521 we find a significant text centred on the Qumranian teachings about the "Messiah of earth and Heaven." Four types of followers are distinguished here: *Anavim* (meek); *Emunin* (faithful); *Hassidim* (holy or pious); and *Zaddikim* (righteous). The shades of distinction that differentiate these virtuous categories are often fine ones. Meekness, in this religious sense, may best be defined as the opposite of assertive aggression: gentleness, unquestioning acceptance, contentment, and a submissive tranquillity of spirit — all the qualities, in fact, which a charismatic Qumran community leader would find admirable in his followers! In all walks of life, leaders with large egos tend to welcome meekness as a highly desirable trait among their disciples. (If it *is* a virtue, as humility is also alleged to be, it's one that's eluded us up to now — and we're definitely not searching for it!)

The Messiah in this Qumran passage will raise the dead, release the captives, heal the sick, give sight to the blind, and lift up those who have been cast down. There are also references in this important section to the concept of "planting a root" or to "a root of planting." The consensus of scholarly opinion seems to be that the Qumran writer thought that God had visited the earth in order to plant this metaphorical Messianic root — and the Messiah of the scrolls is far removed from the Suffering Servant ideas of Isaiah. The Qumran community certainly seemed to be expecting an unbeatable, charismatic warrior-king with Divine powers who would re-establish the State of Israel as a substantial military and political power of the type which it had been in the days of David and Solomon, and, again, all

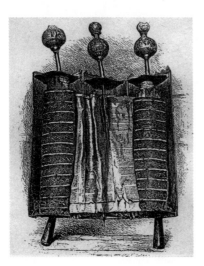

Jewish religious scrolls of the type used in synagogue services.

too briefly, under the aegis of the valiant Maccabees. For the Qumranians, this coming of the Messiah would be the dawning of "the great and terrible day of the Lord" which would mean the beginning of a whole new era of Jewish holiness and independent nationalism. This in turn brings in the subject of the New Jerusalem as depicted in the Qumran fragments.

A section known as 4Q554 is only one of many which make typical references to "The New Jerusalem." Other fragments on the same theme have turned up in caves 1, 2, 5 and 11, but 4 and 5 have provided the best and most extensive evidence. In the fragments, an angel, or archangel, leads the writer around this New Jerusalem which is one day destined to stand on the site of the old one. Measurements are taken using a measuring rod almost 3.5 metres long (seven cubits). This New Jerusalem was to be built on the grand scale: some 32.2 kilometres by 48.3 kilometres in extent. There were to be twelve huge and ornate ceremonial gates in the walls of this great city: one for each of the twelve traditional tribes of Israel. The Gate of Levi (the priestly tribe) would occupy the centre of the eastern wall.

Another significant feature of the Qumran literature is prophecy. Just as Nostradamus, Mother Shipton, and the Brahan Seer always found a ready audience in their day, so prophets, clairvoyants. and fortune-tellers — provided they were holy, of course — could always find a ready Qumranian audience in the centuries immediately before and after the birth of Christ. The gist of such Qumranian "prophecy" is almost invariable similar: the Messiah will come; there will be a great battle; evil will be destroyed; the strictly holy, law-abiding people (especially the Qumranians!) will be rewarded; and there will be a New Jerusalem for them to inhabit.

In addition to these prophecies, many of the scrolls contain what is probably best described as "Wisdom Literature." In the Old Testament this covers the Books of Job, Proverbs, and Ecclesiastes. It is typical of biblical Wisdom Literature to make general semi-philosophical observations about how life should be lived, together with wide-ranging comments on what constitutes prudent human behaviour. Polonius's advice to Laertes in *Hamlet* provides a clear example of Wisdom Literature from a non-biblical source: "to thine own self be true ... thou canst not then be false to any man."

A clear example from Qumran is the *Testament of Levi* contained in 4Q213 and 214. In the fourth fragment, column one, we find: "The essence of each of your works must be truth.... He who sows what is Good shall reap what is Good.... He who sows what is evil finds his harvest is turned against him.... He who teaches Wisdom will find that Wisdom brings honour."

226

As well as Wisdom Literature there are numerous interesting legal documents among the Qumran fragments. With Qumran — as with the Epistle of Saint James — it is action that counts, not abstract faith. The authors of these legal texts were far stricter, more literal and more traditional than Jesus. This applied especially to their quibbling and nit-picking over "working" on the Sabbath. Jesus, above any other religious teacher or leader of his time, understood perfectly what the Sabbath was for and why it was there in the Divine Law at all. Originally it had been a good and humanitarian rule, intended to prevent slaves, servants, and bondsfolk from being worked to death by greedy owners and masters. The Sabbath provided rest for servants, slaves, and beasts alike. It was a wonderful protection for them. Then, later on, in the hands of narrow-minded, legalistic, religious fanatics like the Pharisees, it began to go horribly and grotesquely wrong. What was intended to do good, to bring happiness, pleasant rest, recreation, and refreshment, became a weapon with which to inflict misery. In Shaw's brilliant play *The Devil's Disciple,* the hero so styles himself because he detests New England Puritanism as it was practised in the eighteenth century. Satan, he tells the audience, seemed to him to be the only supernatural being who did not rejoice in the sight of children's tears, whereas the Sabbatarian Puritans would fiendishly smash any much-loved toy that a child dared to take out of the cupboard on what those same Puritans (wrongly!) called the Sabbath.

Typical of these legalistic Qumranian documents are 4Q397/8/9 which deal with "works that are believed to count as righteous behaviour": "Remember the Kings of Israel and let their works be understood ... whoever among them went in search of the law was saved from suffering ... when they followed the law their sins were forgiven."

Fragment 4Q418 brings us to yet another different class of Qumran writings: one which can best be categorized as *Mysteries* in the religious sense. Unfortunately, it is tantalizingly broken, and several important sections of it are missing:

"Why did it exist ... in what did it exist...?
... concerning the knowledge of secret truth
... keep secret your mysteries ... with all the power of your mind search for the Mystery of Existence."

What strange secrets might those missing fragments have contained?

There, then, are a few fleeting glimpses of the Dead Sea Scrolls and their contents. They have, sadly, all too often become a happy hunting ground for relatively harmless religious eccentrics. They have also provided a little damp and unreliable ammunition for the literary guns of anti-Christian sensationalists who have tried to use the Scrolls as sinister indications of first century religious and political conspiracy. Their dark implications have sometimes insinuated that Jesus was really only a political and military Davidic Warrior-Messiah who failed to overthrow Rome and the priestly establishment, and was then judicially murdered by them. According to these theories, it was Paul and his antinomian overseas followers who spiritualized the episode, and deliberately conspired to suppress all the politico-military Jewish aspects of the failed Qumran-style Messianic revolution. Under their influence, Jesus, who had been simply a dynastic descendant of David through his perfectly normal human father, Joseph, was misrepresented as the Son of God instead. This whole line of argument disintegrates once it is realized — as the scholarly Eisenman and Wise have pointed out with such brilliance and objectivity in their superb work *The Dead Sea Scrolls Uncovered* — that there were *two* very different forms of early Christianity: Jamesian and Pauline – pronomian and antinomian.

There was no conspiracy. There were no lies. There was no cover up. There was no deceit. It was the old, old tragedy of *two* religious groups interpreting the same central and eternal truth in different ways to try to make it fit their personal preferences and preconceptions. The Dead Sea Scrolls reveal that there was a fanatical Nazirite and Hasidean style of fierce religious ascetics in the Qumran area. They were Zealots and nationalists as well as obsessive pronomians. They believed passionately in a traumatic and imminent Day of Judgement when a ruthless Messiah with cohorts of invincible and invulnerable angels to assist him, would lead them all to a glorious Armageddon-style victory. After that, with their enemies dead — or better still, screaming in hell with Satan and the defeated demons forever — they would all live happily ever after, and keeping every iota of their beloved law in their New Jerusalem.

This weird Qumran doctrine was just one more obstacle for Jesus and those who really understood him to overcome. Because of the prevalence of their ideas, Jesus had to emphasize in his own teachings that God was a loving and sustaining parent — not a moody punisher and destroyer; that the Sabbath was made for humanity's benefit — not vice versa; and that the Kingdom of God was to be established in the hearts and minds of caring friends and companions, rather than on the battlefield of Armageddon — although that did not preclude its ultimate establishment on earth as well as eternally in Heaven.

As far as we're concerned, based on the data we've seen, there isn't the tiniest scrap of evidence on the minutest fragment of the Dead Sea Scrolls which throws any doubt on Jesus being the Son of God in a unique and vitally important way. There is no evidence that he was not the Miraculous Child of Mary the Virgin. There is no evidence that he did not rise from the dead. The Qumran Scrolls are full of interesting mysteries — but they contain no threat and no challenge to the central truths of Christianity.

Chapter Twenty-five

Was Jesus Married?

One of the many theories advanced about the mystery of Rennes-le-Château was that Jesus was married to Mary Magdalene and that, after the crucifixion, she escaped to the south of France with their children — who eventually married into the Merovingian Dynasty. As an explanation for the Rennes *treasure* mystery, it's not very convincing. When we first began investigating Rennes back in 1975 for the unsolved mysteries lectures which Lionel was giving for Cambridge University's E-M Board at that time, we were inclined to think that Christ's hypothetical marriage to Mary Magdalene and her later involvement with Rennes were unlikely. Certainly, the popular and highly sensational Rennes theories which suggested that Father Saunière (the Rennes priest who became inexplicably rich in 1885) had found Jesus's mummified body near the village and was merrily blackmailing the Catholic Church with it, are as far from historical reality as Peter Pan and the Never-Never Land. That Mary Magdalene might have been married to Jesus, and subsequently fled with their children to the Rennes area could *possibly* have just a little mileage in it.

There are three intriguing women in the Gospels who could, perhaps, all be one and the same person — *and the wife of Jesus*. The first is Mary Magdalene; the second is Mary of Bethany, sister of Martha and Lazarus whom Jesus raised from the dead; the third is the woman caught in the act of committing adultery who was swooped on with ill-concealed delight by the hypocritical, puritanical Pharisees, and dragged off for Jesus's judgement as to whether she should be stoned in accordance with Mosaic law.

That was a particularly vicious and underhanded act on their part — one of those heads-we-win-and-tails-you-lose questions which are the stock-in-trade of barrack-room lawyers. If Jesus had said, "Stone her," the very people who had accused her would have rushed off to the Roman authorities to bleat that Jesus was advocating disobedience to Rome which alone had the right to pass death sentences in occupied Palestine. If Jesus had said, "No, it's wrong to stone her," her accusers would have crowed loudly to their own Jewish people that Jesus couldn't be from God because he was contradicting the law which God had given to Moses. He would also have been accused of being a pro-Roman yes-man, a traitor to Israel and a cowardly collaborator. But what if they had had an *extra* ace in their grubby, sweaty little hands? Suppose the unnamed woman whom they'd caught was Jesus's own wife? Were they counting on his jealousy and anger — the quixotic fury of a betrayed husband — to condemn her to death immediately? If so, they had badly underestimated and totally misjudged their man.

Was it Christ's own wife, Mary of Bethany, or Mary Magdalene, who anointed him?

Jesus was never angered by the frailty of those he loved. He was angered by hypocrisy and deceit. He was angered by the flagrant commercialism that filled the temple with profiteering money changers. He was angered by the narrow, hard-hearted legalism that tried to deny him the right to heal on the Sabbath. Human weakness and human failings never angered him: they only served to increase his fathomless reservoir of love, pity, and mercy.

In any case, wasn't there something totally understandable and readily forgivable in the girl's adultery? How many political or showbiz marriages last the course? How many loving partnerships collapse under the constant pressure of being in the limelight, talking to crowds, making major career decisions, and taking on the responsibilities of leadership? Did she feel that she was being left behind with the children, neglected, playing second fiddle to the crowds who came to be healed, to see her husband's miracles and to hear him preach?

As an alternative theory, how much of a set-up might her accusers' caught-in-the-act scenario have been? Wasn't this exactly the kind of devious cunning at which Christ's enemies were such virtuosos? Send handsome, charming young Sadducee A to flatter her, to listen sympathetically to her feelings of loneliness and neglect, to put a gentle, seemingly innocent, fraternal arm around her shoulders ... and then push her down into a compromising position beside him, just as Herodian B bursts in — exactly on cue — with half a dozen temple guards to act as "witnesses," all ready and willing to swear that things had gone much further than an arm around her shoulders.

Desperately ashamed and embarrassed, she is roughed up by the temple guards, her robes are disarranged suggestively as "evidence" and she is dragged off to Jesus for "judgement." They throw her at his feet, and look up expectantly for his furious, condemnatory response.

It's intriguing to ask at this juncture just what became of handsome young Sadducee A; as soon as the hapless girl was arrested, if he *was* part of a set-up scenario, he simply melted away into the anonymity of the crowded street outside.

Jesus knows perfectly well what has happened. Is he hiding a smile of loving sympathy for his beloved Mary, or a frown of righteous anger at those who had treated her this way, as he stoops and writes thoughtfully in the dust before answering them?

"Let him who is without sin among you cast the first stone at her." Then he ignores them all and turns back to his writing. One by one, each of her accusers looks inside his own mind, and listens to his conscience. *Oh, yes, there was that business with bribing the tax collector last week.... Wasn't it only yesterday that I failed to help my elderly parents to carry food home from the market...? I lied to that customer about the age of the donkey I sold him.... There was that night I spent with my wife's young servant girl last year, before we had to send her away.*

No one throws the first stone. One by one, they think it through — and leave.

Jesus turns to the girl. "Where are the people who condemned you?" he asks gently. She smiles for the first time since the ordeal began. "They have gone," she answers quietly. Her eyes are steadfastly on his. She reads nothing there except love and understanding. Jesus smiles again. "Neither to do I condemn you." He also uses the Aramaic phrase: "Go your way." This simple statement also has a deeper meaning — as many first century Aramaic phrases have. In the old Norfolk dialect — which was both authors' first language — there is a stylized exchange between any two friends or acquaintances who meet each other travelling in opposite directions to or from the field, the market, the shop or the pub.

"Where ya goin'?" (Where are you going?)
"Humm. Where ya goin'?" (I'm going home. Where are you going?)
"Humm." (I am going home as well.)
"Git you humm then." (You'd better get on with your journey home as fast as you can.)
"Ar, an git you humm an all!" (You should, yourself, take the advice which you have given me, and hurry to your own home as soon as possible, also.)

The roots of this apparently meaningless, ritualized, dialect exchange go back to medieval cuckolding jokes. The implication is that while each of the two speakers is away from home, their wives are entertaining illicit

Classical, symbolic study of Mary of Magdala, or Mary of Bethany. Was she the "widow" of Jesus?

lovers in their absence. The first speaker is implying that he knows about the behaviour of the second man's wife. The second speaker is implying that the first speaker should be remedying that same situation in his own household before giving good advice to others. The point of their hurrying home is that, if they do, they may succeed in catching their respective wives with their lovers. This kind of humour goes back to Chaucer's *Miller's Tale,* written well before 1400. The old Norfolk dialect had much in common with Chaucer's Middle English.

So what does "*Go your way*" really mean in first century Aramaic? It's equivalent to a benignly dismissive remark such as: "That's all OK then. There's nothing more that needs to be said about it. Everything's fine. It's sorted. It's settled. It's done with."

Jesus then adds: "and sin no more." What does that mean?

If the accused girl *was* his wife (Mary of Bethany, alias Mary Magdalene) and if the alleged adultery had been *real* — not just a set-up arranged by his enemies — is he telling her: "It's all forgiven and forgotten, but please don't do it again"? If, on the other hand, it *was* merely a despicable set-up on the part of his enemies — the Scribes, Pharisees, and Sadducees — is *"and sin no more"* said with a gentle smile so that it really *means:* "I know perfectly well that you did nothing wrong in the first place"?

Another interesting facet to the mystery of whether Jesus was married or not concerns the famous wedding at Cana of Galilee, where Mary the Virgin asked him to use his miraculous powers to help because they had run out of wine. Christ responded by making enough to keep everyone at the party very happy for at least a week.

Whose wedding was it? The case for saying that it was Jesus's own is not a strong one, but it cannot be dismissed peremptorily. There are just enough clues pointing that way to leave the serious, unbiased investigator wondering — but it is only a long shot at best. What if shocked, celibate copyists of the earliest Gospel manuscripts deliberately omitted a line or two from their account of that wedding at Cana: because for Jesus, their leader and exemplar, to have been married would have completely invalidated the church's own feeble arguments for celibacy.

It may also be asked *why* Jesus and Mary the Virgin had such prestige, power, and influence at that wedding — *unless Jesus was the groom.*

There are just as many — if not more — valid pointers in the opposite direction as far as the Cana wedding is concerned, but such evidence as the Gospel account does provide cannot be dismissed as entirely frivolous or trivial.

Then there is the highly significant conversation between Jesus and Martha of Bethany, sister of Mary and Lazarus. Martha is rushing around madly looking after the guests, while Mary is sitting at Christ's feet, listening intently to every word he says. Martha feels that this is unfair. She wants some help. Curiously, however, she does not simply ask Mary directly to get up and help her: she asks Jesus to tell Mary to help. Before we can analyze this little piece of evidence as fully as it deserves, we need to examine the social hierarchy, customs, norms, and mores of first century Palestine.

A young single woman was at the bottom of the pecking order. A married woman ranked considerably higher. A married woman with children ranked higher still. The mother of sons ranked higher than the mother of daughters. The lowest male ranked above the highest female, and so it went on. Because the male was seen as the head of the household, and had undisputed authority over his wife and children, it was considered bad manners and presumption to ask a married woman to do something *without asking her husband's permission first*. It would be tantamount by first century Jewish standards to borrowing a man's oxen and plough without asking him. If Martha felt that she had to ask Jesus whether Mary could help with the housework, it strongly suggests that Jesus was Mary's husband. His defence of Mary is then even more understandable. If, during his preaching tours, she had been separated from him for long periods in order to keep the children safely at home and look after them, now that she had a brief opportunity to be with him for a few hours in the house that they shared in Bethany, she was clearly going to make the most of it. Jesus tells Martha that Mary has chosen rightly; he is not going to order his wife to get up and help her sister — he would far rather have her here beside him. The shadow of Calvary is already falling across his mind. His time on earth is growing short. He wants to make the most of every moment.

And what of the mystery of the woman with the alabaster box of very expensive perfume, the oil of spikenard, which she pours over Christ's feet, washes them with her tears and dries them with her hair? Why was that girl so emotional? Was it not only repentance that stirred her, but a great tidal wave of love for the husband who had saved her from being stoned for adultery, and then forgiven and forgotten the entire episode; the same husband who had brought her beloved brother Lazarus back from the grave?

On balance then, Jesus *might* have been married to the girl who was variously known as Mary of Bethany, Mary Magdalene, the woman with the ointment, and the woman charged with adultery and brought to him for judgement.

Bethany near Jerusalem where Mary, Martha, and Lazarus lived. Was Mary the wife of Jesus?

There is a theological case to be made for Jesus being married, so that as the Incarnate Son of God in a uniquely special and particular sense, he would have experienced the *full* human condition. When intimate relationships with loving partners, and normal, healthy, human sexual appetites play such a major role in our lives, it is difficult to see how Christ could have been *fully* human *without* being married.

In no way does marriage interfere with his divine mission of salvation: if anything, it enriches, ennobles, and enhances it.

But what happened *after* Christ's death and resurrection? Mary (his wife?) was one of the very first to whom he appeared. Was there a special, personal message for her at that meeting? Could it have been something to do with taking their children to safety far beyond the clutches of Scribes, Pharisees, Sadducees, Romans, and Herodians? Was "Uncle" Joseph of Arimathea involved in this plan? By all accounts he had money, influence, and unswerving devotion to Christ's cause.

So as Jesus re-ascends with clouds to the Heaven from which he undoubtedly came, does Mary of Bethany (Magdalene?) take their children to live with friends of Joseph of Arimathea close to Rennes-le-Château in south-western France? The Romans were certainly at neighbouring Rennes-les-Baines at about this time. Abundant traces of their unmistakable architecture can still be seen there.

The persistent rumours that Jesus and Mary's children grew up near Rennes and married into the Merovingian Dynasty of early France, suggest that whether this is true or not, a strong suspicion persists that there was something more than ordinary mortal blood in the thaumaturgical

Merovingians — and, furthermore — that they never completely faded away when the Carolingians usurped their throne.

Saunière's strange little church at Rennes was dedicated to Mary Magdalene.

Chapter Twenty-six

The Synoptic Problem

The synoptic problem concerns the riddle of the *sources* of the four Gospels in the New Testament: Matthew, Mark, Luke and John. The Greek word *synoptikos* means "seen by the same eyes" or "looked at together." The first three Gospels are very similar indeed. Mark's is the shortest and seems to be the oldest. There is a distinct and probably reliable Christian tradition that Mark became the amanuensis of Peter, and wrote down everything that Peter remembered of his time as a disciple while Jesus was still on earth. Mark has a direct, simple, almost blunt style. Matthew and Luke contain substantial amounts of Mark, almost word for word, with a few additions of their own. These additions are distinctively flavoured. Whoever wrote Matthew's Gospel had Jewish readers in mind. Luke, who was probably a doctor of medicine from Macedonia, knew Paul, and is on one occasion referred to by him as the "beloved physician." Luke also wrote the Acts of the Apostles, and there is reason to believe that he wrote a third volume — presently lost — which *might* have recounted Paul's release from his first imprisonment in Rome and his hypothetical missionary journey to Spain, but that's all speculative.

Matthew and Luke both had access to another source besides Mark, and this is generally referred to as Q which stands for the German word *Quelle* meaning "source" or "origin." The other two sources are called M for material found only in Matthew, and L for material found only in Luke. When we look at the statistics Mark has a total of 661 verses, and six hundred of these turn up again in Matthew. Luke borrowed 350 of them. Only thirty-one verses of Mark's Gospel occur there and nowhere else. Where Luke and Matthew have shared material that is *not* found in Mark, the theory is that they both got it from Q.

Augustine who lived and worked in the fourth and fifth centuries had a different theory, in which there may still be a little controversial life. Augustine thought that Mark was simply a convenient *summary* of Matthew. This removes the problem of theorizing that Matthew *copied* Mark.

There is one very curious little record towards the end of Mark's brief Gospel, which looks almost as though it might be intended to be the writer's modest signature. When Jesus is arrested in the Garden of Gethsemane, there is a young man who is wearing only a linen sheet. The temple guards seem to think that he, too, is one of Christ's followers and they attempt to arrest him as well as Jesus. The unnamed "young man" is fast, athletic, flexible, and well co-ordinated. He leaves the sheet behind in the guards' hands and runs naked into the night. Was that anonymous young man none other than John Mark, the supposed author of Mark's Gospel? Traditionally, he was the son of one of the women disciples, who lived nearby. Had he been lying in bed on the flat roof of his home, with only his bed-linen as covering on that hot Palestinian night when Jesus was arrested? Had the boy been aroused by the shouting of the guards looking for Christ in the garden below? Had he run down clutching his bed sheet for covering, only to be taken for another disciple and pursued by the guards? Compared to all the major events that were going on that night, the narrow escape and embarrassment of one young man seems too trivial to be included: unless that young man is himself the author of the Gospel that bears his name, and this short narrative is his way of saying *"I was there!"*

Another mystery connected with Mark's Gospel is the vital missing ending of Chapter 16.

Prior to this missing ending, verse 7 contains another significant instance of the use of the phrase *"go your way"* which was examined at some length in Chapter 25. Again, it is benignly dismissive — just as it was when Jesus used it at the end of his conversation with the woman who had been brought before him accused of adultery. Whether the mysterious, white-robed speaker in the empty tomb is human or angelic, he uses this same phrase to express clearly to the women (who had brought spices to the tomb to anoint Jesus's body now that the Sabbath was over) that the episode of the tomb is complete. There is nothing relevant for them here now. *Jesus is alive.* He has risen from the dead. He has gone on before them to his much-loved former home: Galilee.

The oldest and most reliable sources end abruptly at verse 8, and do not include verses 9 to 20, which are in a different style, and were almost certainly added by another writer at a later date. There are outstanding New

Testament Greek language scholars who tend to argue that verse 8 (the last piece of the genuine, earliest known manuscript of Mark's Gospel) actually finishes with "for they were afraid of...." This abrupt and unsatisfactory prepositional ending makes it almost certain that the original manuscript was torn or damaged in some way, and subsequently lost.

Fortunately, there is enough of Mark's sound, original record still extant to leave little room for doubt that as the amanuensis of such an important eye-witness as Peter — and as a *probable* eye-witness himself — Mark believed firmly in the historical reality of Christ's resurrection, and that this rational faith of his was founded on reliable data which he had heard and observed at first hand, or had received directly from those who had.

So the synoptic problem as such evaporates in the light of Mark's reliability. It is perhaps an advantage rather than otherwise to know that Matthew and Luke both based their Gospel narratives on the work of someone who was particularly close to first class contemporary sources of evidence. Artists who are striving to improve their own techniques frequently make copies of acknowledged masterpieces. Their copies in no way detract from the power or perfection of the originals. Each man or woman puts something of himself, or herself, into the work on each individual easel. It may well be that a copying artist has background experience or worthwhile additional information to add. For example, the great masterwork being copied may have only wheat and blue cornflowers in a particular field. The copier might recall visiting that same field and seeing fascinating splashes of red poppies in it as well. If he makes a faithful copy of the masterwork but adds a poppy or two from his other source of information, this surely enhances and enriches the work rather than detracting from it. Isn't this something like what seems to have happened with the three synoptic Gospels?

Chapter Twenty-seven

Who was the
"Beloved Disciple"?

Just as the synoptic problem has cast shadows over the authorship of the first three Gospels, and raises the question of the identity of the young man who fled naked from Gethsemane, there is an equal mystery hanging over the identity of the man (or woman?) described in John's Gospel simply as "the disciple whom Jesus loved."

The traditional theory is that the fourth Gospel was written by John the brother of James. These two men were the sons of Zebedee the Galilean fisherman, just as Peter and Andrew were also Galilean fishermen and brothers. Peter, James, and John seem to have been Jesus's close inner circle: they were with him on the Mount of Transfiguration.

It seems perfectly reasonable to accept the traditional theory — yet the author of the fourth Gospel was a theologian, a philosopher, a metaphysician, and a writer of almost poetic quality. This writer, whoever he was, really understood Jesus, his pre-existent divine origin, and his message of love and mercy more clearly than most. There is a mystical dimension to his Gospel. There is perhaps another clue in his modesty — like that of Mark — in saying "I was there" without actually using his own name.

Some contemporary analysts have wondered — on what seems to us to be rather flimsy evidence — whether the beloved disciple was a woman. Could it possibly have been Jesus's *wife* as argued in Chapter 25? Just suppose, for the sake of following the argument, that he *was* married, and that Mary (Magdalene/Bethany?) was the same girl whom he had saved from stoning. Realizing that their time together on earth was now growing very short indeed, did Jesus change his former hypothetical policy of leaving her behind to look after their children — a policy which had exposed her unfairly to the temptation of adultery because of her loneliness? Was he now taking her everywhere with him — even to the Last Supper in the upper room — while someone (her very domesticated sister Martha, perhaps?) looked after the children for her? When they are eating that Last Supper together, is *she* the beloved disciple who is leaning up against him so affectionately, as described in John 13:24–26? Unless there has been an unmitigated lapse of concentration on the part of an early copyist, this is totally impossible. The male pronoun "he" is used throughout when references to the beloved disciple are made. It is used here, too.

On a slightly later occasion, the dying Jesus looks down from the cross and sees his mother, Mary the Virgin, standing there faithfully alongside the mysterious, unnamed, beloved disciple. Jesus's thoughts are with Mary not with his own indescribable agony and imminent death. He looks at them both and says that they are to regard each other as mother and son as from that moment. The fourth Gospel then clearly records that the beloved disciple takes Mary the Virgin home to live as his adopted mother. This piece of evidence assumes that Joseph her husband is already dead. But how does it affect the various theories regarding the physical brothers and sisters of Jesus, such as the James who wrote the controversial pronomian Epistle, and headed the Jerusalem Church — unless that was James the brother of John? Would Jesus have felt it necessary to provide for his mother's welfare if he had had younger brothers and sisters to care for her? Or is it more likely that Jesus would have wanted her safely in the care of a great and loving man like John whom he knew well and trusted completely rather than in the hands of his siblings who seem not to have been followers of his at this stage? Whatever the reason for Christ's choice of the beloved disciple to be his

Peter, James, and John were the inner core of Christ's Disciples.

244

Who was the "Beloved Disciple"? Was it John who wrote the Gospel?

mother's protector and guardian, the text at this point in the fourth Gospel makes it clear beyond any reasonable shadow of doubt that, whoever he is, the beloved disciple is definitely male.

The other candidate who has been put forward to fill the role is Lazarus whom Jesus raised from the dead, Lazarus who could well have been Jesus's brother-in-law. Certainly, Jesus was very fond of Lazarus and wept over his death. So far as the Gospel records indicate together, Lazarus was not one of the Twelve Disciples, and traditionally only the Twelve were present at the Last Supper. It seems unlikely, therefore, that he was the mysterious beloved disciple.

So the weight of evidence returns again to John, the brother of James and the son of Zebedee the Galilean fisherman. Yet a tantalizing trace of doubt still lingers: might the beloved disciple still *just* have been Mary Magdalene, alias Mary of Bethany, or her brother Lazarus rather than John the fisherman?

Bibliography

Allegro, J.M. *The Dead Sea Scrolls*. Middlesex: Penguin Books Ltd., 1961.

Bacon, Francis. *Essays, The Wisdom of the Ancients and The New Atlantis*. London: Odhams Press Ltd., 1950.

Barclay, William. *Jesus of Nazareth*. Collins Fount Paperbacks, 1981.

Bradley, M. *Holy Grail across the Atlantic*. Toronto: Hounslow Press, 1988.

Clayton, Ken *Jesus and the Scrolls*. England: Belvedere Fine Publishing Co., 1992.

Cooper, Rev. Chas. W. *The Precious Stones of the Bible*. London: H.R. Allenson Ltd., Circa 1910.

Eisenman, Robert and Wise, Michael. *The Dead Sea Scrolls Uncovered*. Shaftesbury, Dorset, U.K.: Element Books, 1992.

Encyclopaedia Britannica: Britannica Online: http://www.eb.com

Fanthorpe, Patricia and Lionel. *The Holy Grail Revealed*. California: Newcastle Publishing Co. Inc., 1982.

Fanthorpe, Lionel and Patricia. *The Oak Island Mystery*. Toronto: Hounslow Press, 1995.

Fanthorpe, Lionel and Patricia. *Secrets of Rennes le Château*. U.S.A.: Samuel Weiser Inc., 1992.

Fanthorpe, Lionel and Patricia. *The World's Greatest Unsolved Mysteries*. Toronto: Hounslow Press, 1997.

Fanthorpe, Lionel and Patricia. *The World's Most Mysterious People*. Toronto: Hounslow Press, 1998.

Fanthorpe, Lionel and Patricia. *The World's Most Mysterious Places*. Toronto: Hounslow Press, 1999.

Flem-ath, Rand and Rose. *When the Sky Fell: In Search of Atlantis*. Toronto: Stoddart, 1995.

Fortean Times. London. John Brown Publishing Ltd.

Graves, Robert. (Introduction by) *Larousse Encyclopaedia of Mythology*. London: Paul Hamlyn, 1959.

Mysteries of the Bible

Guerber, H.A. *Myths and Legends of the Middle Ages.* London: Studio editions Ltd., 1994.

Hancock, Graham. *Fingerprints of the Gods.* New York: Crown Publishers, 1995.

Hapgood, Charles. *Maps of the Ancient Sea Kings.* U.S.A.: Adventure Unlimited Press, 1996.

Hitching, Francis. *The World Atlas of Mysteries.* London: Pan Books, 1979.

Inglis, James. *The Bible Text Encyclopedia.* London: Morgan & Scott Ltd., 1922.

LaHaye, Tim and Morris, John. *The Ark on Ararat.* London: Marshall Morgan & Scott, 1979.

Lewis, C.S. *The Abolition of Man.* London: Collins, 1978.

Michell, John. and Rickard, Robert J.M. *Phenomena: A Book of Wonders.* London: Thames & Hudson, 1977.

Sharper Knowlson, T. *The Origins of Popular Superstitions and Customs.* London: Studio Editions Ltd., 1995.

Sinclair, Andrew. *The Sword and the Grail.* New York: Crown Publishers, Inc., 1992.

Smith, William. Editor. *Dictionary of the Bible.* London: John Murray, Walton & Maberly, 1863.

Vermes, Geza. *Jesus the Jew.* London: William Collins Sons & Co Ltd., 1981.

Whitehead, John. *Guardian of the Grail.* London: Jarrolds, 1959.

Wilson, Edmund. *The Scrolls from the Dead Sea.* London: Fontana, 1957.

Zammit, Prof. Sir Themistocles. *The St. Paul's Catacombs.* Malta: Valletta, 1980.